ARCHITECTS AND MAN'S SKYLINE

A Selected List of Books by Lynn and Gray Poole

ARCHITECTS AND MAN'S SKYLINE

by Gray Johnson Poole

Illustrated with photographs

DODD, MEAD & COMPANY

New York

ISBN: 0-396-06435-3
Library of Congress Catalog Card Number: 72-1532
Printed in the United States of America
by The Cornwall Press, Inc., Cornwall, N.Y.

CONTENTS

ILLUSTRATIONS

(Illustrations follow page 84)

ARCHITECTS AND MAN'S SKYLINE

ARCHITECTS AND MAN'S SKYLINE

When primitive man moved out of his cave into a hut, he unwittingly originated the still continuing evolution of architecture. It was to be aeons before architecture as a word was invented and as a profession, formalized. But in those hundreds of thousands of passing years, future architectural problems were compounded with each change in housing and settlement.

Unskilled as laborer, the erstwhile caveman first arranged saplings to support a leafed roof for protection against the elements but, soon after, fashioned walls to keep out human foe and wild beast. He subsequently clustered primordial shelters into a village, the basic community unit of a social order that, when sophisticated, would be complex. Expansion of the village to town to city to megalopolis paralleled the transformation of builder to architect to urban planner.

The architect designing today for tomorrow is said to be faced with unprecedented obstacles which, in fact, are only relative. Whether modern or traditional in his

1

style, the architect has ever been subject to restraints, restrictions, regulations. In the last quarter of the twentieth century, he depends on technology to achieve whatever he imagines, if approved. His forebear in the profession made do with inventive techniques by which to realize his creative plans, when sanctioned. He has been, through the ages, accountable most often to a single client, but frequently to the establishment, the existing bureaucracy.

Certain architects have worked willingly within a conventional framework; others, devious and autocratic, have defied authority. Sir Christopher Wren, renowned for his designs of London churches, himself an individualist, said that however an architect felt about his own major works, he had to provide designs acceptable to the aesthetic taste of the time and place in which he lived. Whether he was right is problematical. Some noncomformists have triumphed, others have been discredited.

This book highlights men, inseparable from their era in history, who are known for their notable contributions to the theory and practice of architecture. The word here is used into its fullest sense, a discipline related to the total environment, the population, the arts and economics, to area development, the availability of materials and the caliber of the labor force, and to the structures.

Dozens of architects, who are not included, range

from Leonardo da Vinci of the fifteenth century to the twentieth century's Louis I. Kahn. Selection of a few from the many who belong in the annals of architecture could not be other than personal. The most arbitrary choice was Baron Haussmann who was not, by training or inclination, an architect. He practiced sanitary engineering before that science was developed, and as city planner, changed the streets and the skyline of Paris.

Alternates were possible for several men, an example being Inigo Jones, predecessor in England of Wren whose mark on London seemed to be the more indelible. Worldwide influence was the reason for choosing the American Frank Lloyd Wright and the Greek Constantinos Doxiadis, the opposite in scope from his ethnic ancestors who concentrated their skills and talents on the geographical pinpoint that is the Acropolis of Athens. Lacking the genius of Brunelleschi, Stanford White was no less a man of his social environment, designing monuments and public buildings, constructing and decorating lavish homes for influential patron-clients.

Tomorrow's history of architecture will indubitably provide lasting testimonials to imaginative contemporary architects, wherever they are today: Japan, the United States, South America, Scandinavia. One can only hope that their works will be spared for posterity, as too many great works of architects of the past have not been.

3

Inflated land values are too often the excuse for demolishing buildings that, at any cost, should be preserved. Air pollution is increasingly eroding, to the point of irreparable damage, structures of historic and aesthetic import. Small wonder that area development and total environment are within the province of the present-day architect. He has a vested interest in the survival of structures.

The realistic architect knows that a certain number of detractors will assail his theories and his works. That will be so whether he builds cities half a mile high or designs domes to cover controlled-atmosphere communities. Architects have been a hardy breed, producing memorable buildings in spite of the necessity to make concessions to clients and officials. No architect of fame has been spared from venomous attacks by laymen and professionals. Each has borne the criticism with fortitude, but some, in rebuttal, have been scathing in denouncement of their critics.

Walter Gropius, founder of the German Bauhaus which uniquely integrated arts and crafts, thought that ideally architectural criticism should be delayed until evaluation could be made in reasoned perspective. He wrote: "Styles in my opinion should be named and outlined by the historian only for past periods. In the present we lack the dispassionate attitude necessary for impersonal judgment of what is going on. As humans, we are vain and jealous and that distorts objective vision. Why don't we leave it, then, to the future his-

4

torian to settle the history of today's growth in architecture—and get to work and let grow?"

Here then are several men of "past periods," and from the present epoch, a few as yet to take their place in long-range architectural history.

Artists and day laborers dedicated to
a community project produced a structure
praised for 2400 years.

ICTINUS, Fifth Century B.C.
CALLICRATES, Fifth Century B.C.
PHIDIAS, c. 500–432 B.C.

BUILDINGS erected on the Acropolis of Athens in the second half of the fifth century B.C. influenced architecture of the Western world into the first half of the twentieth century. The ancient Greek structures, measured and sketched through the ages, have been lauded in poetry, described in travel journals, and analyzed for treatises, scholarly journals, and professional papers. Minute architectural details of the edifices are a matter of record, but biographies of the men who designed, ornamented, and engineered the Acropolis complex are either scanty or so contradictory as to be undependable.

Lack of vital statistics about the private lives of the architects Ictinus and Callicrates and of the sculptor Phidias precludes definitive biography. But their work has revealed to posterity what manner of men they were: observant, creative, imaginative, dedicated, each

7

and all. The very fact that they were selected to assume their respective responsibilities for the projected beautification of the Acropolis attests to their capabilities.

Ravage and reconstruction of the Acropolis alternated in the centuries preceding the time of peace and prosperity in which the Athenian leader Pericles, previously acknowledged as statesman, became a patron of all the arts. For thousands of years before the fifth century B.C., the Acropolis was a command post and temple site. A natural fortress, more than five hundred feet above sea level, it had a gradual approach from the west, and in other directions, sheer drops to the plain below. Although its defenders could observe enemy forces advancing from inland and could sight ships on the distant Aegean Sea, the fort was not impregnable, a fact proved by Persians and earlier invaders.

Before their final rout at the Battle of Salamis, 480 B.C., the Persians laid waste to the Acropolis, razing buildings and smashing statuary. Themistocles, Athenian commander of the sea victory off Salamis, masterminded the postwar construction of a long wall to the Piraeus, seaport of Athens, and the rebuilding of ramparts of the Acropolis. Marble sections from damaged structures were set in the north wall that was visible to all men viewing from below the prominence of their Sacred Rock. The marble remains were deliberately placed to remind proud Athenians of the triumph over the hated Persians.

Themistocles was exiled in 471 B.C. but restoration of the Acropolis continued. More walls were raised to contain an increased surface area, and some new statues were set in place. Site-clearing in preparation for future construction was a useful preliminary to the artistic development of the Acropolis in the Periclean Age. Its flourishing was made possible not only by the Greeks' decisive defeat of the Persians but by the cessation of conflicts among Greek states and the transference of tribute moneys from member states in the Delian League to the treasury of Athens.

The occasional written assertion that Pericles drew up the architectural plans for the Acropolis and its several buildings is without historical confirmation. It is more consistent with his reputation as master executive that he commissioned works from experts to whom he then gave financial support and operational freedom.

Phidias was a long-time friend and contemporary of Pericles, both being middle aged when plans for the Acropolis were begun. The architects Ictinus and Callicrates, probably some years younger, were obviously experienced and sufficiently well known to have been chosen over several architects of established reputation.

Of the four men, only Ictinus has failed to be the subject of historical confusions. Unanimously accepted as having been the chief architect of the Parthenon, he is known to have coauthored a book that gave the dates of construction: 447–432 B.C. Had that book survived through the ages, it undoubtedly would have made pos-

9

sible the sifting of fact from contradictions which, derived from ancient writings, persist in scholarly works and guidebooks. Notable among early contributors to still existing discrepancies were Philochoros, fourth century B.C. into the third; Strabo, first century B.C.; Pliny the Elder, first century; Plutarch, late first century into the second, and Pausanias, late second century.

At this distance from the fifth century B.C., it seems of small consequence whether, as sometimes written, Phidias held the position of overseer and general manager of the entire Acropolis project, or whether Callicrates was the contractor for the Parthenon. Reason indicates that, as a team, the two architects and the already famous sculptor harmoniously conferred about plans, and with singleness of purpose, subsequently executed them with the enthusiastic assistance of Athenians by the hundreds. What matters historically is that the planners, and those whose work they directed, produced beauty which has, for twenty-four hundred years, continued to excite, delight, fascinate, and attract men from every continent.

The Parthenon was the signal achievement of the collaborators. They created a phenomenon of architecture and art by their innovations in the design of the building and for its embellishments.

Greek temples, extant at the beginning of the Periclean Age, although columnar in structure like the post-and-lintel temples of the Egyptians, were markedly

smaller in size. The precision of Greek temple construction resulted in distortions caused by optical il-
lusions that were taken into consideration by the sophisticated planners of the Parthenon. Their departure
from the previous uniformity of column shapes and
sizes gave the Parthenon its appearance of being a perfectly balanced building, which it is not. It just seems
that way, from every angle and at every time of day,
because of the perception and originality of its designers.

Their numerous variations in design were small in
scale but enormous in impact. By the addition of an
inch here and the subtraction of an inch there, harmonious effect was achieved throughout the Parthenon.

In earlier temples, the "canopy of skies" over Greece
made corner columns seem smaller than others. The
bright blue dome overhead tended to reduce in size
both buildings and their separate parts when they were
silhouetted against the intense color. In compensation
for the inescapable diminishing by nature, corner columns of the Parthenon were made imperceptibly larger
than others and in addition were inclined to a greater
degree. Those central columns that would be optically
enlarged by a backdrop of shadowed inner walls were
reduced in size. The Doric shafts were distinguished by
an entasis, or curving bulge, that prevented the appearance of concavity.

Doric, then the most common order of architecture
in Greece, is identified by simple block capitals and by
columns without bases. The Ionic order, more elaborate

in every way, was not to flourish in Greece until the sixth century B.C., although Callicrates expertly used the style, particularly for the Temple of Athena Nike on the Acropolis.

Inside the Parthenon, the floor was sloped from a central curve eight inches high. That refinement, far from being not noticeable, made the floor look perfectly flat, free of the illusionary sag often resulting from the architectural combination of horizontals with verticals.

The temple steps, slightly convex, conformed to the curve of the foundation so engineered as to prevent the accumulation of standing water. Drums of marble were fitted with such precision to make up the columns that the joining remain imperceptible although the Parthenon has been rocked by gunpowder explosion and shaken by earthquakes.

Scholars for centuries have tried to determine the mathematical theories used by the architects of the Parthenon to achieve the perfection of design. Oddly, the designers actually attained their aims by discarding the calculated symmetry that caused the visible distortion and monotony of decoration of earlier temples.

As Ictinus, Callicrates, and their associate architects deliberately corrected for the distortions, by changing structural components, Phidias departed from the conventional static friezes and sculpture placements. Instead of setting identical figures on either side of pediments, he contrasted male with female, the clothed body with the nude. Sizes of figures were subtly varied and certain draped clothing was made to look windblown. Some humans and animals were carved to simulate motion.

A precedence for the bulldozing of twentieth-century buildings to make way for more modern structures was set by the Greeks who beautified the Acropolis in the Periclean Age. The Parthenon itself was placed on a site occupied by earlier temples. One was razed in the early fifth century B.C. that the first, or Old, Parthenon might be constructed. It was not yet complete when its destruction, unplanned, was effected by the Persians.

The temple site was approached from the west through an entry built in the sixth century B.C. on ruins of a Mycenaean gateway. The Periclean Propylaea, an elaborate entrance building, was not begun until after the construction of the Parthenon because a large access was essential for the passage of supplies and materials.

All manpower available in Athens and its environs was recruited for work on the Parthenon. The lowliest day laborer, no less than the skilled craftsman, applied himself with pride and zeal to the specific task set for him. Only an all-out effort could have resulted in the completion of so mammoth a project within fifteen years.

Strong men transported marble from nearby Pentelicus, where newly opened quarries made available building material that previously had to be shipped to the mainland from quarries on the islands of Paros and Naxos. Lumbermen dragged wood from the countryside into Athens and up to the Acropolis, where carpenters fashioned the interior roof, long since disintegrated. Artisans, the metalworkers, marble polishers, and others spent long hours at their various specialities, whether on the Acropolis, noisy and crowded, or down in Athens at workshops, quiet and secluded.

In most Greek states, sculptors were then classed as artisans, but the status, social and economic, differed in Athens. Sculptors there were recognized as artists and their pay was appreciably higher than that of artisans. Dozens of sculptors unquestionably were required to produce the hundreds of figures that decorated the metopes, frieze, and pediments of the Parthenon. It seems equally safe to conjecture that Phidias not only created the sculptural designs but directed the execution of the sculptures which, although characterized by the variances of individuality, were neither inferior nor amateurish. What has to remain forever undetermined is how many relief figures, if any, Phidias himself sculpted.

The artwork was to embellish a peripteral temple about 235 feet by 110 feet, with eight Doric columns at either end and seventeen on each side. Such a temple usually had an exterior columned colonnade and windowless walls enclosing a single room, the cella. The Parthenon was designed with an inner enclosure for treasure given in honor of the goddess Athena, whose cult statue was to be placed in a larger, separate room. Bronze doors opened from the interior, at the east and west.

Long blocks of marble formed the architrave above the Doric capitals of the columns. The architrave was topped by an entablature of triple-channeled triglyphs alternated with four-foot square metopes sculpted with high-relief figures that were two-thirds life size. Mythical figures dominated the metopes, the scenes on them depicting highlights of the Trojan War and conflicts between gods and giants, Athenians and Amazons, centaurs and Lapithae. Pediments, triangulated above the entablature at the east and west ends of the Parthenon, showed respectively the birth of Athena and the contest of Athena and the god Poseidon for domination of Attica. The larger-than-life sculptures of the pediments were freestanding.

Just below the colonnade roof, an Ionic frieze, more than three feet deep, decorated the outer wall of the cella. The low-relief sculptures of the frieze, more uniform and finer in artistry than the exterior sculptures, depicted a procession of the Panathenaic festival with which, every four years, Athena was honored.

Instead of sculpting one continuous procession, the designers imaginatively planned two groups going in opposite directions from the southwest corner of the building and converging above the main entrance at the east. In the dual procession were horsemen, priests, musicians, warriors, maidens with offerings to the goddess, sacrificial animals, and gods. One priest was shown receiving the elaborate, ornamented peplos, or sacred cape, especially woven for the goddess and presented at the time of the Panathenaic festival.

Like other ancient Greek temples, the Parthenon was crudely painted with stark colors. Remaining fragments of paint indicate that black may have been profusely used, probably to prevent the glare from sunlight striking marble, and that colors were limited to a few basic shades. The consensus is that on the Parthenon, as elsewhere in Greek temple paintings, there was a lack of subtlety in both shadings and application of paint. Scholars have long conjectured about the chemistry of the paint that obviously was not resistant to climatic conditions. For lack of humidity, the paint dried and cracked in hot weather and cold, and flakes were either washed away by downpours or scattered by violent seasonal winds.

By a freak of nature, long-held theories about the paint colors seem to have been confirmed in 1970 by tombs excavated at Paestum, in southern Italy. More than one hundred tombs, with over two hundred painted walls, were identified as Greek and dated as fourth century B.C. by the Italian archaeologist in charge of the excavation.

Black, the predominant flat paint, was highlighted by a very few uninteresting shades: green, red, terra cotta, and yellow ocher. The tomb paintings were preserved through thousands of years by swamp moisture from a silted river. After 1944, when the marshland was drained for agricultural use, roots from artichoke crops, planted on the land, fortuitously continued, for another quarter of a century, to provide protective moisture for the subterranean frescoes.

How true the frescoes' colors are to those applied to the Parthenon must forever be debatable. However, as examples of intact paintings by ancient Greeks, the tomb art does seem to verify that colors, limited in number, were lackluster in quality and brushed on without finesse.

There is no uncertainty about the brilliance of the Athena Parthenos, the chryselephantine cult statue for the cella of the Parthenon. A masterwork of Phidias, that colossal figure with its base stood a full forty feet. Draperies of the full-length peplos were overlaid with beaten gold, and the flesh parts of the goddess were made of ivory. Components of the sculpture, a large shield, a spear, and a Nike figure, were also gold. Athena balanced the spear in her left hand, and on the same side, the shield rested against her knee. At the right was the Nike, goddess of victory.

Relief sculptures decorated the base of the statue, and relief decorations covered the shield, the crested helmet of the goddess, and even edges of the soles of her sandals. The statue symbolized beauty, religion, victory in wars, and achievements in times of peace. Athena

Parthenos, resplendent within the extraordinary temple that enshrined her, was dedicated during the Panthenaic festival of c. 438 B.C.

The Athena Promachos, an earlier statue by Phidias, was a triumphant twenty-nine-foot metal figure that dominated the Acropolis. When brightened by direct sunlight, the tip of the statue's spear and the helmet crest reputedly could be seen by sailors on the Aegean Sea as far off as Cape Sounion, forty miles to the south.

The Bronze Athena, consecrated 454 B.C., is said to have been the inspiration for the Statue of Liberty. The latter quite obviously was not a copy because the hand of Athena's outstretched right arm grasped a rested spear while Liberty has a flaming torch in the hand of her upraised right arm.

No authenticated orginal work of Phidias is extant, but some Roman copies are accepted as being faithful to his designs, if not exact in materials. Since neither of his Athena statues of the Acropolis endured, posterity must be grateful for the small-scale reproductions of them on coins, Roman and Greek, and to those who, having seen the two statues, *in situ,* wrote graphic descriptions of them.

Accusations of embezzlement and thievery were made against Phidias in connection with the Athena Parthenos. Conflicting rumors, not substantiated, have come down through the ages. Supposedly, jealous sculptors claimed Phidias speculated in the purchase of ivory

for the chryselephantine statue, and that he actually stole gold from the figure.

Plutarch, centuries later, refuted the accusations. He wrote that, on order of Pericles, all gold of the Athena was removable for weighing should theft ever be suspected. When, according to Plutarch, the gold was weighed in defense of Phidias, the full amount was present.

Phidias was also charged with blasphemy for having put his own likeness and that of Pericles on the shield of the Athena. Who is to know whether either was represented on the shield? The Phidias described by Plutarch was a bald old man, hefting a stone in both hands, while on the Strangford Shield, a copy in the British Museum of the Athena Parthenos shield, the bald old man, identified as Phidias, is wielding an ax. Nowhere is there even a reputed portrait bust or statue of Pericles.

Neither Ictinus nor Callicrates were mentioned in connection with the scandal that, justly or not, raged around Phidias. What disposition of his case was made is no more known than how or when he died, soon or late after allegedly stealing and committing a sacrilege.

Equally shadowy in history are the fates of the sculptor's two glorious Athenas. Both may have utimately been destroyed in Constantinople although, while still on the Acropolis, the Athena Parthenos was more than once mutilated by vandals. She may have been removed to Turkey in the fifth century and burned there five centuries later. The Promachos statue reputedly was taken in the sixth century to Constantinople, where it was destroyed in 1203.

Freestanding sculpture on the Acropolis, whether indoors or out, was vulnerable to devastation by nature and by man. At the height of the Periclean Age, statues were crowded on the Sacred Rock, from which there was no such panoramic view as today awes visitors from around the world. Protective high ramparts towered at the perimeter, and interior walls supported and divided terraces and courtyards. Their floors and pathways were studded with large vases, single sculptures, and statuary groups. The art objects of the exterior, as well as the cult statues in temples, were destroyed by earthquakes, or smashed by enemy warriors, or carted away by plunderers. As a result, most surviving Acropolitan sculpture of the period is architectural.

Nature spared the Parthenon, but man's destruction, occupation, and plundering of the temple are matters of historical record. It became a place of Christian worship in the sixth century and was consecrated as a Catholic church in the thirteenth. Turks made a mosque of the building in the mid-fifteenth century but later turned it into a gunpowder warehouse. In September 1687 the long sides of the Parthenon were blown out by an exploding shell blasted at the Turkish stronghold by attacking Venetians.

Further damage to the Parthenon was inflicted by the successful Venetian besiegers after their commanding general, Francesco Morosini, directed the removal of a sculpted chariot group from the west pediment. A tackle, installed to dislodge the pediment sculptures, failed in operation, and in the resultant fall, the sculptures were shattered.

Thomas Bruce Elgin, seventh earl of Elgin, after being appointed British ambassador to Constantinople, in 1799, acquired permission from the Turks for removal of some sections of the Parthenon and other buildings of the Acropolis. There is a wide difference of scholarly opinion about the motives and intentions of Lord Elgin. It is variously held that he organized an expedition to the Acropolis for the sole purpose of obtaining drawings of architectural details and casts of sculptures, or wanted sincerely to protect the art works from further decay caused by neglect and deliberate mutilation, or foresaw considerable profit to be realized from the sale of his acquisitions.

Indisputably, at his own expense, Lord Elgin shipped to England large sections of the Parthenon and marbles from the Erechtheion and the Temple of Athena Nike. The Parliament, in 1816, paid thirty-five thousand pounds for the entire collection of Elgin Marbles, ever since on exhibit at the British Museum. Whether those art objects should rightly be returned to the Acropolis is a subject of continuing controversy.

The total cost of the Periclean beautification of the Acropolis cannot be closely approximated but, in five years, the equivalent of several million dollars was spent on the Propylaea that never was finished, its construction being halted by the diversion of funds for expenses of the Peloponnesian War. There are extant some building accounts for the constructions on the Acropolis because those records were inscribed on marble, durable through the ages that took their toll of other records. Designs and worksheets presumably were drawn on materials with no resistance to destruction by fire and natural disintegration.

Sketches of the Parthenon were made by an artist in the company of the French ambassador to Turkey shortly before the explosion that severely damaged the building in the late seventeenth century. Measured drawings were made within the following century. Ironically, those structural records are not as essential to a reconstructed view of the original Parthenon as designs for the sculptures would be.

The building itself, in spite of damage, stands today as a monument to the genius of Ictinus and his associates whose architectural innovations remain for all to see. Missing are the designs by Phidias for carved figures and their placements and for the Athena Parthenos, all impossible for man's imagination to recreate.

The few remaining sculptures of pediments, metopes, and frieze, even now only in fair state of preservation, are endangered by future weathering and so-called progress. In late 1970, the Greek Antiquities Department warned of accelerated decay of buildings on the

Acropolis. Increasing industrialization in and near Athens was recognized as a threat to the structures and their decorations, and erosion, to foundations of the ancient Greek buildings. A thick lawn of heavy grass that would retard the erosion was proposed by the inspector-general of the Antiquities Department. No one has yet suggested what measures can be taken against the industrial fumes that scientific experts say will eventually damage the columns of the Parthenon.

The supreme example of ancient Greek architecture may all too soon be one more victim of the modern day scourge: air pollution.

*Florentine architecture was enriched by
a determined man who chose to fight
bureaucracy and to engage in private feuds.*

FILIPPO BRUNELLESCHI, 1377–1446

Bureaucracy was an irritant to Filippo Brunelleschi whose knowledge of classical structures and genius
for inventive construction immeasurably influenced
architecture of the Italian Renaissance. His achievements, recognized since the fifteenth century, were
realized only through persistent confrontations of the
establishment in Florence, his birthplace.

Son of an ambassador of state who was a member of
the legal guild, Filippo was expected to apply himself
to studies that would prepare him for a profession similar to or the same as his father's. But, excelling only
in mathematics, the son disregarded other school subjects, and spent class hours drawing houses and sketch-
ing geometric designs. With commendable wisdom, the
elder Brunelleschi permitted Filippo to follow his own
interests which, in time, led to his graduation as a gold-
smith and to membership in the guild of goldsmiths.

In the arts, Filippo was an enthusiastic student. He
became expert at the cutting and setting of gems, and

in the execution of various kinds of metal design to which he added mathematical dimensions. While very young, he sculpted two of the finest silver pieces for a Pistoian high altar to which many established sculptors contributed their works. His were exquisite half-figures in high relief. It is bootless, if irresistible, to speculate about what reputation as metal sculptor Brunelleschi might have enjoyed had he not, while in his early twenties, been incensed by the decision of judges of a competition open to sculptors.

Florence at the turn of the fifteenth century was ideally conditioned for its role in the Renaissance that, in Italy, burgeoned in the previous century. Peace and prosperity gave influential Florentines a sense of well-being, general confidence, and a self-assurance about their knowledge of all things cultural. Scholars and poets, as well as artists and craftsmen, were supported by affluent families or by individuals who, as patrons, participated in the intellectual and artistic life of their city.

Architects and artists commonly had to submit models in competitions for architectural design and for the decorative components of buildings. Committees of selection, serving as both judge and jury of works under consideration, were made up of experts and lay representatives.

After receiving a commission, by award, an architect or artist or craftsman had to cope with advisors in his guild, to which membership was mandatory. A man who did not belong to the guild of his profession or trade had no vote or any other citizen-rights. The balance of power in the guild hierarchy being unequal, there was a continual tug of war between members of the major and the minor guilds.

In addition to the participation of guild officials in structural projects, there was an administrative council of citizens, known as the opera, for every architectural project. Those serving on the council were patrons and master builders, including, almost always, the chief master. The administrative council was in charge of construction funds, inspection of work progress, and of revision of plans deemed to be essential

It was against the red tape of the guilds and what he considered to be interference from the administrators that Brunelleschi revolted when he became an architect.

The decision to replace doors of the Florence baptistery, planned in the fourteenth century by Andrea Pisano, led to the announcement in 1401 of a design competition. By specification, the doors were to show scenes from the story of the sacrifice of Isaac, and models, cast in bronze, had to be submitted within a year.

Seven sculptors accepted the challenge of a difficult subject that required the depiction of landscapes, animal forms, and human figures, clothed and nude. One of the seven was Brunelleschi and another, Lorenzo Ghiberti, his contemporary and fellow member of the guild of goldsmiths. Their respective methods of working on the required models reflected differences in their character.

Ghiberti, cautious and unsure, experimented with several designs after consulting with experts invited to his workshop. Brunelleschi, secretive and certain of his own judgment, worked rapidly without consultation. The models of Ghiberti and Brunelleschi, now exhibited in the Bargello, the national museum at Florence, were both so outstanding that the thirty-four judges suggested a joint award. When Brunelleschi refused to cooperate on a collaborative commission, Ghiberti unanimously was voted first place, and he began on the baptistery's elaborate doors that were not to be completed for more than twenty years.

Only Giorgio Vasari, sixteenth-century architect, writer, and painter, gives a different version of the award in his *Lives of the Artists,* sprightly but gossipy biographies. He wrote that Brunelleschi, after seeing Ghiberti's model, privately conferred with his much younger friend Donatello and decided Ghiberti should have the commission for the doors. Other sources agree that Brunelleschi, angered and hurt by the decision of the judges, left Florence in a huff. Whether he deliberately planned to change professions that Ghiberti might never again be his rival is questionable. Accompanied by Donatello, Brunelleschi went to Rome where they explored the art treasures, separately developing interests that were to establish them as innovators respectively in sculpture and architecture. Donatello, the first to return to Florence, briefly worked with Ghiberti on the baptistery doors before taking on independent commissions for sculpture.

In and out of Rome, over a period of several years, Brunelleschi studied, inspected, and measured the ruins of classical structures. He familiarized himself with every aspect of the ancient architecture and adapted it to the Renaissance architectural concepts that were to emerge in Florence. On all fours, he dug through Roman rubble, examining building materials and construction techniques. Scrambling to the roof of the Pantheon, he removed a section of tiles in order to have a close look at the dovetailed marble blocks that formed the dome. He selected a special parchment on which to draw plans of Rome's major classical buildings and to sketch not only architectural remains but his own imaginative reconstructions of original structures.

Even when living in Rome with Donatello, Filippo typically did not share every discovery and idea with his young friend. It was not until long after, in Florence, that, as architect, Brunelleschi revealed an invention that resulted from his study of square holes in large stones of the Roman classical buildings. Puzzled by the stones, he eventually decided they were for insertion of a square instrument that would facilitate lifting and placement. Since no such device had survived through the ages, Brunelleschi designed one, a sort of grappling iron, strong enough to lift weighty stones by a crane, without cords.

That invention and numerous others were to distinguish Brunelleschi's construction of the dome for the Florence cathedral, the Cathedral Santa Maria del Fiore, that had been started more than a century ago. Its cornerstone was laid in 1294, and two years later, work was begun under the direction of the architect Arnolfo di Cambio. He died, probably within a decade, but his plans were sporadically carried forward throughout the fourteenth century.

Inevitably, with the existent system of supervision by committee, changes were made through every stage of construction, and the cathedral was still unfinished at the turn of the fifteenth century. Florentines were quite understandably possessive about their now-famed Duomo. It was literally a community project, having been financed through several generations by funds from the city treasury and from a poll tax levied on every adult male with the status of citizen.

Engineering of the dome, major superstructure of the cathedral, had long been discussed by the building council. The method of placement of Gothic domes had been to support them with wooden scaffolding and curved wooden planks prior to installation of keystones. But that technique was known to be impractical for the Florence Cathedral because the exceedingly large dome of Arnolfo's scale model had caved in when the supports gave way. The previously dependable framework system obviously would not do for the Duomo's pro-jected dome with its two-hundred-foot diameter.

Well-aware of the technical difficulties presented by the size of the dome, Brunelleschi had deliberately and carefully studied various domes in Rome. In 1417, again in Florence, he talked to the council about the cathedral dome, assuring members that he had evolved both an artistic design and practical techniques for construction.

There was acrimonious exchange about Brunelleschi's plans between him and the council, and between him and other architects. In general terms, he told the council of his intention to build a marble dome with-out pillars or other supports or even, except at the very top, scaffolding. Since he cavalierly failed to reveal the details of his design or to explain the original devices by which the superstructure was to be engineered, his proposal was questioned by the council and derided by architects.

He, in turn, scoffed at those architects who variously suggested a porous or lightweight material, instead of marble a central column up to the oversized dome, or, for support during construction, a tremendous mound of earth that could be shoveled from the tribune it filled, when the dome was safely in place.

In the late summer of 1418, a prize of two-hundred gold florin was offered for the award-winning design for the dome. Within a matter of days, Brunelleschi was at work on a brick model. Although he had four masters of the building guild to help him, the time allotted for completion of the model was too short, and the deadline was extended.

His design was accepted after he submitted specifics for building materials and measurements. He was vague about construction techniques, neither telling nor showing anyone his inventions for facilitating certain parts of the operation. As indicated by his model, the work of Brunelleschi was to be from the octagonal tribune of the Duomo to the base of the lantern that would eventually be placed above the dome.

Restrictions set by the council so infuriated Brunelleschi that only his determination to be the architect of the dome restrained him from once again leaving Florence. The council commissioned him to complete the dome only up to twenty-seven feet, a limitation afterwards rescinded. But the bitter circumstance for him was the council's stipulation that his associate was to be, of all people, Ghiberti.

The council was influenced by the guild of builders, a prominent group that included architects in its membership. The guild did not want recognition for the dome to go to Brunelleschi, who belonged to the guild of goldsmiths, but not to theirs. In addition, Ghiberti was then much in favor because his doors of the baptistery, nearing completion, were the talk of Florence. A sculptor, he also was a member of the guild of goldsmiths, but cannily had joined the guild of builders as well.

Brunelleschi accepted the terms of the council but

apparently from the first was determined to have sole credit for his original design for a dome-within-a-dome. It was said he envisioned a dual structure from the time he scrutinized, close to, the roof of the Pantheon in Rome. He foresaw that inner and outer domes, each of dovetailed sections, would be mutually supporting. He did not reveal, until the construction was well under-way, that the area between the two domes would con-tain steps for easy access to the top.

Such details as he did offer were entered in the records of the council in 1420, the year the dome was started. In amendments of 1421, the diameter of the dome was reduced to just over 138 feet, and the building material was changed, from marble only, to marble and bricks. The bricks were shaped for dovetailing to Brunelleschi's specifications. Freed from the earlier restriction, Bru-nelleschi was responsible for the entire dome to the base of the projected lantern.

Early on, Brunelleschi was relieved of the onus of having to defer to, or confer with, Ghiberti about the dome. The sculptor, inept as supervisor, said, long after, that for sixteen years he worked side by side with Brunelleschi, a claim not supported by records. They showed that, for a number of years, Ghiberti did re-ceive some remuneration for the dome project. But from the beginning, the dome was incontestably Bru-nelleschi's very own, and his alone.

* * *

The dome, crown of the Cathedral Santa Maria del Fiore, attests to Brunelleschi's mastery of lineal design. Hardly less remarkable were his achievements as engineer and overseer of the construction.

For a machine lift that, in 1421, replaced a previous invention of his, Brunelleschi received not only a handsome bonus but full expenses for supplying pulleys and wheels, balances and beams, leather and glue, ropes and chains, and the yokes of oxen required for operating the lift. The same year, he applied for and obtained the equivalent of a patent on a raftlike boat for transporting marble, complete with hoisting cranes. The terms of his permit were for three years, during which no similar craft should ply the Arno River with marble from Pisa to Florence.

Brunelleschi planned a marble channel for draining water from the dome to pipes in the wall below, and invented numerous devices for the raising of weighty materials, including marble. Paid an honorarium for his design of an intricate chain with which the double domes were to be strengthened, Brunelleschi was impatient about the length of time, two years, that it took to secure the heavy retaining lines to the superstructure.

Irked by guild rules that hampered construction, Brunelleschi, a perfectionist, also found fault with the quality of some work. When, once too often, he carped about delays and workmanship, the building masters made no effort to prevent a laborers' walkout. The strikers, demanding a pay raise, claimed their jobs were exhausting and hazardous. They resented having to stay all day on the platform where they worked and had to spend their lunch hour. That restriction and another about wine drinking were imposed by the guild, not Brunelleschi.

There was unquestionably danger that a man, unsteady from imbibing too much strong wine, might plummet from the platform to the tribune floor, far below. As a precaution against such a mishap, water diluted the wine that, raised by pulley, was issued at the masters' discretion. To further insure the safety of workers, high up in the structure, Brunelleschi had drawn the specifications for their sturdy scaffold and personally supervised its carpentry.

In the matter of the demands of the strikers, Brunelleschi was concerned only with the pay raise, about about which he promptly consulted the council. Its members turned down the request for higher wages and dismissed every building master. With pickup crews, Brunelleschi continued the construction until he thought masters and strikers had been taught a lesson. The original workers were then returned to the payroll for less money than they had received before the strike.

Work thereafter went forward rapidly and without interruption, but Brunelleschi was to be once more harassed by the guild of builders. He was ever opposed to their tactics, and they were resentful of his attitude. He not only wanted full credit for his work but held that no man should be anonymous under the aegis of a collective group which interfered with designs or, worse yet, altered plans in committee.

In 1434, the guild officially ordered Brunelleschi to pay the fee required of their graduate masters and the annual tax paid by members. Although the ultimatum was opposed by the council, the guild proceeded legally and had Brunelleschi jailed for nonpayment of dues. Defying the powerful organization, Brunelleschi refused to become a member, on any terms, and his decision being honored, continued to function as architect.

The dome of the cathedral was closed on August 31, 1436, the year Brunelleschi completed his model for the lantern to top it. His winning design had been submitted with several others, including one by Ghiberti. After years of discussion, Carrara marble was decided on as the lantern's material, and in December 1444, measurements were made and carving details settled.

Brunelleschi died before the lantern was finished, and his design for its base was never executed. The beautiful and ingenious dome, which, as John Symonds wrote, "remains a *tour de force* of individual genius," was to be Brunelleschi's major but not sole contribution to the completion of the cathedral.

Following two years of conference, Brunelleschi and Batista d'Antonio, cathedral council member and long-time chief master of the building project, were commissioned, in 1430, to design an altar for the tomb of St. Zenobio being sculpted by Ghiberti. The now-famous sarcophagus was placed above the altar, which was in a small, undecorated chapel. Ironically, it is Ghiberti's masterpiece, set under an arch facing the choir loft, that is commonly seen. The chapel with its altar is open only once a year, on St. Zenobio's Day, May 25.

With his engineering skill, Brunelleschi overcame a technical problem that involved the installation of decorations for the organ gallery and choir loft of the cathedral. For sculptured groups of young maidens and children, by Donatello and his pupil Luca della Robbia, an access to the music center was essential. But no one could decide where to build a stairway that would neither violate the privacy of a cathedral sacristy nor destroy the aesthetic proportions of the building.

Instead of steps, Brunelleschi designed a flat arch, in effect a bridge made of smooth stone blocks, slanted on either side of a keystone. It was again, like the dome, a construction of self-supporting components. The unobtrusive passageway, after serving its initial purpose, was used by singers to reach the choir loft without disturbing priests in the sacristy or detracting from the beauty of the cathedral.

No sooner was Brunelleschi awarded the commission for the dome than he became the most sought-after architect in Florence. His output was prodigious, particularly in light of the fact that no building detail was too slight for his attention and no construction technique unworthy of his attention. Although his commissions frequently overlapped, he somehow kept abreast of the progress of each structure.

By the time the dome was started, Brunelleschi's Foundling Hospital had been under construction for a year. Columns of its impressive colonnade were Corinthian, the order most felicitous to Brunelleschi who, from building to building, varied only ornamentation of columns. For the Foundling Hospital colonnade, terra-cotta medallions were set in spandrels of semicircular arches on the colunms. His use of the supported series of arches was an innovation which found immediate favor among architects.

Brunelleschi's designs were distinguished by freshness and variety, and many, through adaptations by others, became representative of Florentine Renaissance architecture. He was as much master of pure line as of scientific precision in the delineation of every plan. When possible, as for churches and chapels, his buildings had delicacy, lightness, and an openness typical of the classical styles that engrossed him in Rome.

The originality of his design for the Church of San Lorenzo shocked certain Florentines, who summarily had the work stopped. Construction was resumed after church officials, undoubtedly abetted by wealthy donors of funds for family chapels, announced that any citizen heard to criticize San Lorenzo would be exiled for life. Brunelleschi's controversial plan was for a basilica with nave and aisles separated by columns, supporting entablature blocks. That novel combination of features, like many another pioneering concept, architectural or otherwise, was opposed by those to whom it was unfamiliar.

Giovanni de' Medici underwrote the tribune, sacristy, and his family chapel in San Lorenzo, with the provision that other families should pay for their chapels. Following the death of Giovanni, Brunelleschi finished the sacristy under the patronage of the heir, Cosimo de' Medici. One hundred years later, Michelangelo designed the New Sacristy, or Medici Mausoleum, that conformed with the fifteenth-century one.

In every way, the Church of Santa Spirito seemed more spacious than San Lorenzo. The chapels of the latter opened onto aisles that were lower than the nave, from which inner arches looked to be smaller than the upper, a view that diminished the grandeur. The chapels of Santa Spirito, uniform in pattern and structure, as was not customary, were on the level with the nave, so there was no optical illusion of disproportion of columns. Effective double colonnades, dividing nave from aisles, appeared to flow through tribune and transept.

The Pazzi Chapel in the Cloisters of Santa Croce was a becolumned miniature of a Roman temple. Brunelleschi deliberately intended the tiny gem of a church to exemplify how art could be revolutionized through study of classical architecture. The building was ornamented by dome decorations of Luca della Robbia, whose medallions of majolica were set on a central arch. Luca, earlier wearied by the arduous task of sculpting stone and metal, invented the clay-with-glaze technique that produced majolica. His family was to become famed for that pottery, particularly for their della Robbia cherubs and wreaths and swags of fruits and flowers.

Of necessity, most of Brunelleschi's *palazzi* for prominent citizens had solid façades that households might be protected from marauders or feudal assailants. Even so, the architect managed to give airy elegance to the Palazzo Quaratesi, built for the Pazzi family. Above the essential heavy masonry at ground story, Brunelleschi placed double-arched windows, a refinement of the conventional low, utilitarian openings. Single pillars, or columns, supporting the arches, added height and grace to the windows set off by handsome moldings.

Large arched windows and balustrades somehow managed to lighten the upper façade of the Palazzo Pitti, that otherwise resembled a huge rock pile. Florentines, then oriented to art and its expression, were critical of the ostentatious Luca Pitti who wanted his palace to be not only the most elegant of its time, but the largest. Brunelleschi admirably met the challenge with a tremendous symmetrical structure that was later literally fit for a king, and second in size to only one other palace in Italy: the Vatican.

Following the death of Brunelleschi, many changes were made in his Palazzo Pitti and even in the sections of the building that he had finished. As in almost every other part of the *palazzo,* additions were made to the

39

cortile that opened to the Boboli Gardens, also enlarged through the years. The lower part of the façade remained, as originally, solid enough for defense of the owner whether monarch or merchant prince.

Brunelleschi built strongholds, not only for family living but for garrisons. Recognized as an expert in military architecture and engineering, he was consulted about various fortifications throughout Italy. He is said to have contributed plans for forts at, among other places, Ferrara and Milan, and did design two fortification towers at Pisa.

In the first half of the fifteenth century, the cultural atmosphere in Florence and the attitude of her citizens, whether patrons or artists, provided the ambiance for limitless expansion. The de' Medicis and their peers supported, with both money and intellectual understanding, the projects and ideas of creative fellow citizens. In the arts, men in spite of inevitable dissension and occasional rivalry, enthusiastically engaged in collaborative projects. Their works remain as monuments, honoring their names: Donatello, Masaccio, Ghiberti, the della Robbias, and Brunelleschi.

Those deservedly famous Florentines were the immediate precursors of other Italians also destined to make invaluable contributions to the history of art and architecture.

A distinguished scientist turned to
architecture and earned world
renown for the churches of his design.

SIR CHRISTOPHER WREN, 1632–1723

St. paul's Cathedral, London, one of the most famous buildings in the world, had an origin unprecedented in the history of architecture. Its designer was a
distinguished scientist who turned to architecture only
three years before he became involved with the proposed rebuilding of St. Paul's, that was in a state of
deterioration. How Christopher Wren, Savilian Professor of Astronomy, Oxford, happened to become an
architect is a known fact; but why that should have
come about must forever remain a mystery.

When not only inexperienced but untrained, Wren
was almost simultaneously chosen by his uncle Matthew
Wren, bishop of Ely, to design the chapel of Pembroke
college, Cambridge, and by Gilbert Sheldon, archbishop
of Canterbury and chancellor of Oxford, to design the
Sheldonian Theatre, Oxford.

Pembroke Chapel was the realization of a continuing
dream of the bishop of Ely while a prisoner in the
Tower of London. The Sheldonian Theatre was the

result of Archbishop Sheldon's determination to separate ecclesiastical services from secular ceremonies at Oxford. Among scholars there is still disagreement about which of the two structures was the first designed by Wren. Neither was in any way unique, which is hardly surprising in consideration of Wren's immaturity and his lack of experience in the field of architecture.

A prolific architect, once started, Wren designed fifty-two London churches in the two decades following the Great Fire of 1666, and in the course of a long career in architecture, had for clients many private citizens and monarchs of three dynasties: Stuart, Orange, and Hanover.

Lack of records makes it impossible to confirm, as Wren's, numerous buildings attributed to him, and biographical data are equally wanting. Voluminous writings about the architect and his work, published by his grandson Stephen Wren, are suspect by most scholars and art historians who find Stephen often in error or mistaken in an interpretation. Wren Society publications provide some information about Wren's architecture that is revelatory, if mostly secondhand. Wren's own written statements on the subject survive in a limited number of treatises and of letters, chiefly to clients.

He left even fewer personal communications, none informative. There is little to learn about Wren, as a person, from a letter in Latin, written when he was only nine years old, to his clergyman father, Dean Christopher Wren; from a note to his first wife, or a much later one to his son.

In an epoch when quilled pens flowed freely with facts, gossip, and philosophical observations, neither his long-time friends nor British diarists gave linage to Wren that might have illuminated his character and fleshed out his biography. Inexplicably unknown are the dates of Wren's marriages to the two wives by whom he was widowed, and the name of the political party which elected him to Parliament for two short and widely separated terms.

After taking a science degree at Wadham College, Oxford, Wren was professor of astronomy at Gresham College, London, from 1657 to 1661, the year he returned to Oxford as Savilian Professor. There is extant a list of fifty-five subjects which commanded his attention in the years from 1649 to 1657, and on it are four items about the construction of buildings, including forifications "in the sea."

It may have been on the basis of those studies that Charles II asked Wren to go on a mission of inspection to Tangiers, a fortified port that was part of the dowry of the king's consort, Catherine of Braganza. In 1662, the year of his marriage, King Charles made Wren assistant surveyor of works and public buildings, following the appointment with a request that Wren inspect the fortifications at Tangiers. Wren, who was to recommend whatever strengthening he deemed necessary,

43

begged off, giving ill health as an excuse that, to be acceptable to the king, must have been valid.

The monarch's interest in Wren as a potential architect is no more bewildering, in retrospect, than the contemporaneous choice of Wren as designer of the Chapel at Cambridge and the theater at Oxford. Only thirty years old at the time, he held a prestigious chair at Oxford, had a well-deserved reputation as mathematician, but in architecture was a tyro. That circumstance failed to deter him from accepting the offered commissions from Bishop Wren and Archbishop Sheldon.

Matthew Wren, the bishop, following his arrest at the beginning of the Puritan revolution, was incarcerated for eighteen years. During his imprisonment, the clergyman vowed that, on release, he would have a chapel built at Cambridge. His nephew's design neither conformed to the Gothic style of other buildings at Cambridge nor incorporated Renaissance refinements that were later to distinguish Christopher Wren buildings.

Apparently the bishop of Ely approved the plan for Pembroke Chapel, which is a simple blocklike rectangle with classical elevation. On the façade of the chapel, two pairs of Corinthian pilasters frame a central window with a rounded top, a window style used in the Sheldonian Theatre. Wren placed carved swags at either side of the chapel's façade window, and mounted urns, with sculpted flames, on the front corners of the slanting roof pinnacled by an octagonal lantern.

The Sheldonian Theatre's façade, as well as the entire structure, was more imposing. In his role as Oxford chancellor, Gilbert Sheldon wanted a building specifically for academic functions which previously, and as he thought, unsuitably, were held at St. Mary's Church. The theater was primarily to be for the Encaenia, the academic procession for commemoration exercises. When designing the theater, Wren took into consideration the interior traffic and the engineering problems it posed, not specifically the aesthetic effect.

Sixteen sixty-five was an important year in Wren's life. He spent upwards of six months in Paris and its environs, meeting French scholars and architects and, with perception, viewing churches, palaces, public buildings, and gardens. Unlike most intellectuals and dilettantes of Restoration England, he had not previously traveled on the Continent, nor did he ever again. Whatever the influence of Italian architecture on his work, it was gained through major volumes in the important library he collected through subsequent years. But even the young Wren, as associate of professors and friend to scholars, had an interest in antiquities and classical architecture which, at the time, was a prerequisite of the educated man.

Before leaving for France, he may have designed, in 1664, the storehouse of the Tower of London, although documentation is missing, and did discuss a plan for the quadrangle at Trinity College, Oxford. On his re-

45

turn from his only trip abroad, Wren designed the chapel and gallery of Emmanuel College, Cambridge, and undertook the renewal of the restoration of old St. Paul's, a project started by England's great architect Inigo Jones, who died in 1652.

Jones had traveled extensively in Italy, where he was much influenced by the work of the Renaissance architect Palladio and by the theories of his inspirator Vitruvius of the last century B.C. and the first century A.D. Consequently the alterations of and additions to the old cathedral, as specified by Jones, were Renaissance in concept. One hundred thousand pounds had been awarded to him for modernization of the old St. Paul's, long in a state of disrepair.

Wren, honoring the work of Jones, as he did not always thereafter, intended to follow many of the precursor's plans. A notable exception was to be the addition of a large dome to replace the cathedral's steeple, destroyed a century earlier. Wren's plans, submitted for approval to the committee for restoration of the old St. Paul's on August 27, 1666, were never to be implemented.

London burned on September 2, 1666. The old cathedral, like many another landmark, was ruined in the holocaust.

Five plans for the rebuilding of London were presented within two days after the fire, the first being Wren's. He proposed a grid of rectangles arranged to incorporate the major buildings that were not seriously damaged and in several cases were not subject to relocation. New structures, including churches, were set on Wren's plan with geometric precision. Contemporary adherents hailed Wren as a master of town planning, and even in the early twentieth century, the map of his proposal for post-fire London was offered as proof of his genius as pioneer city planner and innovator of urban development.

Although Wren's plan was not accepted, he was commissioned to rebuild the city's churches, an assignment that was to last twenty years. By 1688, Wren had designed fifty-two parish churches and, as a separate project, the cathedral that was not completed until well into the eighteenth century. The rebuilding of London did not go according to the accepted proposal of Robert Hooke, the scientist and inventor, then city surveyor, nor did it follow all of those made by Charles II. The monarch urged the widening of streets to prevent such spread of flames as had all but leveled the city, and the denying of Thames River locations to industry, "those trades" responsible for waterfront smoke and noxious odors. Some thoroughfares were widened and certain narrow lanes were done away with, but there appeared no broad, straight avenues that would have facilitated traffic and beautified London. The citizenry, impatient to return to normalcy, pushed for immediate and even makeshift construction of homes and churches, shops

47

and factories, public houses, livery stables and other service centers.

Wren, relieved of the necessity to restore the old St. Paul's, suggested a temporary structure for worship until such time as a replacement could be commenced. A little over a year after the fire, the collapse of a hastily repaired section of the old cathedral's ruins that some had thought to be salvageable convinced everyone of the need for a brand-new diocesan church.

Crown, clergy, and commissioners agreed on Wren as architect for a new St. Paul's. In the summer of 1668, a royal warrant was issued for the specific demolition of walls and other ruins of the cathedral to prepare for new construction "neare or upon the old foundations." Then began seven years of travail and frustration for Wren. Before the laying of the cornerstone of the cathedral, he revised several designs and their variations, and submitted at least two models that were not approved. Through that period nothing about the project was free from complication but the budget.

In January 1670, Wren, by then surveyor general of the royal works, was paid a hundred guineas for one cathedral design, and in May, the Parliament voted a coal tax that was to cover expenses for ensuing years. More than three decades earlier, Inigo Jones, observing that the smoke of London was affecting the stone of the cathedral, suggested a coal tax as only proper for use in the restoration of the ancient building. The coal tax of 1670 was allotted at one-quarter for the building of

St. Paul's and three-quarters for parish churches, where Wren occasionally did encounter budgetary problems.

The design for Wren's Great Model, now in St. Paul's, marked a revolutionary departure from the conventional. The building he envisioned was in the form of a Greek Cross with certain modifications. A circular center offered a spaciousness and grandeur pleasing to Charles II but not to the cathedral's dean and canons. They insisted on having a cathedral with nave, crossing, transept, and choir, or in other words, the traditional medieval style suitable for religious processions.

Similarities in the Great Model to the earliest buildings by Wren indicated his individuality as architect and the consistency with which he approached design. In the Great Model, there were again the rectangular windows with rounded tops, as in Pembroke Chapel and the Sheldonian Theatre. The same self-assurance about his work was evidenced later when, already renowned for his church spires, he interchanged steeple designs at will. A notable example was the shifting of both steeple and tower of a design for St. Edmund, Bloomsbury, to the church of St. Peter's, Cornhill, when that building was nearing completion.

It was characteristic of Wren that he never wasted an idea or a design. Every creative conception was filed, at least in his mind, for use at another time on some other building. Distinguishing features of his work could be traced, however altered, from structure to structure, and those recurrences in part accounted for mistaken

49

attributions after other British architects fell under Wren's influence.

He not only borrowed from himself and from Inigo Jones when preparing the approved plan for St. Paul's, but also he had to include chapels insisted on by the Duke of York. The design shaped in a Latin cross to placate church officials received a royal warrant in mid-May, 1675.

On paper, the building lacked the originality of the Great Model, and little resembled the cathedral as completed in 1711. The warrant permitted Wren considerable leeway for modifications that he continued to make for more than a quarter of a century, although by no means always getting his own way about changes. Some of his decisions were made when construction was well advanced, and in the final stage, he was forced to make concessions to the cathedral committee.

If early on Wren made detailed sketches of various parts of the cathedral, he kept his counsel. Having learned his lesson from criticism of previous designs presented *in toto,* he revealed the St. Paul plans, area by area, ordering models in sections and only as needed.

Had Wren known from the beginning how weighty the cathedral eventually was to be, he might have had second thoughts about the composition of its piers and walls. Made of Portland cement casing filled with rubble, they settled prematurely on shifting earth and had to be continually reinforced for years before the heavy dome was even designed.

A considerable part of the choir was already built by the time the last of the ruins was cleared away. The whole cathedral on the site was to be 64,000 square feet in area, and 463 feet in length, including the apse. The chapels, "forced on" Wren by the Duke of York, projected on the outside and opened into a square bay at the west. The crossing was sufficiently vast to hold enormous numbers of people, congregations large by any standards. The springing of the twenty-six-foot arches gave the first indication that the piers were not strong enough to support the building as planned. Moreover, certain components, as built, were thicker, and so heavier, than Wren intended.

At its exterior top, the cathedral was markedly at variance with the Great Model. It had featured a squat dome below a large lantern supporting another dome, slightly tapered, above which rose a six-stage spire. That superstructure had none of the felicity recognized as Wren's signature in various spires, already designed, one of the most beautiful and now famous being on the church of St. Mary-le-Bow, Cheapside.

The cathedral's eventual triple dome, ever since extolled, was not finally planned until 1702. It consisted of a brick cone, with supporting chains, an inner dome and the outer. It had been Wren's intention to cover the 138-foot dome with copper, but the committee was adamant that the material be lead. Wren wanted the dome's interior to be either coffered or lined with mosaics; his preference is not historically certain. The committee unequivocally ordered figure-painting decorations, and when choosing the artist, opted for Sir James Thornhill rather than Wren's supposed choice, the Italian Pellegrini.

The choir of St. Paul's was consecrated in 1697 and the entire structure, complete with dome, lantern, and west towers was finished in 1711. The completion of the "greatest church in Christendom" in no more than thirty-five years was a remarkable accomplishment made possible by the architect. Wren meanwhile had completed most of his other major works, in all, 116 buildings. Yet to come was the restoration of Westminster Abbey's north transept.

Inconsistency of design was anathema to Wren. When commissioned to restore the old St. Paul's, he observed that since "we cannot mend this great Ruine, we will not disfigure it." For Westminster Abbey, he designed in "a Style with the rest of the Structure, which I would strictly adhere to throughout the whole Intention." He held that "to deviate from the whole form would be to run into a disagreeable Mixture, which no person of a good taste would relish." His plan for the north transept restoration were "such as I conceive may agree with the original Scheme of the old Architect, without any modern mixtures to show my own Inventions . . ."

The style was Gothic quite unlike original concepts of his own inventions, then ultramodern. Wren was well past eighty when approval was given to Westminster Abbey's north transept design, but he followed the "original Scheme" with the flexibility and enthusiasm of an eager young architect whose reputation was not yet established.

Four decades earlier, Wren had originated a structure in Gothic style and for the same reason that he used it at Westminster Abbey. His gate tower for the unfinished quadrangle of Christ Church, Oxford, was Gothic because he "resolued [sic] it ought to be Gothick to agree with the Founders worke . . ." Tom Tower, as the dominant structure of the quadrangle was called, harmonized with other buildings of the college but was distinctly Wren in its resemblance to his tower of the Church of St. Antholin, c. 1677.

Although himself an astronomer, Wren resisted a suggestion by the dean of Christ Church College that Tom Tower be topped by an astronomical observatory. In a letter to the dean, the architect explained in detail why a rounded top, or dome, would be inconsistent with the Gothic style characterized by spires and pyramidal effects. He would not revise his design to include an observatory because, as he wrote, "I feare wee shall make an unhandsome medly that way."

No such conflict of architectural styles affected his work on the Greenwich Observatory, for which a warrant was issued in June 1675, almost immediately after the one for St. Paul's. The Thames River site for the observatory was in London's Greenwich borough and placement was on the prime meridian. Geographic longitude calculated at the location became the basis for worldwide standard time. As astronomer, Wren knew exactly how to plan for the functional purposes of the observatory's central room, an octagon, and its two domes. As architect, he added to the beauty of the exterior with the use of scrolled buttresses, for which he had a predilection, and the addition of charming little domed pavilions, complementary to the two domes of the main building. Availability of materials from a demolished palace facilitated construction, which was completed in little more than a year.

It took nine years, 1948–1957, to relocate the Greenwich Observatory in this century. The move to Sussex from the borough on the Thames was necessitated by industrial contamination of London's atmosphere.

Almost twenty years after the issuance of the warrant for the Greenwich Observatory, Wren became associated, as treasurer and surveyor, with the Greenwich Hospital. He submitted several designs over a period of years but the building, unlike St. Paul's, was not his alone. Greenwich Hospital, completed after Wren's death, was a major collaborative undertaking and only fragments and suggestions of his designs are discernible.

His first and finest design for the hospital was the more remarkable because, had it been approved, the Queen's House, built by Inigo Jones, would have had to have been razed. Previously Wren had been respectful of the work of Jones even to the point of adapting some designs and often preserving others. Specifically

54

Wren's first design for the Greenwich Hospital was rejected because Queen Mary would not countenance the demolition of the charming little palace, the Queen's House, by Jones.

Wren's work was well known to Queen Mary, Mary II of England, joint ruler with her cousin and husband, William of Orange, William II. For the two monarchs, the architect had made designs for three palaces, Whitehall, Hampton Court, and Kensington where, after its remodeling by Wren, William of Orange stayed when in London.

Following a second disastrous fire that swept Whitehall, its rebuilding was assigned to Wren, who had been knighted in the previous decade. A diarist, Narcissus Luttrell, wrote that "Sir Christopher Wren has taken a survey of the ruins of Whitehall and measured the ground, in order to rebuild the same: his Majesty designs to make it a noble Palace . . ." For some reason, perhaps the disinterest of William of Orange, the ambitious project was never started and only a dozen of Wren's sketches survive. But once again, Wren intended to tamper with an Inigo Jones building, Whitehall's Banqueting House, left intact by the fires. The elaborate plans for rebuilding would have doubled the size of the Banqueting House, while reducing the effectiveness of the design by Jones.

Major demolition of Hampton Court to make way for his building was in Wren's original plan, and in that instance, the monarchs apparently did not protest the proposed destruction. However, a totally new palace was never realized, probably due to the death of Queen Mary, 1894. The limited work of Wren at Hampton Court marked his first design of brick walls with stone quoins for a massive structure. On a smaller scale, both Jones and Wren had used the brick construction that was to have its prime vogue in Georgian architecture.

Wren designed a new tower, c. 1715, for St. Michael, Cornhill, one of his early churches, commissioned in 1669. By the time the new tower for St. Michael was finished, Sir Christopher, a victim of court intrigue, had been dismissed, 1718, as surveyor general after half a century of service under five sovereigns. During the last years of his life, Wren was aware of open criticism of his works in certain London circles. He must also have known that, throughout England and on the Continent, he was receiving profuse praise for St. Paul's with its extraordinary tower, for a dozen of his city churches, for the Library at Trinity College, Cambridge, and other secular buildings—indeed for all the major works, his personal monuments.

To the end, Sir Christopher remained a revered member of the Royal Society. When not yet thirty, he had been a founding member of that august body which he served as vice-president, 1674, and president, 1681, for a two-year term. In the charter, he was listed as a medical doctor, and an extension of medical research he had done at Oxford was later carried forward at the Royal Society.

The Society wanted Wren to be its president again in 1693 but, although only in his early sixties, he declined because of his "age and infirmities." What precisely was wrong with Wren's health that it served as an excuse throughout his life is another imponderable. Nothing is more definite than one reference to him as a "delicate man," and another hint that he might have been consumptive as a child. Whatever his physical problem in 1693, it must have been minor because he was then working concentratedly on designs for St. Paul's and other buildings, and the following year accepted the Greenwich Hospital commission. Sir Christopher's stamina may have had its limitations, but not his mind, which was alert until 1723 when he died at the age of 91.

St. Paul's Cathedral was severely damaged by air-raid bombing during World War II, and its rebuilding, according to Sir Christopher Wren's plan, was completed in 1962.

Early in 1971, officials of St. Paul's ominously opened a fund-raising campaign for seven million dollars needed to repair the cathedral. Restoration was essential in one section because the material Sir Christopher used was three parts lime to one of sand, which is exactly the reverse proportions recommended in the twentieth century. But elsewhere the three-hundred-year-old building, decrepit and bomb shaken, is deteriorating from the effects of London's fog, smog, and smoke. Like the Parthenon, St. Paul's Cathedral is threatened by a contemporary hazard: air pollution.

A city planner made maximum use
of available land when designing
the capital of the United States.

PIERRE CHARLES L'ENFANT, 1754–1825

CHERRY trees that once a year riotously blossom along the Tidal Basin in Washington, D.C., would have delighted the designer of the city, Pierre Charles L'Enfant. Although he was responsible for planning neither the Tidal Basin nor the monuments to great Americans mirrored in it, L'Enfant was a proponent of "far-distant points of view" and of water enhancements for well-planted landscapes.

Gardens, a waterfall, and numerous impressive vistas for the permanent capital of the United States were described in a report, dated June 22, 1791, that L'Enfant presented to President George Washington. The Parisian designer of the federal city thought in large-scale terms, emphasizing his ideas by frequent repetitions of the adjective *grand*. L'Enfant specifically mentioned a grand locale, a grand navigation canal, a grand and majestic avenue, and future grand improvements of the city.

Not all of his grandiose plans were to be realized, but L'Enfant's master design is discernible in much that is imposing about present-day Washington. His inspiration can be traced to his native France where formal gardens, built for royalty, were in every way large scale: outsized terraces, reflection pools, and fountains complemented huge palaces. Avenues were broad and vistas long. Extensive woodlands balanced proportionate wide-open spaces.

The influence of French landscape architecture on L'Enfant was manifest by his bold and imaginative adaptation of its best features for his federal city plan. Although unschooled as city planner, engineer, and architect, L'Enfant undertook projects requiring the respective skills of those professionals. Self-assured to the point of arrogance, he was not the least deterred by his lack of qualifications for positions he sought in the United States or for commissions he accepted. He was, however, trained in the graphic arts and well qualified to draw portraits of fellow officers in the Continental army of which he was a volunteer.

In the fall of 1771, Pierre Charles entered the Académie Royale de Peinture et de Sculpture in Paris. He studied there with his own father, Pierre L'Enfant, a painter and designer of Gobelin tapestry. The elder L'Enfant depicted countryside panoramas and battle-front scenes, done in the field. From his father, Pierre Charles learned the technique of expansive representations and to draw military fortifications, a practice that later benefited him in the United States.

When George Washington made his decision about the designer for the federal city, he had known Pierre Charles L'Enfant for more than a decade. Washington was aware of L'Enfant's war record; his reputation as "artist of the American Revolution"; his designs for several medals; his plans for the hall to house a major fete, and the reviewing stand for a political parade; and his success as architect in New York in the immediate postwar years. Washington's own inauguration took place in a New York building reconstructed on architecural plans made by L'Enfant.

L'Enfant, made a captain in the Corps of Engineers in 1778, was frequently at the Valley Forge headquarters of General Lafayette and made for him a pencil sketch of George Washington. After Valley Forge, L'Enfant was stationed in Philadelphia before moving south with the troops. He took part in the siege of Savannah, Georgia, where he was wounded. Later, at a date not authenticated, he was with the Continental forces on the Hudson River. His drawing of the army's encampment is at West Point.

In a long letter to General Washington written in February 1782, L'Enfant requested a promotion. He cited the prior advancements of others and stressed his own dedication as an officer who "sought to distinguish myself by love for the Service." He was promoted to brevet major in 1783 and retired from the army with that rank.

The spring following his petition for promotion, L'Enfant, with General Washington's sanction, designed a Philadelphia hall to accommodate more than a thousand celebrants of the birth of the dauphin of France. The hall, open-sided like an enormous pavilion, was surrounded by temporary greenery strung with lamps to illumine the scene at night. Honored guests at the fete included General Washington and the Comte de Rochambeau, hero of Yorktown, the engagement that ended the American Revolution.

Shortly after the Philadelphia festival, George Washington established the Badge of Military Merit which in his bicentennial year, 1932, became the Order of the Purple Heart. The decoration ordered by Washington was not specifically for the wounded but included all men of valor and "extraordinary fidelity" in both war and peace. L'Enfant is generally credited with the design of the Badge of Military Merit, a purple heart made of fabric and variously trimmed with contrasting binding.

There is no question that L'Enfant designed both the medal and order for the Society of Cincinnati, to which Revolutionary War officers and their male descendants were eligible. At an organizational meeting held in June 1783, Washington was elected President-General of the Society, and by letter, L'Enfant submitted medal designs he had been asked to make. The Society adopted his design of a bald eagle "which is peculiar to this continent," with emblems on its breast, and approved the same motif for the parchment certificate of membership.

L'Enfant was dispatched to Paris to see to the striking of the medals in silver; to present honorary memberships to French officers who had served in the Revolution, and to organize a branch of the Society in France. In a bon voyage letter to L'Enfant, Washington enclosed two hundred and fifty dollars for "eight of the bald eagles." L'Enfant returned to the United States in April 1784, and was reimbursed to the amount of $1,548 he personally spent in France. His expenditures were for silversmith creditors and for his own keep which "produced expenses far beyond the sum I had first thought of." That was not the last time L'Enfant was to solicit for money due, by his reckoning.

In post-Revolution New York, L'Enfant was a sought-after and popular architect. During 1787, he built an academy in Flatbush and a house in Brooklyn while, at the same time, his embellishments were being added to St. Paul's Chapel, a building dedicated in 1766. Over a period of years, L'Enfant was architect for dozens of houses in town and country, including the residence that, later enlarged, was to be Gracie Mansion, official home of New York's mayors. He designed the home of Duncan Phyfe and also was associated as decorator with that cabinetmaker who was to become world-famous.

Three days before New York ratified the Constitution to become the eleventh state on July 26, 1788, a parade celebrating the newly formed republic was held in the city. L'Enfant, director of the event, designed the dome that sheltered Washington and other dignitaries. In the parade's line of march were uniformed men, including members of the Society of Cincinnati in full regalia; bands; floats, several bearing workers engaged in their respective trades; a frigate model named the *Hamilton;* and Christopher Columbus on horseback. L'Enfant's dramatically staged procession was greeted by cheering crowds.

Later that year, L'Enfant was commissioned to do a major rebuilding of New York's old City Hall which, as Federal Hall, was turned over to the "New Government." The elegantly remodeled building was extolled by a visiting Boston architect who wrote, "We cannot close our description without observing that great praise is due to Major L'Enfant, the architect, who has surmounted many difficulties, and has so accommodated the additions to the old parts, and so judiciously altered what he saw wrong, that he has produced a building uniform and consistent throughout . . ." Federal Hall elsewhere was described as being "on the whole superior to any building in America."

Among the "many difficulties" encountered by L'Enfant were disagreements with the contractor, who did unsatisfactory work under pressure of the time schedule necessitated by the inauguration of 1789. In 1790 Congress moved to Philadelphia, and the hall, federal in name only, served other purposes until, in the early 1800s, it was demolished because of its faulty construction.

L'Enfant, originally offered ten city acres for his work, turned down the land fee as inadequate. He also declined $750 voted to him in 1801, and in 1820 petitioned for compensation. At that time, thirty years after the commission, disinterested authorities refused to consider his request. L'Enfant never was paid for building handsome Federal Hall, in which George Washington was inaugurated as first president of the United States, April 30, 1789.

In September 1789, President Washington received a letter from Major L'Enfant asking that he might design the capital city of "this vast empire," wherever it might be. The site for the headquarters of the federal government was not yet settled, but the president was in no doubt that L'Enfant was capable of carrying out his promised plan. It was to be "on such a scale as to leave room for that aggrandisement & embellishment which the increase of the wealth of the Nation will permit it to pursue in any period however remote . . ."

The residence Act of July 16, 1790, established the site of the federal city on the banks of the Potomac River. The area was confined to ten square miles, most of the land being ceded by the State of Maryland and the rest by Virginia. President Washington made the final decision about the location and was personally responsible for the acquisition of property from individual owners.

In January 1791, the President chose three federal commissioners who ultimately designated the capital as Washington and the territory as Columbia. They also made the decision to name the city's streets by letters and numbers. Washington's appointee for a survey, Andrew Ellicott, began his boundary measurements in February 1791, and in March, L'Enfant started his design of the city.

When making final arrangements with the landowners, Washington had a lengthy recommendation from L'Enfant, and from Thomas Jefferson, Secretary of State, a memorandum with a small rough sketch of the proposed city. Jefferson's plan for the ten-square-mile limit had streets at right angles like those in Philadelphia. He suggested, however, that the federal city's houses should not be equidistant, a regularity that produced "disgusting monotony." It was Jefferson's idea that no house should be built of wood and, while distance between houses was to be optional, a "limit on height be set."

L'Enfant thought square blocks bound by parallel and uniform streets, as in Jefferson's plan, made for a "tiresome and insipid" pattern. But he and Jefferson agreed about the importance of parks and other open areas. Spaciousness was in part achieved by L'Enfant's very wide roadways that displeased landowners when they saw his plan. At their meeting with President Washington, landholders agreed to the price of just under sixty-seven dollars an acre for land needed by the government and to donate property for streets. In the official agreement, signed March 30, 1791, the remainder of the area was to be divided into lots for sale, with proceeds from every other one going to the government.

The land acquired for the capital mushroomed from a narrow stem between the Potomac River and Eastern Branch, now the Anacostia River. It was L'Enfant's intention to make use of Tiber Creek flowing through the town and to provide for a commercial canal because he and others fully expected the capital to be a flourishing port. The only height within the city boundary was Jenkins Hill at eighty feet above sea level, and L'Enfant chose that prominence, now Capitol Hill, as the site for the "congressional building."

His plan, as has been noted, reflected his own familiarity with the large-scale dimensions of French landscape architecture. In addition, he had at hand detailed maps of a dozen European cities, requested from Jefferson, who had collected them while Minister to France. Whatever L'Enfant's reference sources, his originality warrants recognition, particularly for his imaginative use of available land.

Soon after his arrival at the federal city site, L'Enfant wrote to Jefferson describing the area "most advantageous to run streets and prolong them on grand and far-distant points of view." His grid was a rectangular system of long and short blocks and right-angle streets, north-south and east-west, which other crisscross roadways "to and from every principal place." The purpose of the radial avenues was to make the "real distance less from place to place" while at the same time establishing a reciprocity of sight from any three streets meeting at a single point.

A considerable number of L'Enfant's vistas were destroyed by underpasses built in the nation's capital to accommodate twentieth-century automobile traffic. Previous tree planting had considerably restricted the "far-distant points of view."

The sizes of L'Enfant's large squares and smaller centers were proportionate to the number of streets converging on them. He suggested that in certain squares, allotted to the states of the new nation, there should be raised "Statues, Columns, Obelisks, or any other ornaments." He placed the squares to be "most advantageously and reciprocally seen from each other," and expected their neighborhoods soon to "be connected." His ideal for normal urban development was not to be realized for many years because residential sections became separate self-sustaining communities.

Vistas and parks in mind, L'Enfant designed a triangle with the president's palace (the White House) and the congressional building (the Capitol) at two points connected by what is now Pennsylvania Avenue. The vista of his plan is somewhat blocked by the Treasury

Building. L'Enfant designated the third point of his triangle as "proper for to erect a grand Equestrian figure," such a statue of Washington having been voted in 1783. The equestrian figure never materialized, and the present Washington Monument, an obelisk just over 555 feet high, is a hundred yards from L'Enfant's triangle point.

He planned a "grand and majestic avenue" that was to be about a mile long and 400 feet wide to connect the garden of the Congress with the park of the President. That tremendous roadway, with its vistas, was to "bordered with gardens, ending in a slope from the houses on each side." The famous Mall of present-day Washington replaces his avenue but provides impressive vistas of memorials and public buildings, gardens and parks, all typical of the city's original design.

East of his congressional building, L'Enfant envisioned an arcade of stores, forerunner of the modern shopping center. One of the radial avenues of his plaza is blocked by the Library of Congress. Another is dominated by the Supreme Court Building. He had located the Supreme Court at one of his largest cross axes, now Judiciary Square.

At Jenkins Hill, he proposed to harness the headwaters of Tiber Creek into a grand cascade forty feet high and more than one hundred feet wide. The water was then to fill the proposed canal, finally emptying into the Potomac. Only a short section of the canal was ever built because the capital did not develop into a maritime port. Where the original plan indicated an extensive public market on the canal, the National Archives Building, completed in 1935, now stands. Powerful pumps, electrically operated, protect its foundations from erosion by Tiber Creek, running underground.

The master plan of the federal city was shown to the President at Mount Vernon on June 22, 1791. A few days later, he presented the general proposal to the landholders who were taken aback by the number of acres they were to give for roadways. They questioned the necessity for streets 100 to 110 feet wide; for one broad avenue 400 feet wide, and others uniformly 160 feet wide. The appropriately designated broad avenues were to have ten feet of pavement on each side, thirty feet of gravel walk with trees on each side, and eighty feet in the middle for horse-drawn vehicles.

Of the 6111 acres encompassed by the city boundary, 3606 acres were for roadways; 541 acres for the government, and the remaining 1964 acres for partition into 20,272 city lots. By prior agreement, profits from the sale of lots were to be equally divided by landowners and the government. In spite of their immediate objection to the number of acres to be donated, the proprietors quickly capitulated and signed over the required land.

L'Enfant very much disapproved of selling the city lots at public sale that year, and made clear his ob-

jections to the President. The designer thought the land
would bring higher prices at a later date when the plan
was known to the "whole continent." He warned that
the sale might not be a success, and feared that those
who bought might be speculators uninterested in im-
proving the lots. L'Enfant could not tolerate the prospect of having his design ruined by the construction of
inferior structures at prime locations. He advised float-
ing a million-dollar loan as the alternative to selling
off lots to finance the government's buildings. His suggestion of borrowing money for implementing the project was not acceptable, and the date for the sale was
set for October 17, 1791.

As far as was known, L'Enfant had previously been
amiable and cooperative with clients, and had never been
autocratic about his work. He had not been blamed for
the arguments with the contractor of Federal Hall, and
the disastrous consequence of the resultant poor construction had not yet come to light. But, by the time
the lot sale took place in the capital, L'Enfant was being
difficult and domineering. His relationship with all officials, including President Washington, steadily deter-
iorated for the next five months.

Well in advance of the public sale, the commissioners
requested ten thousand maps of L'Enfant's city plan for
distribution to prospective buyers. Delivery was delayed,
according to L'Enfant, because the engraver had failed
to live up to his contract. No maps were available before or during the sale which, as L'Enfant had predicted,

was unsuccessful. He was blamed for the poor results by commissioners who were annoyed by his refusal to pass around even a single copy of the plan. One commissioner wrote to Washington, explaining that the weather had been "much against us," and adding that he thought an exhibition of the general plan "would have aided the sale considerably . . ."

Washington, although conciliatory about the maps, sent word to L'Enfant that, as requested by the commissioners, he should have shown the plan at the sale, and "must in future look to the commissioners for directions." The President took much less kindly to L'Enfant's next defiance of the commissioners.

L'Enfant's work crews, on November 20, 1791, began to tear down the partially constructed manor house of Daniel Carroll of Duddington, the largest landowner within the city boundaries. His site had been chosen in 1790, and the house started in June 1791, at about the time that L'Enfant was revealing his master plan to the President. No sooner did L'Enfant realize that the Carroll mansion was to obstruct a vista and to be in the center of a projected major square than he advised the owner to demolish the structure.

Unwilling to wait for compliance, the impatient L'Enfant himself ordered the demolition over the protests of Carroll and the commissioners. They stopped the destruction in the absence of L'Enfant from the city, but on his return he issued contrary orders. Thereafter, he received a stern reprimand from President Washington, who wrote, ". . . the Commissioners stand between you and the President of the United States—they being the persons from whom alone you are to receive your directions."

Even the President could not restrain L'Enfant. On December 2, 1791, he warned another owner of a large estate that his home eventually would have to be torn down, but said a grace of seven years might be expected. There followed two months of conflict between the commissioners and L'Enfant's assistants. The designer was in Philadelphia supervising the engraving of city maps while his loyal associates, continuing with various projects, refused to meet with the commissioners.

Washington and Jefferson conferred at length about the recalcitrant designer of the city. Then, in an attempt to clarify the situation, Washington sent his private secretary to call on L'Enfant for a discussion about his relationship with the commissioners. L'Enfant said he "had already heard enough about this matter," a reply that, when repeated to the President, hurt and displeased him.

A letter of dismissal from Jefferson to L'Enfant followed, on February 27, 1792. The Secretary of State explained to L'Enfant that the President wanted to "preserve your agency in the business," but because of the repeated refusal to accept the authority of the commissioners, "your services must be at an end."

L'Enfant was thirty seven years old.

* * *

Unlikely as it may seem, L'Enfant designed the federal city without signed contract or verbal agreement about fee. In October 1791, the commissioners asked him about financial terms on a yearly basis and suggested six-hundred pounds, but he chose not to discuss money with them. At the termination of his services, he refused an offer of twenty-five hundred dollars and a city lot, and did not raise the question of adequate compensation until after the death of President Washington.

L'Enfant requested, and in December 1802 was refused, more than ninety-five thousand dollars for his services. He eventually received about three thousand dollars by vote of Congress but when final payment was made, in 1810, L'Enfant was so heavily in debt that creditors took almost the entire sum.

From Washington, L'Enfant had gone to New Jersey to design the industrial city Paterson, but financial and labor problems prevented execution of his plan. Once again, he was unable to profit from his efforts.

He was subsequently architect of a never-completed mansion for Robert Morris, Philadelphia financier, who was imprisoned for debt. In Philadelphia and New York, L'Enfant added rooms or embellishments to buildings. He designed Fort Mifflin on the Delaware River in the late 1790s and more than a decade later had some part in the redesign of Fort Washington on the Potomac. Records of that reconstruction are missing, so it is impossible to credit L'Enfant with the star-shaped design of the fortification completed in 1824.

74

By that year, L'Enfant had been destitute for about a decade and reduced to living with friends in Prince Georges County, Maryland. He died there on June 14, 1825, and was buried in a family graveyard.

During the thirty-three years following L'Enfant's dismissal from the federal city project, he saw his grand plan temporarily abandoned, and here and there debased by tumble-down houses.

A return to his plan and to general improvements of Washington were instituted in the early twentieth century by a commission named for Senator James McMillan of Michigan, chairman of the Senate's committee on District of Columbia affairs. Experts on the McMillan Commission were Daniel H. Burnham and Charles F. McKim, architects; Augustus Saint-Gaudens, sculptor, and Frederick Law Olmsted, Jr., landscape architect. The 1902 report of the members recommended a restoration of L'Enfant's plan and adaptation of it suitable to the times.

The revival of the city plan of 1791 resulted in national recognition of L'Enfant. His body was exhumed from its modest grave in the Maryand countryside, and on April 28, 1909, memorial services were held for him in the rotunda of the Capitol. In attendance were high officials of the country, including President William Howard Taft, with his wife. A military procession, with burial in Arlington National Cemetery, immediately followed. On the table tomb, dedicated in 1911, there is a carved section of the Washington plan designed by Pierre Charles L'Enfant, architect, city planner, long-neglected man . . . and his own worst enemy.

He redesigned the surface streets
of Paris, planned its sewer system,
and changed its skyline.

GEORGES EUGÈNE HAUSSMANN, 1809–1891

Paris was modernized in the nineteenth century largely through the efforts and dedication of Georges Eugène Haussmann, prefect of the Seine—in effect, mayor of the city—from 1853 until 1870. In those years, urban development, in its twentieth-century sense, became a reality with the construction of new parks, thoroughfares, sewage and water-supply systems, public buildings, and private residences. Experienced engineers and technicians were recruited by Haussmann, whose architect-associates were less competent.

For the seventeen years of his tenure as prefect, Haussmann had to employ a succession of inept architects. He was required to choose them from the École des Beaux Arts, which he sometimes openly berated for the poor caliber of its architectural training. The prefect agreed with a contemporary critic who noted that only dull buildings were erected in the new city. Even more emphatically, the same critic wrote, "Here is the wonder of the nineteenth century which perhaps no other epoch has seen: Paris and nearly all of France has been re-built without bringing forth a single architect worthy of the name."

Haussmann resignedly accepted the burden of an inferior architectural staff because, to him, structures and their design were of only secondary interest. His zeal was for the clearing out of slums, the construction of roadways, drains, and sewers, and the provision of pure water to Parisians.

Opportunity to make a modern city of Paris was presented to Haussmann the very day of his installation as prefect of the Seine. Following a celebration lunch, Napoleon III, Emperor of France, showed to the new prefect a general map of the city, indicating projected and in-progress improvements. While a political prisoner in the 1840s, Louis Napoleon Bonaparte, later emperor, had planned the future of himself and his country. For Paris, he envisioned a new city that would make him a second Augustus, "for he made Rome a city of marble."

Stone was of less interest to Louis Napoleon than parks, which, two centuries earlier, had also been of major importance to Louis XIV. In his reign, André Lenôtre had established himself as a brilliant landscape architect by designing, among others, the glorious gardens of the Tuileries and at Versailles. Lenôtre's grand-scope designs initiated the correlation of structural with landscape architecture, and depended for effect on contrived vistas.

A park, designed by Napoleon III, was on his imprecise map of Paris that incorporated, albeit sketchily, reconstruction plans drawn by a committee of artists after the 1789 revolution and actual improvements made under Napoleon I. Napoleon III had several identical copies of his map and kept one wherever he was in residence. Four crayon colors provided keys to his priorities.

No detailed map of Paris then existed and to obtain one, Haussmann added a cartography section within his department. Demolition, construction, and other work went forward during the preparation of a dependable, inclusive map. The working set, on a 1/5000 scale, was nine feet by fifteen, and Haussmann sent copies to all personnel in the modernization program. His own map, framed and set on castors, for mobility, was in his study where "Many an hour I have spent in fruitful meditation before this altar-screen."

By 1853 Haussmann had been in civil service for twenty-two years, the last five as prefect in the provinces. Born in Paris and educated there as a lawyer, he was very close to his father, a journalist, and to his paternal grandfather. The latter, in commerce before becoming a municipal and government official, may have encouraged Georges to enter the prefecture service. From his mother's family, Haussmann took the title baron, a presumption for which he was widely criticized, since titles were traditionally passed on through paternal lines.

While working his way up from his first appointment

as secretary-general to the prefecture at Poitiers, Haussmann kept in touch with Paris officialdom by post and in person. Ambitious and self-confident, he made use of friends and family to widen his acquaintanceship with influential men. Except at Poitiers where, at age twenty-two, he was more social than diligent, Haussmann concentrated on the public works of his various prefectures.

By carriage and on horseback, Haussmann traveled every main road and byway of each of his successive districts, afterwards making plans for the rebuilding of roads that, whenever possible, were straightened. And with regional engineers, he endlessly discussed water-supply problems.

In November 1851, Haussmann was appointed prefect at Bordeaux, the home city of his wife. The following October, Louis Napoleon Bonaparte, then president of France, made an official three-day visit to Bordeaux, where gala festivities were arranged by Haussmann, already known to Louis Napoleon. At a banquet the President publicly indicated his willingness to become emperor, which he did when the Second Empire was voted in by plebiscite, November 1852. In his speech at Bordeaux, October 9, 1852, Louis Napoleon had specifically outlined the public works projects necessary in France: "We have uncultivated areas to develop, roads to build, ports to construct, rivers to make navigable, our whole network of railroads to complete . . ."

The soon-to-be emperor was thinking of the whole of France, but Haussmann was totally focused on Paris and what he could do there. Only weeks before, he had turned down the position of prefect of police in Paris, an office considered to be more important than prefect of the Seine. Haussmann, when refusing the first position, explained that no one had yet fully understood the potential scope of the second, which he referred to as the mayoralty. His singlemindedness was rewarded in June 1853 by the appointment he had coveted.

Haussmann's concept of what should be done for the city was quite different from that of his emperor. Napoleon III had stated his views on the need for public works programs elsewhere in France but, for Paris, wanted changes that would be visible to all and aesthetically pleasing. Haussmann looked forward to a city rebuilt literally from its foundations.

He frequently met with official resistance to his comprehensive plans that were not all to be realized. What he did accomplish was phenomenal and not subjected to major revisions until the late 1930s. Aerial views of Paris disclose broad boulevards running in the straight lines that were Haussmann's obsessions. Close up, the houses and apartments built during the Second Empire attest to the mediocrity of the era's architects, who were Haussmann's encumbrances. Under the city are mazes of conduits and drains, and miles of sewers that were his signal achievements, masterminded through persistence.

But, in 1853, other projects took precedence over those of water supply and sewage disposal. One of the first was the replanning of the Bois de Boulogne, the only program initiated by Napoleon III. Other priorities, predating the presidency of Louis Napoleon, were the completion of the Louvre and of the Halles Centrales, the wholesale food market, and the extension of the rue de Rivoli. Without complication or delay, work proceeded on the Louvre, which was completed and officially dedicated in August 1857.

The Halles Centrales, familiarly known as Les Halles, was another matter. It was ultimately built on architectural plans originally drawn by two amateurs: Napoleon III and Haussmann. The emperor, having ordered that work be stopped on a well-advanced market building, personally rough-sketched an umbrella-shaped substitute. He specified a structure made entirely of iron instead of stone, the material of the partially completed market.

After seeing the emperor's plan, Haussmann, as the first order of business, mapped a suitable access street for the market. He then adapted the royal sketch before assigning a staff architect to do the blueprints. A couple of preliminary designs were discarded before Haussmann permitted construction of a scale model that Napoleon III enthusiastically approved. Property needed for the market was obtained at such inflationary prices that nearly twenty million francs, or two-thirds of the total cost of the whole market, were spent on expropriation.

For nearly a century the market was an attraction not

only for Parisians but for tourists drawn to Paris, following the city's beautification in the period of the Second Empire. But with passing years the market area became overcrowded, its traffic snarled, and the streets rat-infested. In 1969 the wholesale market was moved to an area near Orly airport. A modernization project of the mid-nineteenth century, Les Halles was a victim of twentieth-century population growth, automobile production, and enforcement of public health laws.

The extension of the rue de Rivoli became part of Haussmann's master plan for facilitating traffic movement within the city and at its perimeter. He made the rue de Rivoli a major transverse street, running east-west, and established a north-south route, the boulevard de Strasbourg-Sébastopol. By their crossing, the two thoroughfares quartered Paris and long served as fast routes to suburbs under development.

Although the grand crossing was an acclaimed success, Haussmann met resistance to and criticism of several road proposals. He had to justify, to citizens and officials, each separate plan for rerouting and widening streets, and for building new ones.

He boldly doubled the width of most streets, built seventy-one miles of new ones, had four hundred sidewalks laid, and ordered the planting of fifty thousand trees to beautify boulevards and to shade side streets. He closed off a few streets, impassable to carriages and wagons, that were previously no more than walkways for pedestrians and passageways for tandem-borne sedan chairs, the jinrikishas of Europe.

The center of Paris was made accessible by streets from the several railways on the outskirts, and by radial highways from outlying industrial areas. No longer able to support crosstown traffic, an inner ring of boulevards was improved and a new outer ring constructed.

None of the great intersections, *places-carrefours,* designed by Haussmann was more challenging than the place de l'Étoile. When he faced its problems, old streets converged on the location any which way, and new streets traced on the emperor's general map of Paris were obviously inadequate for the inevitable increase of through-traffic. Extant and proposed streets numbered seven, irregularly placed.

The prefect added radial roadways to achieve regularity, as of wheel spokes, with the Étoile as the hub. He balanced opposite streets and built an ingenious side street to draw traffic away from the Étoile. That street, the rue de Tilsitt-Presbourg, which circled at the back of houses overlooking the Étoile, was for the passage and parking of private carriages.

As Haussmann expected, the rue de Tilsitt, funneling neighborhood traffic from the Étoile, perfectly served its purpose. But an auxiliary plan did not come off so well. He foresaw on the rue de Tilsitt a symmetrical row of houses, precursors to twentieth-century townhouse complexes. The houses, uniform in appearance

Portrait head of Phidias (?)
from the Strangford Shield

British Museum

The Parthenon (center) on the ancient Acropolis, Athens, Greece

Greek National Tourist Office

Brunelleschi's Dome on the cathedral in Florence, Italy

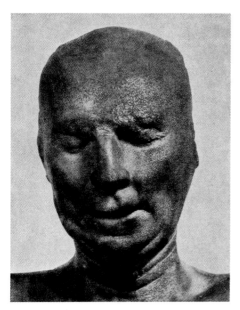

Death mask of Filippo Brunelleschi by Andrea Cavalcanti

Sir Christopher Wren

National Portrait Gallery, London

Saint Paul's Cathedral, London

Major Pierre Charles L'Enfant

Aerial View of Washington, D.C., 1930

Paris, France, with surface streets redesigned by Haussmann

Baron Georges Eugène Haussmann, with his daughter Valentine

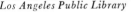

Stanford White

LEFT: Madison Square Garden, designed by Mc-Kim, Mead and White, and completed in 1890

BELOW: Annie Pfeiffer Chapel, designed by Frank Lloyd Wright, on the campus of Florida Southern College, Lakeland

News Bureau, Florida Southern College

United Press International
Frank Lloyd Wright

United Press International
Le Corbusier

The Marseilles Block designed by Le Corbusier

United Press International

Doxiadis Associates,
Athens, Greece

Charles Center-Inner Harbor Management, Inc.

ABOVE RIGHT: Ludwig Mies van der Rohe

ABOVE: One Charles Center, Baltimore, Maryland, designed by Mies van der Rohe

RIGHT: Constantinos A. Doxiadis

Ecumenopolis in the World, 2060

Doxiadis Associates, Athens, Greece

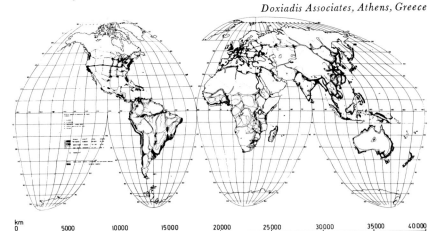

from eaves to foundation, were to have, at street level, identical grilles and small gardens. In theory, the concept was effective and pleasing, but as executed, the architect's design so upset Haussmann that he had trees planted to conceal the row of houses.

The Étoile, opened to a free flow of traffic, was only one of several similar intersection centers planned by Haussmann. It was a prime example of his grasp of immediate needs, his vision of future development, and his sensitivity to well-ordered perspective.

Like Lenôtre, Haussmann related buildings to their natural settings. He arbitrarily positioned buildings where they would dominate their sites, and deliberately aligned boulevards with impressive landmarks. For example, the spire of Sainte Chapelle, on the Île de la Cité, was the point of perspective for the boulevard St. Michel, and the dome of the Tribunal de Commerce for the boulevard de Strasbourg-Sebastopol.

Haussmann wanted the pont de Sully to be slanted across the Île de St. Louis so the two boulevards linked by the bridge would be in a straight line that afforded a view of the column of the Bastille at one end and of the Pantheon at the other. Napoleon III was adamant that every bridge had to be at right angles with its river banks. Rather than give in, Haussmann postponed the project. The bridge was built, according to his plan, in 1874, when he was no longer in office and Napoleon III was dead. But during Haussmann's administration, four conventionally placed bridges were built and then, rebuilt.

In spite of the disagreement over the pont de Sully, Haussmann's proposed changes in the configuration of Paris were generally more acceptable to Napoleon III than to most citizens and to many officials of state and city. The emperor was a reasonable man, more often than not amenable to a revision of plans, to a new idea. Albeit with regret, he even permitted alterations in his own design for updating the Bois de Boulogne, first laid out in 1679. When President of France, Louis Napoleon described the Bois as he wanted it to be, arranged for financing of the work, and assigned a family gardener to supervise it. At that time, the eleven-hundred-acre park was a shambles. More than once it had been a bivouac for the military and following the February Revolution of 1848, had been overrun by untrained lawn crews. More than a thousand unemployed Parisians, hired to work in the park, did no more than weed and water, the only gardening of which they were capable. There was little drainage, no organized planting, and a lack of perspective from straight paths radiating from only two focal points.

The emperor saw the Bois de Boulogne as a showplace with flower gardens, an expanse of greensward, bridle paths, carriage drives, a serpentine for strollers, and a river flowing between two vehicular and pedestrian traffic circles. He planned it as a recreation area

86

similar to London's Hyde Park, which he had much admired while exiled in England.

Recognizing the emperor's design as impractical, Haussmann ordered a survey of park land and water sources. An engineer, confirming the artificial river as not feasible, designed two lakes, at different levels, connected by a waterfall. Meandering roads replaced the straight ones, and an irrigation system provided water for grass, shrubs, and trees, expertly thinned to open up vistas.

The Bois was extended to the Seine and a barren area became the famous Longchamps racecourse. Haussmann, who by his own admission could take or leave park projects, gave the emperor the Bois of his dreams, and several other parks. One biographer of Haussmann has called them the "English whimsies" of Napoleon III. The Bois de Vincennes, the emperor's park for the poor of Paris, cost four times as much as the Bois de Boulogne, or so Haussmann stated in his *Memoires.*

The *Memoires,* in several volumes, were written late in Haussmann's life, primarily to define his achievements as prefect of the Seine, but the comprehensive details suggest that he long kept a daily diary. He had complete geologic, geographic, economic, and sociologic records of every provincial prefecture in which he served. His accounts and statistics of the Paris projects are today invaluable because many official documents were burned during the political upheaval of 1871.

*　　*　　*

The demolition for which Haussmann was most criticized was on the Île de la Cité where he had three-quarters of the medieval houses razed. Their sites provided space for official buildings, including the Palais de Justice, the Tribunal de Commerce, and a complex for the prefecture of police.

In order to extend the rue de Rivoli, Haussmann had the temerity to clear out a congested area that Napoleon I, for fear of public censure, had hesitated to demolish. The predictable outcry that restrained Napoleon Bonaparte rose in the city as soon as Haussmann's work crews moved into the unsightly neighborhood. Dilapidated warrens, occupied by the uncomplaining poor, political malcontents, and undesirables of both sexes, lined narrow streets, easy to barricade against police or soldiers.

To Haussmann, his slum clearance was as much a matter of social reform as of redevelopment. He wrote of the "shameful mass of low cabarets that used to dishonor the Cité, and which I later had the pleasure of razing to the ground—hideouts of thieves and assassins who seemed to defy justice and the police." The prefect brought about only impermanent social reform by chasing denizens from the slums. The criminal element, returning to the city, settled in Belleville and Montmartre, along with thousands of workers who, attracted to Paris by job offers, stayed on as potential revolutionaries.

The more lasting results of Haussmann's destruction

of the slums was the construction of the place du Carrousel. To open garden space between the Louvre and the Tuileries, Napoleon I had wanted to lay waste to the crowded hovels, but did not dare. Haussmann dramatically claimed that "Since my youth the broken-down state of the place du Carrousel, in front of the court of the Tuileries, seemed a shame to France, an admission of impotence on the part of her Government, and it stuck in my throat."

Permitting no sentiment to interfere with his plans, Haussmann did not hesitate to demolish historic buildings. He even ordered the destruction of his birthplace on the rue Faubourg le Roule. That house and others were sacrificed for a broad avenue, none other than the boulevard Haussmann. In all fairness, Haussmann's record shows that he would have been insouciant had the street carried another name. In his administration, 27,-500 houses were torn down, and 102,500 raised or restored. Several hospitals were enlarged, one new one was designed and constructed. Also built were fifteen houses of worship; buildings for business, recreation, and the military; three secondary schools; dozens of elementary schools, and numerous nursing homes.

Paris was a growing city. Its population of 1,200,000 in 1853 spurted in 1859, and at 1,700,000 in the early 1860s, was still on the increase.

The necessity for an adequate water supply for such numbers of people was patent to Haussmann. Statistics of the Paris water board informed him that, as of 1850, one house in five had piped water and less than a hundred and fifty residences had running water above the first floor. The daily supply available was 112,000 cubic meters.

Drinking, cooking, and bath water had to be fetched from the city's seventeen hundred public fountains or bought from door-to-door water carriers. Most of them filled their containers from the contaminated Seine, but some cheated by tapping neighborhood fountains. As of 1853, water came primarily from a canal built by Napoleon I; 20 percent from the Seine, and a lesser amount from a Roman aqueduct. Every drop was polluted.

The only pure water, in short supply and unpalatably warm, was piped into Paris from a small artesian well.

Setting up a water supply for Paris was not to be easy. Samples of water were chemically analyzed and available sources explored. New distribution pipes were laid and old ones rerouted. But bureaucracy interminably delayed appreciable progress. In 1860, Haussmann presented a water-supply program to the state council, which took almost a year to appoint a study commission. When, after twelve months of deliberation, the commission approved the plan, it had to be revised to meet the needs of greater Paris. The area of the city had been doubled and its population increased by four hundred thousand through annexation of a ring of townships.

Following the commission's favorable report on the proposed program, work was begun on conduits and reservoirs. Pure spring water for household use first filled reservoirs in August 1865, and poured through distribution pipes in the amount of 28,000 cubic meters a day. By 1869, there were 311,000 c.m. available from previous sources; 24,000 to 30,000 c.m. from the Dhuys and, in prospect, 100,000 c.m. from the Vonne district.

Although Haussmann left office in 1870 before the whole system was operative, it was acknowledged as one of his major contributions. He was justifiably proud of "this considerable piece of work, because it is really mine. I did not find it in the program of transformation of Paris drawn up by the emperor, and nobody in the world suggested it to me. It is the fruit of my observations, of my assiduous researches as a young official, and of my mature meditations. It is my own conception."

No less his own conception was the system of sewers that became sightseeing attractions. He was determined that unprocessed waste should not gush into the Seine within the city. The ideal disposal of the sewage for which underground pipelines were being laid "occurred to me suddenly." It was during a sleepless night he spent studying the map of Paris, his "altar-screen."

When he became prefect, the system consisted of one big unfinished sewer below the existing section of the rue de Rivoli, and one uncovered collector, running along an old roadbed. Haussmann immediately planned a large corridor with sewage pipes under the boulevard Strasbourg-Sebastopol, and for continuation of the one under the rue de Rivoli. In 1858 he proposed the major program that came from the attack of insomnia. It was for operation through a *cloaca maxima,* a central collector, under the place de la Concorde. Bureaucracy once again caused delays, and the project was not entirely finished in 1869. But in Haussmann's administration three-hundred-twenty miles of sewer were laid; collectors, large and small, constructed; and wastes deposited in the Seine beyond the center of Paris, not far from the gare de St. Lazare.

The prefect, supported by expert opinion, promoted the use of separators for treatment of liquid and solid waste to produce fertilizer. In his *Memoires,* Haussmann explicitly describes the corridors and collectors, and the methods for cleaning the whole sewage network. For inspection of Haussmann's model sewers, sightseers were seated in specially equipped cleaning trucks. Along the route, surface streets overhead were identified by porcelain plaques set into the corridor walls.

Haussmann's cemetery program was a failure. Hoping to reduce health hazards caused by overcrowded cemeteries within the city, he wanted to establish one "giant necropolis" beyond suburbia. But he was balked by the emperor's disinterest and by political opposition.

Cemetery stench pervaded the neighborhoods and, through open windows, even houses. Lack of space made the common grave a necessity that increased air and water pollution. At Père Lachaise, seventy-five of every one hundred burials were in the common grave that was often awash with water that speeded decay. The cemetery in Montmartre contaminated a nearby well, and during the 1865 cholera epidemic, the highest death toll was in that putrid section. Even shocking statistics failed to give impetus to Haussmann's cemetery plan. It was a total fiasco.

Funding projects for the prefecture of the Seine was very complicated. Money was allotted by state and municipal councils and obtained through taxes and bank loans. By an individual robbing-Peter-to-pay-Paul system, Haussmann managed to finance public works programs by means that were at once arbitrary and effective. But officials and bankers increasingly questioned his methods, and in 1870 the emperor refused to stand by the prefect. He had not misappropriated funds for personal profit, but had juggled books for the public good, as he knew it to be.

Forced in 1870 to retire, Haussmann, for the remaining twenty years of his life, was a neglected man, personally discontent. The widespread recognition he craved came too late to solace him.

An architect attuned to his epoch,
its artists and tycoons, brightened
the façade of New York.

STANFORD WHITE, 1853–1906

Success for the American achitectural firm of McKim, Mead, and White, established 1879, was accompanied by frequent criticism from their American contemporaries in architecture. It was popular in certain circles of the profession to belittle the prestigious firm for accepting as clients none but rich social leaders, and for producing mansions and other buildings that were no more than copies of European landmarks.

There was no question about the status of the clients of McKim, Mead, and White, for the three architects were friends with many distinguished men. But the firm did not, as some said, primarily construct palatial residences. It also designed monuments, banks, bridges, and office buildings, as well as two important public centers: the old Madison Square Garden and the New York Pennsylvania Station completed four years after the death of White.

In spite of statements to the contrary, there was not an exact replica of any structure in the list of buildings designed at the McKim, Mead, and White office. Several styles of European architecture familiar to and favored by clients were adapted with originality by the members of the firm: Charles F. McKim, William R. Mead, and Stanford White. The individuality of each man was reflected in his work.

Retiring and cerebral, McKim was quietly effective in public affairs and in his profession. For years, he patiently worked toward the establishment of the American Academy in Rome, of which he was the first president. A member of the McMillan Commission, he contributed to its 1902 report that led to the reactivation of Pierre Charles L'Enfant's plan for the nation's capital.

In Washington, through McKim's associations, the firm built the Arlington Memorial Bridge, designed the main building of the National War College, and at an estimated cost of half a million dollars, made major improvements to the White House when Theodore Roosevelt was president.

The balance of McKim, Mead, and White was provided quite fittingly by the middle man, William Mead, a well-trained and experienced architect. His instinctive sixth sense about the logical and natural developments of the elevation of buildings was an invaluable asset. But Mead's prime contribution to the firm was his down-to-earth understanding of the other two partners, so disparate in character, and his forthright dependable judgment of their plans. Stanford White, the exuberant and most vital member of the architectural firm, was a man of many talents. He was born on November 9, 1853, into a family with broad cultural interests. His musical father, early active in medicine, then passed his bar examinations in 1854, and later became a recognized Shakespearean authority.

Deciding against a career as artist, the son, in 1872, became an architectural draftsman for H. H. Richardson, prominent Boston architect. Vagabonding through Europe in 1878, on the first of many trips abroad, Stanford White made stunning sketches of buildings and landscapes surrounding them. Throughout his life, his correspondence was illustrated by caricatures, in signature or salutation. His natural facility for writing was evidenced by the charm of his informative letters, whether social or business.

Concurrently with his work in architecture, White established a considerable reputation as the designer of jewelry, gravestones, bindings of limited-edition books, and magazine covers for *Scribner's, The Cosmopolitan,* and *The Century Illustrated Monthly Magazine.*

White disliked naturalistic art in every medium. In architecture, he personally disregarded rules and standards, being more concerned with effect than with conformity, an insouciance reflected by his lifestyle. For commissions of his firm, as an entity, White went along with the master plan.

Few of his own independent structures were architecturally imposing, but all were impressively ornamented.

He had a strong conviction that art should be available to everybody, no less to the man in the street than to the affluent collector. By intent, White's public buildings and monuments highlighted the works of artists. In numerous collaborations, he designed ideal backdrops for the art of Augustus Saint-Gaudens, the sculptor, and of John La Farge, the muralist and designer of stained glass.

Many residences by White were interior-decorated with fabrics, furniture, and *objects* selected by the architect, who often made specific purchases in Europe for his American clients. He avidly collected foreign art treasures, including mantels, paneling, doors, and grillwork removed from chateaus and chapels, and justified the practice by saying it was an age-old custom. He pointed out that, historically, dominant nations took over the works of art of earlier civilizations. It was his contention that America, leading country of the world, had the right to enrich its culture with valued and beautiful objects wherever they were found and could be bought.

When White joined the Richardson office, he and Charles McKim worked on plans for Boston's Trinity Church, commissioned by the Reverend Phillips Brooks. Mural decorations of the chancel were by John La Farge. Thirty-two years later, White and McKim, by then long-time partners, designed the Phillips Brooks Memorial at Trinity Church. The church, completed in 1877, was in a style that became known as Richardson Romanesque, which influenced American ecclesiastical architecture, and marked the departure from the Gothic previously in vogue.

McKim, who had left Richardson to start his own firm, was with White during some of the latter's 1878 European trips, and for part of the time, they were accompanied by Saint-Gaudens. The sculptor was then at the École des Beaux Arts where Richardson, La Farge, and McKim had also studied.

After White's return to the United States, he carried on an extensive correspondence with Saint-Gaudens about a joint commission for a monument honoring Admiral David Glasgow Farragut, naval hero of the Civil War. Preliminary sketches were shuttled by transatlantic mails, and what evolved was too elaborate for execution on the assigned budget. Rather than compromise their plan, White and Saint-Gaudens made up the deficit, although neither, at the time, was financially established.

An inspiration to designers of later monuments, the Farragut memorial, dedicated in 1881, was an outstanding example of White's creativity. His setting for the sculpture of Saint-Gaudens was a great stone bench reached by three steps from a landscaped walkway. The statue's pedestal was centered above a curved seat with carvings in bluestone along its back.

The Farragut memorial gave impetus to the career of the twenty-eight-year-old White, as the Washington

Arch at the entrance to Greenwich Village was later to enhance his reputation. He originally donated a design for a wooden arch to be constructed for the passage of a patriotic parade, held in 1889. That temporary structure sparked such public interest that White was commissioned to execute a permanent one in marble. He referred to it as classic, as opposed to Renaissance, but his variations, particularly of the proportions, distinguished it from ancient triumphal arches.

When not yet thirty, White designed his last Romanesque building, the Tiffany house at Madison Avenue and Seventy-seventh Street in New York. He thereafter designed in the classic tradition that was the trademark of the firm. Tiffany house was described, in 1885, by a visiting British critic, as the most beautiful modern domestic building." Built for occupancy by two families, it was unique as a town house, and its entryways and service areas solved some problems for builders of subsequent multiple dwellings, the apartment houses of the future.

White's favorite building materials for town houses were white stone and yellow brick. Commenting on his introduction of the light-colored substances for metropolitan buildings, a newspaper noted that White had changed the face of brownstone New York. He further brightened the city by the frequent use of terra-cotta facings.

The Century Club, one of three clubhouses he designed, was distinguished by its terra-cotta color and a

99

wrought-iron loggia which attested to the influence of Florentine architecture on White during a tour of Italy. He also designed the Lambs Club and the Metropolitan Club, founded by J. P. Morgan, the financier whose library was the work of McKim. Decades after the Metropolitan Club was built, it was referred to as the most successful example of pure Renaissance architecture in New York.

White had clients in Washington and Baltimore, and in New York built homes for dozens of notables, including Charles Dana Gibson, illustrator; Joseph Pulitzer, publisher, and William K. Vanderbilt, philanthropist and yachtsman. For Pierre Lorillard, the tobacco tycoon and sportsman who established an exclusive colony at Tuxedo Park, close to the New Jersey line, White drew plans for the millionaire's private mansion in the park.

With his partners, White designed several buildings for New York University, including its Hall of Fame. At Charlottesville, they reconstructed University of Virginia buildings designed by Thomas Jefferson, and supplemented his original campus plan.

The firm's Pennsylvania Railroad Station in New York was a major undertaking. It cost 25 million dollars to excavate the site, and 112 million dollars to construct the gigantic terminal that was finished in 1910. The station's main staircase was 40 feet wide and its grand concourse, longer than the nave of St. Peter's in Rome, had a vaulted ceiling that was 138 feet high.

In 1890, McKim, Mead, and White completed Madison Square Garden, for which their fee was two million dollars, half the amount commonly rumored around New York. The vast arena was for horse shows, circuses, concerts, prize fights and other sporting events. There was a roof-garden restaurant and theater, and, at ground level, an arcade intended for fashionable shops that did not materialize.

The heavily ornamented exterior of Madison Square Garden was done in yellow brick with terra-cotta, so typical of White's style. Against the opposition of the Garden's board of directors, he forced the approval of a large and imposing central tower that was his adaptation of the Spanish Giralda Tower adjacent to the cathedral at Seville. To crown the tower, Saint-Gaudens sculpted an eighteen-foot Diana whose left foot was poised on a ball.

A beautiful figure with wind-tossed drapery blowing behind her, the Diana caused a furore when placed atop the tower, three hundred feet above the sidewalk. Her body of beaten copper was harmonious with the terra-cotta facings of the building, but her nudity offended puritanical citizens. Their vehemently expressed outrage forced the removal of the statue, and White personally paid for a thirteen-foot replacement that was not only smaller but more decorous.

White was a stockholder of the Garden, which operated at a deficit year after year and in his lifetime failed to pay a common stock dividend. A member and one-time vice-president of the board of directors, he kept a treasure-filled studio on the top floor of Madison Square Garden. In those sumptuous quarters, at the base of the tower, White was gracious host at frequent lavish and lively parties.

In 1903, for an addition to St. Bartholomew's Church, an edifice underwritten by the Vanderbilt family, White went back to 1878 for inspiration. He had then written to his father that the triple-arched portals of the church at St. Gilles made it the "best piece of architecture in France." And its influence was to be seen in his marble arches at St. Bartholomew's.

In the following three years, he worked on five build-ings that some considered to be his very best: Gorham's, the Colony Club, Tiffany's, the Knickerbocker Trust Building, and the Madison Square Presbyterian Church. Florentine in style, the Gorham building had a ground-level arcade and a colored cornice of a type shortly barred by New York City law for the safety of pedes-trians. It was feared that cornice decorations, if loosened, might fall and strike some passerby below.

The Colony was ladylike in appearance, as befitted a club with an exclusively female membership. The building's columns were slender, and its brickwork was of headers, or exposed short ends of the bricks, set parallel to the structure, giving it a light, delicate look. Without ornamentation, unusual for White, the shop of Tiffany & Company depended for its beauty on rhythmic spacing. It reminded world travelers of the Renaissance palaces of Venice.

The Knickerbocker Trust Building was a sensational departure from accepted architecture. Its façade appeared to be without walls because spaces between the Corinthian columns and the pilasters were filled with bronze grilles and glass. A conventional frieze topped the columns, but the total effect was so unique that crowds gathered to gawk at the strange structure.

There was almost as much brouhaha over the Madison Square Presbyterian Church as about the first Diana of Madison Square Garden. The church dome was made of green glazed tiles, its portico was fronted by polished green granite columns, again of the Corinthian order, and reliefs were carved with della-Robbia-like figures. Fascinated by White's polychrome design that included cornices of glazed terra-cotta and walls of yellow bricks incised with crosses, contractors for the construction donated the colors for the glazing. Some people, finding the completed church much too modern in lines, proportions, and colors, attacked it vocally and in letters to the editor.

White answered his critics by saying that the design had been a deliberate "protest against the idea so prevalent among laymen that a building to be churchlike, must be built in the Medieval Style." He claimed that the edifice was "in a style natural to and belonging to the religion which it represents and the country in which it is built."

Apparently the public was more swayed by his reference to their country than to the religion because the church was widely copied and by many denominations. The first reproduction, approved by the congregation of a California synagogue, was even constructed of the bricks with Christian crosses.

In 1907, for the design of the Madison Square Presbyterian Church, White was posthumously awarded the Medal of Honor of the New York Chapter of the American Institute of Architects. The church, completed in 1906, was razed in 1919 to make way for a skyscraper. A British visitor said that tearing down the magnificent church was analogous to destroying one of Sir Christopher Wren's London churches, an act which, to the English, would be an unthinkable desecration. In New York, protests from the public and in newspaper editorials failed to save the building that, generally recognized as White's masterpiece, was his last work.

On the night of June 25, 1906, while attending a premiere performance at the roof-garden theater of Madison Square Garden, Stanford White was shot and killed by Harry K. Thaw, who subsequently was found "not guilty as charged in the indictment on the ground of the defendant's insanity."

St. Bartholomew's Church was crowded for the funeral

service of the fifty-two-year-old architect who, having changed the face of New York, had begun to experiment with original and imaginative concepts of architectural design.

Prolific in prose and in his
innovative architectural designs,
he had no doubt about his own genius.

FRANK LLOYD WRIGHT, 1869–1959

CHILDHOOD toys and architect Louis H. Sullivan were acknowledged by Frank Lloyd Wright as major influences on his work.

The playthings, always referred to by Wright as the *gifts,* were first seen by his schoolteacher mother in the Friedrich Froebel Kindergarten exhibit at the Philadelphia Centennial of 1876. Froebel, German inventor of the system for educating preschool youngsters, thought children should learn by doing. His own observations of nature inspired the educator to design games and gadgets for the development of a child's creativity through reconstruction of nature's shapes, rhythms, and color compositions.

One set of the *gifts* to the young Wright included cardboard triangles, and maple wood blocks in three shapes: cube, triangle, and circle. Other *gifts* were fine quality colored papers with slits for making whatever patterns were fancied, and construction sticks, sliver thin, to be jointed with dried peas. In his *A Testament,*

1957, Wright described the *gifts* and asserted that all "are in my fingers today."

Conditioned by experimentation with Froebel toys, Frank Lloyd Wright freely adapted their forms and shapes to his own designs in architecture. He credited to the *gifts* his ability to understand and view nature in depth, even from the inside out. His experience with observation of nature in its totality began when, as a teenager, he had to go to work on an uncle's farm in a Wisconsin valley.

The same locale provided Wright with roots that remained more than seven decades. There, at Spring Green, Wisconsin, he built his first house for his aunts, the Misses Lloyd Jones. In 1896, also for them, he designed an unusual windmill and water tower. Its hollow-stemmed shaft was enclosed and its polygonal exterior, covered with wooden shingles.

Adjacent to his aunts' Hillside School, 1902, Wright built his home Taliesin I, 1911. Beginning in 1933, the school buildings were remodeled and incorporated into the complex of the Taliesin Fellowship.

Years before the first Taliesin was even a dream, Frank Lloyd Wright left the farm for Madison, Wisconsin, where he briefly studied engineering at the University of Wisconsin. Long after, he wrote that, in 1888, a few months before graduation, he ran off to Chicago to find work in an architect's office. Actually, in 1888, Wright had been in Chicago for at least a year, and, at

Wisconsin, he never was close to earning an engineering degree.

Discrepancies in Wright's biography, resulting from deliberate omissions and casual inconsistencies in his own writings, appear in books of others unable to sort facts from the fiction of biographic dates that vary, this way or that, by a year or two.

After about a year in Chicago, Wright became a draftsman with the architectural firm of Dankmar Adler and Louis H. Sullivan, who designed residences and commercial buildings, the latter marked by Sullivan's unmistakable style. When Wright was hired, the firm's major commission-in-work was the Chicago Civic Auditorium. His first assignment was the drawing of detailed plans of the auditorium's interior decorations.

In 1914, Wright stated that, while he was with architecture's two "great moderns," Sullivan was "my master and inspiration." During those years, Adler and Sullivan undertook, among other important commissions, the Wainwright Building in St. Louis, Missouri, and the Transportation Building for the World's Columbian Exposition, or Chicago World's Fair of 1893.

The Wainwright Building, 1890, was a notable example of pioneer skyscrapers constructed of all-steel frames strong enough to support curtain walls. Those walls, having no structural function, were, in effect, partitions between indoors and outdoors. The curtain wall was to be refined and popularized by renowned architects of the twentieth century.

Sullivan, onetime student of the École des Beaux Arts, Paris, received one of its gold medals for his Transportation Building at the Chicago Exposition. The exterior was attention catching, in part, because of the glittery gilding of its handsome façade. The interior was typical of Sullivan, who held that, in architecture, "form follows function." That expressed ideal was not realized in every building by Sullivan, but his innovations led to originality of design, and his integration of decoration with form was ever distinctive. For example, the unbroken lines of his flowing friezes were often accented by intertwined leaves, plant stems, vines, and grass blades. Wright excelled at drafting Sullivan's ornamentations.

Although pleased to be a "good pencil in the master's hand," Wright was not for long limited to drafting. Given increasing responsibility, he contributed to many commissions, especially those for residences. He was the prime architect for Charnley House, 1891, a palatial three-story town house. The balance of its floor plan and windows, while effective, was not typical of Wright's later work. More often than not, as an independent architect, he boldly combined symmetry with asymmetry.

Wright always used building materials with ingenuity and imagination, as at Charnley House. Its base was given appropriate solidity by smooth-cut random ashlar, building stone irregularly set. Above, variety of texture was achieved by thin Roman brick. Ornamentation of a tiny balcony over the entrance and throughout the interior was Sullivanesque.

Charnley House and other buildings indicate that Wright and Sullivan, in their relatively brief association, worked in harmony and with mutual respect. They had, in common, individualistic styles and definite points of view. Both were not only articulate about their profession's relationship in and to society, but wrote voluminously on the subject.

Sullivan and his young assistant designer parted company, in 1893, because Wright had worked on after-hours commissions. The moonlighting, for economic reasons, displeased Sullivan, and Wright's employment with the firm was terminated. Ever after, he referred to the homes built without the master's knowledge as the "bootlegged" houses.

Wright chose to call the Winslow House, River Forest, Illinois, 1893, his first, although it was just the first built after he was forced into private practice. It had the unobtrusive chimney and sheltering roof of the Prairie house style introduced by Wright and some few of his contemporaries in Midwestern architecture.

Except for the conventional balance of its façade, the Winslow House evidenced the burgeoning of Wright's invention. Instead of dominating the entry, his staircase was off-center. His double fireplace heated both the reception room and, on the opposite side of the building, the dining room. At the exterior-rear, the dining-room bay and a tower, enclosing parts of the upper floor, reflected Froebel influence. The asymmetry foreshadowed many of Wright's subsequent designs.

Winslow House was the last residence for which he used double-hung, or "guillotine," windows. To Wright, casements provided the ideal link between the indoors and nature. He said his insistence on that window style cost him a number of commissions from people accustomed to being separated from nature when within their homes.

Nonetheless, between 1893 and 1900, Wright did not lack for clients. He completed many buildings and designed numerous projects never constructed. Among the latter were an amusement park, a yacht club, a beach resort, and the Luxfer Prism skyscraper, its steel skeleton authoritatively designed by Wright, then only in his middle twenties.

Finished works included many residences, a golf club, row houses, apartments, and one low-cost housing development. The multiple dwellings had defined boxlike rooms totally unlike Wright's upcoming designs characterized by a free-flowing relationship of main floor living areas.

In the decade between 1900 and 1910, Wright did dozens of Prairie houses, large and small. Each house, like the local terrain, was flat and low. He substituted the horizontal for the vertical by reducing the height of the building through elimination of the basement, the attic, and the tall, thin chimney.

The typical Prairie house, instead of rising from a masonry base inset with cellar windows, was placed, at ground level, on a stone or cement water table, the foundation platform. Servants' quarters, until then customarily cramped in a garret, were moved to the first floor, adjacent to service areas. The lowered and broadened chimney squatted on the flattened roof, which had projecting eaves. Their flat undersides were colored to brighten the interior, by reflection. Gloom in rooms was anathema to Wright.

His "light screens," the casement windows, side by side in a series, opened onto carefully planned vistas. Landscaping was an integral part of Wright's designs, and where nature did not supply the proper setting, trees, shrubbery, and garden plots were drafted at the drawing board and accordingly planted. No less important to him than light and views was air flow, a freedom of openness achieved by keeping partitions and doors to a minimum, except as needed for bedroom privacy.

As an architect in the machine age, Wright was determined to put the machine to work, producing structural components to be combined with artistry and simplicity. By his definition, simplicity was a "perfectly realized part of some organic whole." He avoided multiple combinations of materials in any one house, but chose to unite natural woods with quarried stone or with the man-mades: brick, concrete, cement, plaster. Unadorned wood bands, mass-produced, followed the lines of Wright's doors and windows. The slim bands, flowing around a room above the tops of openings and, again, at the floor line, emphasized what he termed plasticity. Vertical bands divided walls into so many colored planes.

Human scale, or man's height, was the guide to the lowering of windows and of the few doorways of a Prairie house. The "integral fireplace," often double, had no mantel high above the hearth. Ceilings were brought down into rooms by the simple technique of keeping them the same color as the plaster walls above the upper band of wood. The resultant effect of spaciousness seemed to open up and enlarge even small rooms.

For increase of simplicity, Wright planned built-in furniture as also integral to the Prairie house and recommended that movable furniture be custom-made. It was "painful" to him to see a house after clients, disregarding his advice, moved in with a clutter of old furniture that was in no way complementary to their new environment, to the home he had designed for them.

Built-in metal filing cases and the first metal office furniture, desks and chairs, were designed by Wright for a commercial commission, the Larkin Administration Building, 1904. He made the structure light and airy but, in that exception, shut out the landscape, an industrial section of Buffalo, New York. An air-conditioning system of sorts kept the temperature equable in all seasons.

Monumental is the adjective commonly applied to the interior of the building. A central court, lighted from above, was flanked by parapets and by four tiers of gallery offices which had windows high above the built-in files. Abstract carvings embellished the interior tiers, and other decoration was provided by greens and flowers growing in planters on the parapets. Exterior walls were smooth brick, a material most effective up the blank faces of two squared-off towers of the façade. A carved fountain was to the right of the steps leading to entrance doors of plate glass set in flat metal frames.

The Larkin building, with its practical innovations of the interior, enhanced Wright's reputation and influence, particularly with European architects.

More important to Wright personally was Unity Church, Oak Park, Illinois, designed in 1905. For economy, he dared to build with poured concrete, until then commonly limited to small structures. Facing the concrete with brick and stone would have increased construction costs that Wright circumvented. He exposed, for texture of the mass, the concrete's own fine pebble aggregate. Since the expense of the poured concrete process was proportionate to the variety of wooden forms or molds used, Wright confined himself, as much as possible, to a single block mold. That form, adaptable for a building alike on four sides, predetermined the square shape of the church and of the adjacent parish house, a smaller cube.

The church outside was a mono-material building. It was also a prime example of instant architecture because, when in place, the structural material required no surface finish.

The interior was consistent with Wright's flair for combining ambiance with function. Seats for four hundred were placed on a raised floor above a foyer that had entrance steps at its opposite ends. That arrangement prevented those entering the auditorium from disturbing worshippers already seated. After service, the congregation exited through wide doors opening out to the foyer.

Four freestanding hollow posts supported the overhead structure: roof, skylight under it, and a grid formed by interlocking concrete beams. Clerestorys were directly under the roofline. Daylight was filtered through amber glass ceiling lights so that, even on cloudy days, a soft sunny glow might suffuse the place of worship.

The concrete supporting posts set off double tiers of seats on four sides of the auditorium. Each lower-level alcove was slightly sloped, the balcony above, sharply raked. Again, as in the Prairie houses, unadorned wooden bands defined vertical lines, and along the balconies, flowed horizontally.

Wright's disposition of utility components was as unique as his use of poured concrete for so large a structure. Heating units were enclosed in the hollow posts and lighting wires were associated with the beams, as part of the design.

From 1889 through 1909, Frank Lloyd Wright designed a hundred and forty constructed buildings and about seventy projects. He went to Europe in 1910 and for several months lived in Italy, near Florence. In the half century following his return to the United States, he was to complete nearly four hundred designs, in all, six hundred in the course of his seventy years as architect.

In the early 1920s, Wright worked in California, producing a number of blockhouses, his breakaways from the area's mission style. He developed an original textile-block slab construction for the Millard House, Pasadena, 1923, and built a miniature Mayan temple, the Barnsdall House, Hollywood, 1920. That building is now part of a municipal art center.

Wright's Broadacre City was never built, and its model, exhibited in 1935, showed his lack of enthusiasm for urban living. Broadacre, with some concessions to community needs, was a country sprawl with one acre of ground allotted to each small house.

Only a few of the experimental low-cost Usonian houses that Wright designed at about the same time were ever built. A few of the type were constructed on commission. The initial cost of $5,500 was to range, with improvements, from $7,000 to $10,000. On the

Usonian plan, flexible at the construction site, the conventional garage gave way to the carport, a term generally credited to Wright.

World-famous works, designed after 1911, reflected certain constants established during Wright's first two decades in his profession: Every design hinged on environment, producing what he called organic architecture. Natural light was a structural dimension. Existent materials were put to new uses and even processed in different forms. Ingenuity with engineering made reality of the seemingly impossible.

The Imperial Hotel, Tokyo, 1917–1922, a showplace and luxurious haven for travelers, was a triumph of engineering skill over earthquakes. In a city daily exposed to temblors, Wright floated his spacious hotel on filled ground, layered above marsh mud.

The foundation, an ingenious invention, consisted of thousands of small concrete piers. Pillars and cantilevered floors supported the structure's weight, at the center, not at the meeting of the floors and walls where damage might result from shock-stress. Concrete, brick, and green lava were combined in specially made masonry. The fireproof material was a rarity in a city where wood and paper were the common, and flammable, construction materials. Lightweight, sheet-copper roof tiles were substituted for the local heavy tiles that, easily loosened, had killed countless Japanese in every severe quake.

Wires, pipes, and mains for power and plumbing were installed in covered concrete trenches at basement level. That placement of utility components was to prevent snapping or breaking during a major quake. The entrance court's decorative pool was, by design, an immense reservoir connected to the hotel's water system. Wright, in a showdown over the pool's cost, forced through construction. He expected the pool to be functional should a quake disrupt the city's water supply.

Tokyo was devastated by a 1923 earthquake that did not structurally damage the Imperial Hotel. It withstood violent shocks which razed buildings at the perimeter of its ground. And when the quake's afterfire neared the hotel, the window sashes and frames, the only exterior wood, were drenched with water drawn by a bucket brigade from the entrance pool. Wright's reservoir saved the hotel's interior from being gutted by flames.

A natural water source dominates the site of Fallingwater, Connellsville, Pennsylvania, 1936. It was designed for Edgar J. Kauffmann and is one of the most photographed buildings of the twentieth century. Horizontal in line, the Kauffmann house is cantilevered over the waterfall of Bear Run, a woodland stream. The structure is securely anchored to natural rock and heavy masonry, at the rear, and at the front, resembles a giant bird in flight.

To support the beams and several terraces at three levels, Wright needed strong slabs, and for the first time in a residence, used reinforced concrete. Steel sash that "came within reach also for the first time," is the almost imperceptible framework for the glass wall-screens of the living room.

Glass, in quite other shapes, was used structurally and decoratively for the S. C. Johnson and Son Administration Building, Racine, Wisconsin, 1936–1939. On the exterior, continuous bands of glass tubing glow at night, accenting the building's upper outline. Translucent interior walls of glass tubing silhouette passersby in office corridors. Pyrex glass tubes crisscross the ceiling of the tremendous central office. Desks, chairs, and filing cabinets of steel and magnesite were the first office furnishing designed by Wright after the Larkin commission of 1904.

The Johnson complex was completed, 1950, by the Laboratory Tower, a dramatic seven-story glass shell. The central core houses elevators, stairways, and utility components. Cantilevered floor slabs spread out "like tree branches" from the center stack toward the glass-tube shell that is lined, for insulation, with a plate-glass screen.

Earlier, Frank Lloyd Wright had spiraled the V. C. Morris Shop, San Francisco, 1948. The two-story shop was lighted by a circular dome above the spiral ramp from the main floor to the mezzanine. The design was similar to a planetarium project, 1925. Wright's final spiral was the controversial Guggenheim Museum, New York City, finished the year he died.

That same year, 1959, a major commission was still in progress at Florida Southern College, Lakeland, Florida. It was undertaken in 1938 when sixteen buildings were planned for the West Campus where the chapel and three administration buildings were constructed in 1940. Those four and two other Florida Southern buildings constitute the world's largest concentration of Wright architecture.

The hundred-acre campus, once an orange grove, borders Lake Hollingsworth. The Wright buildings, asymmetrically placed, are connected by his covered esplanades, shades against hot sun. Hanging plants and flowers are integral to the total design, and with clusters of trees provide the campus with additional shade. The flower-topped Annie Pfeiffer Chapel has a trellis lining to the tower that opens to the sky. Light also filters into the chapel through wall inserts of colored cast-glass.

Frank Lloyd Wright's homes, the two Taliesins, one at Spring Green and the other on the Arizona desert, near Phoenix, are probably familiar to anyone who has ever heard the architect's name. A self-styled romanticist, he lyrically described, in his autobiography, the origin and plans for Taliesin I. Rebuilt, after two disastrous fires, it became the headquarters of the Taliesin Fellowship where student-apprentices worked on the farm and in the architecture office.

Like most architects, Wright not only made occasional concessions to clients, compromising his ideas and ideals, but experienced some unproductive years. His were from 1925 into the mid-1930s, partially due to the Depression.

In 1932 his work was included in an international architecture show at the Museum of Modern Art, New York City. Wright denied being influenced by European coexhibitors, but numerous architectural experts noted a change in his subsequent designs, a felicitous new approach to architecture of the twentieth century.

Wright, who confidently said he expected to go down in history as the greatest architect of all time, was not spared the indignity of having some of his buildings demolished in the name of progress.

Midway Gardens, Chicago, designed in 1913 as a restaurant and concert complex, was razed in 1923, to make way for a car wash. The Larkin Administration Building was torn down for scrap in 1949. The Imperial Hotel, after two decades of slow deterioration, was closed on November 15, 1967. Demolition followed. Unpredicted settling of the unique foundation had weakened and cracked the structure of the hotel. And its soft stone facing had been disintegrated by industrial atmosphere: the smog of Tokyo.

A major twentieth-century architect made
impact through the written word and
evoked dissent with his city plans.

LE CORBUSIER, 1887–1965
(Charles Édouard Jeanneret)

BY understatement, Le Corbusier is often identified as a French architect. He was much more: a sometime craftsman, carpenter, and interior decorator, a dedicated if arbitrary teacher, a painter and sculptor of some invention but little distinction, a city planner fated for major disappointments through rejection of all but one of his designs, an author of widespread and incontrovertible influence.

Le Corbusier thought talent must be coupled with strong character and was himself an outstanding example of that combination of traits. A man of definite and unequivocal opinions, he aroused vehement reactions from those critical of his ideas, theories, and work. Charles Édouard Jeanneret was the real name of Le Corbusier who, in 1920, delved into family history when choosing a pseudonym.

He was born in 1887 at La Chaux-de-Fonds, Switzerland, a community famous for its watchmaking, the craft of his French forebears. His father was a dial enameler, and the son showed an early aptitude for watch design. At the Turin Exhibition of Decorative Arts, 1902, Le Corbusier won a medal for a watchcase decorated with an Art Nouveau design. He was soon to revolt against all Art Nouveau elaborations in favor of purism, a style dependent on geometric forms and simplified images.

When Le Corbusier received the Turin award, he had been for two years at the art school of La Chaux-de-Fonds, where he was well trained in manual techniques and stimulated by an erudite teacher. School experience with construction materials was to benefit Le Corbusier for life. Nearly half a century after leaving Switzerland, he personally constructed the framework for hollow reliefs of his famous Marseilles Block, an apartment building. At about the same time, he sawed wood for his studio-cabin at Cap-Martin on the French Riviera.

The first house designed by Le Corbusier was built in his home town in 1905. He was eighteen years old. Two years later, Le Corbusier began extensive travels during which he became acquainted with noted European architects. In that time of creative ferment, Le Corbusier was attuned to all artists experimenting with new forms and new materials.

His first trip was through northern Italy, Hungary, and Austria. There he spent six months in the atelier of Josef Hoffmann, decorator, architect, and founder of the Vienna Workshops. The next year, Le Corbusier was in France, where he became friends with the Paris architect Auguste Perret and with Tony Garnier, urban planner and architect for the city of Lyons. Garnier had designed a much-talked-about industrial city that proved him to be inventive and prescient. Le Corbusier was impressed by Garnier's early awareness of the birth of a new architecture "based on social factors." In 1909 Le Corbusier went to work with Perret who, having foreseen the future of reinforced concrete, designed the first house with framework of that material, 1902–1903.

Following fourteen productive months with Perret, Le Corbusier, in 1910, on a fellowship, went to Germany to study its arts and crafts. For five months he was an apprentice in the Berlin office of Peter Behrens, teacher also of Walter Gropius, organizer of the Bauhaus art school and of Mies van der Rohe, renowned architect and onetime director of the Bauhaus. Behrens, architect and industrial designer before that term was known, made his reputation with designs of factories and workers' homes.

Time spent with Behrens and Perret was no more meaningful to Le Corbusier than the architecture he was to see in 1911, when he traveled for seven months through Central Europe, the Balkans, Italy, Turkey, and Greece. The architecture of Greece, particularly the buildings on the Acropolis at Athens, were an inspiration and challenge to Le Corbusier. He spent three weeks observing the Parthenon, which he sketched and studied from every angle. The Parthenon was to him a "pure creation of the mind."

He wrote, "The Greeks built temples on the Acropolis which answer to a single conception, and which have gathered up around them the desolate landscape and subjected it to the composition. So from all sides of the horizon the conception is unique. This is why no other works of architecture exist which have this grandeur."

Various aspects of Greek architecture are traceable in the work of Le Corbusier. Grandeur was often his aim and loftiness his state of mind. For every building or complex, he attempted to gather up the surrounding landscape. Unlike Frank Lloyd Wright, who linked the indoors with nature, Le Corbusier said, "The plan conquers landscape."

His masterful use of light, including the deflection of it, was as much Greek in concept as the concern for integration of human scale in every structure. He later wrote, "Architecture is the masterly, correct, and magnificent play of the forms of light." And he insisted, "One must try to find the human scale."

Following the pilgrimage to Greece, Le Corbusier returned to La Chaux-de-Fonds. There he directed the art school's curriculum of architecture and furniture, and was in charge of interior decoration for a regional workshop of related arts.

During World War I, Le Corbusier remained in Switzerland where he designed his never-built Domino houses. But, for them, he proposed prefabrication techniques and structural standardizations that presaged his later work. "Let us admit pre-fabricated *elements* of the house but not pre-fabricated *houses.*"

Le Corbusier established residence in Paris in 1917 and in 1930 became a French citizen. He was by then so well known outside of France that foreign students crowded his Paris architect's office, opened in 1922. There were many more apprentice-applicants than he could accept in spite of his reputation as a stern and exacting teacher.

He painted his first pictures in 1918, the year he and Amédée Ozenfant held a joint exhibition entitled *After Cubism.* Their purism form was less abstract but no more representational than cubism. Ever after, painting and architecture were inseparable to Le Corbusier, whose style in both subtly changed with passing time. Eventually he painted icons, designed tapestry, and sculpted. He once posed the question, "Where does sculpture start, or painting, or architecture?" And he then answered, "The body of the building is the expression of the three major arts in one."

Ozenfant and Le Corbusier, in 1920, started an avant-garde magazine, *L'Esprit Nouveaux,* in which city-planning and industrial-design articles were bylined *Le Corbusier,* the first appearance of the name he was to make internationally famous. His writing, complex, recondite, and lacking conventional organization, elicited pro-and-con opinions. Adverse criticism caused him neither to improve his method nor to be more lucid in statements that, however abstruse, were always expressed with passionate personal conviction.

Throughout the 1920s, Le Corbusier primarily designed and built mansions and villas when he wanted to get on with housing developments related to town planning. He did do workers' houses at Pessac near Bordeaux, 1925, but local officials, violently opposed to the residential complex, withheld a water-supply system for six years. After occupancy was finally made possible, successive tenants changed the houses to suit their needs and taste.

Le Corbusier went to Russia, in 1928, prepared for a lecture tour to South America, and with others, organized an architectural congress, the first of eleven held in the following three decades. The Russian trip was minor to Le Corbusier's professional life, the second two events were of great import to twentieth-century architecture.

In Russia, Le Corbusier undertook a commission for a Moscow building, 1929–1935. However, like other distinguished foreign architects, he lost out in the 1931 competition for the Palace of the Soviets that was designed, finally, by minor local architects.

While in South America, Le Corbusier visited Argentina and Uruguay and, in Brazil, lectured at São Paulo and Rio de Janeiro. One Brazilian already familiar with Le Corbusier's writings and works was the young architect Oscar Niemeyer, who was to be much influenced by the French architect. When Le Corbusier returned to Brazil in 1936, he collaborated with Niemeyer and his mentor-teacher, Lúcio Costa, on the design of the Palace of Ministry of National Education at Rio.

Niemeyer and Costa, with P. L. Wiener, were the architects of the Brazilian Pavilion at the New York's World Fair, 1939. In 1957 Costa laid out the city plan for Brasilia, the new capital of Brazil, for which Niemeyer designed the buildings.

Le Corbusier had said mass production "must be made to serve mankind in newer and more creative ways," as Niemeyer knew. But ever an individualist, he never wanted to use, nor could he rely on, mass-production methods of construction, building techniques of Brazil being restricted by lack of industry for prefabrication. While well-aware of other potentials, Niemeyer adapted for Brazilian architecture only the fluid elements proposed at the architectural congresses masterminded by Le Corbusier.

Urbanism in all its aspects, including low-cost and multiple housing, was the prime consideration of the International Congresses of Modern Architecture (Congrès Internationaux de l'Architecture Moderne), CIAM, organized at Sarraz castle in Switzerland, 1928. By the time CIAM was disbanded in 1959, it had been a vital force in architecture and to its outstanding professionals.

CIAM was dominated by Le Corbusier, whose city

plans and concepts of design and construction were integral to specific themes of the group's various assemblies. At the 1934 CIAM Congress, in Greece, members precisely set forth town-planning theories that were chiefly those of Le Corbusier. The principles passed on by CIAM were secretly edited by Le Corbusier, during the German occupation of France, and published, without credit, as the Athens Charter, 1942.

Four functions in the Charter represented its general theme: living, working, recreation, circulation. Le Corbusier often substituted "cultivation of mind and body" for the word *recreation*. Zoning was specifically outlined in two consecutive articles of the Charter: "We must insist that the distance between home and place of work be reduced to a minimum. And that the industrial sectors should be independent of the living quarters and separated from each other by verdant zones."

Dimensions were added to the Charter's rules by ASCORAL (Assemblée de Constructeurs pour une Renovation Architecturale), founded in 1943 by members of CIAM-France. ASCORAL was expanded, under Le Corbusier's leadership, "Into an organization covering all branches of knowledge . . ."

After extensive research into the "places and conditions of work in a technical civilization," one ASCORAL committee published its study of three human establishments, based on an early concept of Le Corbusier. His revision listed "three natural establishments: (1) The unit of agricultural production. (2) The linear industrial city (manufacturing industries). (3) The radio-concentric change-over metropolis (government, thought, art, commerce)." Service roads and passenger automobile routes were bordered by the "verdant zones." The pedestrian way was to be "separated from motor traffic."

On the ASCORAL map, 1943, the linear industrial cities were linked from the Atlantic Ocean across to China. At that time, such a future possibility was as radical as the 1949 sociopolitical predictions in George Orwell's novel *Nineteen Eighty-Four*.

When, in 1921, Le Corbusier had described a house as a "machine to live in," many branded him a disciple of functionalism, of the totally impersonal. In reality, Le Corbusier was concerned with the comfort and happiness of man in his home, and thought of the living-machine in terms of mass production. He foresaw a new architecture made possible by the assembly-line methods that were turning out the "flying machine" and the automobile.

As early as 1914, the basic frames for his Domino-houses project were designed to be "made of standard elements which can be fitted together, thus permitting a great diversity in the grouping . . ." As required by "town-planner or customer, such frames, oriented and grouped, can be delivered by a manufacturer anywhere in the country."

The architect recognized no dichotomy in his statements that others found to be contradictory and inconsistent. Considering architecture and the graphic arts to be interrelated, he said, "Art has no business to resemble a machine." Yet, he designed a project as Citrohan, an adaptation of Citroen, the name of an automobile. The first Citrohan house was not built until 1927, when Le Corbusier was invited by Mies van der Rohe to participate in the International Housing Exposition at Stuttgart, Germany. The house, planned for additions of prefabricated units, had "free-standing supports (*pilotis*), free plan, terrace-roof, free façade, ribbon windows."

The design was in some ways eclectic. Certain of the elements outlined had been previously seen in the works of other architects. Frank Lloyd Wright had, long before, introduced the free plan. Adolf Loos, the Austrian architect, had used the free façade by which external emphasis was minimized, and the ribbon window, in unbroken double or multiple numbers. The terrace-roof was a major feature of Tony Garnier's designs.

"An argument for modern housing is put forward here," Le Corbusier wrote of the Citrohan house with its two-storyed living room. Sleeping rooms were no more than cubicles, individual cells like those "in sleeping-cars" of trains. Space was given where the family gathered in the "vast living room, in which one spends most of the day, well-being ensured by large dimension and plenty of air and light . . ."

Like Frank Lloyd Wright, Le Corbusier was resentful when people took treasured furniture from a former home into one he had built for them. Furniture to him was synonymous with equipment, and he developed "machines to sit in, machines for classification purposes, lighting machines . . ." In 1926, with two partners, Le Corbusier began the design of assembly-line beds, tables, and chairs. Eventually he made poured-concrete furniture close enough to sculpture for it to be impossible to decide "Where does sculpture start?" (*see* page 125)

Le Corbusier lifted single dwellings, apartment houses, and public buildings off the ground with the *pilotis* that were to become his signature. As later adapted by outstanding architects, the pillar supports were aesthetic; when commonly adopted by inexpert imitators, the shafts were hackneyed contrivances. In Le Corbusier's hands, the pilotis evolved from the stilts of the early 1920s to slabs and finally, with no more purpose than roof support, to pure enhancements of a structure.

To overcome drawbacks of glass walls, Le Corbusier invented the sunbreak, which was first "put to the test of practice" in the Ministry of Education palace at Rio. The sunbreaks were of two types, movable and fixed. The adjustable sunbreak shaded an interior, provided privacy to those within, and interrupted the monotony of glass walls. The permanent sunbreak was planned to control sunlight and to effect circulation of air.

Committed to geometric precision and mathematical

measurement, Le Corbusier chose the human form as his unit of dimension. He considered the entire man: height, span of limbs, gestures of hands and arms, and even, for the design of a doorknob, thumb shape.

Le Corbusier worked for six years on his Modulor system of design, based on human dimension in double-scale proportions. The principle was applied to a total plan and to mass-produced components. The Modulor was first used in Le Corbusier's Marseilles Block, 1947–1952, the partial realization of a 1922 project. That "Plan for a Contemporary City of Three Million Inhabitants," and the slightly later "Radiant City" project, included vertical dwellings, each for upwards of fifteen hundred people.

The Marseilles Block contains 337 apartments within a free framework 430 feet long, 80 wide, and 185 high. The reinforced-concrete skeleton rests on pillar supports through which run utility wires. Separate living units on two levels are slipped into the framework, like bottles in a winerack . . . The apartments, grouped in twos, overlap head to foot, with the living room of one apartment next to the adjacent bedroom level. No two units touch, being insulated with intermediary lead boxes to insure total soundproofing. The resultant silence has disturbed many tenants, who object to the feeling of isolation.

Standard elements of apartments of various sizes and arrangements include a ladder staircase, inset bookcases, and kitchen built-ins. Every living room opens to a terrace with sunbreak. Lack of uniformity of the terraces gives interest to the façades on three exposures; the north façade is a blank wall.

Access to each floor is by elevator and to the individual apartments from an interior street, stark as the passageway in a prison cell-block. Interior street and corridor street, the latter describing suburban roads, were terms originated by Le Corbusier. His additional contributions to the vocabulary of architecture were: living units, for rooms; classified cities; free plan; and, of course, the living-machine.

On levels seven and eight of the Marseilles Block, the interior streets were planned for commerce use, to serve an eighteen-room hotel, food markets, clothing and beauty shops, laundries, a post office, and a pharmacy. Level 18 is the terrace-roof designed as an activity center with swimming pool, three-hundred-meter racetrack, adult gym, open-air theater, kindergarten, and day nursery which has concrete benches set in streetcar rows.

Le Corbusier theorized that collective living was the ideal for human beings, and promised, in his muli-storyed dwellings, "seclusion, silence and rapidity of 'inside-outside' contacts." He could not accept man as a social animal who, in isolated habitation, would miss the over-the-back-fence communication and the normal sounds of a residential community. But both tenants and observer-experts criticized Le Corbusier's alternatives to suburbia.

When, in a scathing article, an American authority

on urban planning denounced the Marseilles Block, Le Corbusier had long been subjected to verbal abuse. His concepts and his structures had been equally reviled in the press and from the lecture platform. He was called the "Trojan horse of Bolshevism" in a Swiss architect's pamphlet published in 1928 and, in 1933, was assailed by another architect in "Is Architecture Going to Die?" A French public meeting, 1932, was organized to "protest against the baneful influence of Le Corbusier."

Vertical dwellings were incorporated in all of Le Corbusier's town-planning projects. He decried the removal of families to the outskirts and said, "The garden-city is a will-o'-the-wisp." Horizontally-grouped houses, so he claimed, created suburbs which "become tentacles of the town."

To make way for urban living in high-rise buildings, he proposed center-city demolition except for major historic monuments. "When the old is destroyed, the new can be re-thought" meant destruction within existing cities. Like Baron Haussmann, Le Corbusier advised the leveling of unsanitary, if colorful, sections of Paris. He also stressed the necessity to tear down certain skyscrapers of midtown New York, and of cutting deep into the Casbah for his town planning of Algiers.

The plan for Algiers was rejected as revolutionary, impractical, and inhuman, as were a number of others. Officials summarily turned down his town-planning projects for Paris, Saint-Dié, La Rochelle; for Rio,

Buenos Aires, Bogotá; for Stockholm, Geneva, Antwerp, and Berlin.

Le Corbusier's only accepted town-plan was for Chandigarh, the new capital of the Punjab in India. With architect-associates under his supervision, he began, in 1951, to work on the massive building set on a remote plain with the Himalaya mountains as backdrop.

The city plan and the rough concrete buildings of the Capitol complex were designed by Le Corbusier, who produced exciting buildings in spite of limitations imposed by unskilled local labor and by lack of industrial sources of construction materials. *Pilotis,* sculptural in effect, support the parasol entrance roof of the Assembly Hall. Permanent concrete sunbreaks, like so many giant squared-off holes in a honeycomb, dramatically lattice the Palace of Justice. The Secretariat, nine storys high and long as a city block, has a terrace-roof that serves as town square and playground; the structure is climate-conditioned by an ingenuous system of shuttered boxes set into the undulating glass wall. Vast expanses between the government buildings are minimized by expertly positioned water tiers.

Chandigarh has not escaped criticism. The budget exceeded all estimates and the per capita cost was exorbitant. And, when designing residential buildings, the staff architects disregarded Le Corbusier's onetime statement, "it is essential that the customs of the people be fully understood." Emphasis at Chandigarh was on the prestige and requirements of officials, not on the needs and habits of the half a million Punjabi who were to live in the city.

At Chandigarh, Le Corbusier fully developed his system of roads, as suggested first in the Athens Charter and afterwards in the ASCORAL plans. He called it the V system, the V for the French *voie,* meaning road. V 1 and V 3 are interurban routes, and V 2 is the main axis of urban traffic. V 4, the commercial street, channels off "the city traffic from points of intense activity." V 5 and V 6 serve the houses, and V 7 is the pedestrian walk, a "green linear zone which irrigates the different sectors of the city."

Unfortunately the V 7 system cannot be properly evaluated at Chandigarh, for the traffic and size of the capital do not warrant so involved and complicated a network of roads.

The completed works of Le Corbusier range from residences to university buildings, from industrial plants to the Ronchamp Chapel, 1950–1955, which is widely praised with adjectives normally applied to poetry. The distinguished buildings to his credit are, unfortunately, outnumbered by his projects in notes.

Le Corbusier was never free from discouragements in his professional life. He built a museum in Tokyo but never his Museum of Unlimited Growth. His design for the League of Nations Palace at Geneva, 1927, won first prize but, because of a technicality, the award was not honored. Jealous art academics contested the judging on the flimsy excuse that Le Corbusier's plan was not drawn in India ink, as stipulated in the rules of the competition.

Although Le Corbusier had two major art exhibitions in the United States, and was a member of the committee of architects for the design of the United Nations Building, New York City, he completed only one American commission: the Carpenter Center of the Visual Arts, Harvard University, 1961–1962.

In his seventy-eight year, Le Corbusier drowned while swimming at Cap-Martin. He had been working on major designs at his tiny studio-cabin which for him exemplified the theory that the development of every site should contribute to the "joy of living."

Building was an art to Mies,
who spent a lifetime refining and
confirming his own early concepts.

LUDWIG MIES VAN DER ROHE, 1886–1969

A FOUNDER of modern architecture, Mies van der Rohe was an incontestable genius in the profession for which he had no formal training. He, who was long after to say, "Architecture starts when you put two bricks together," was early in his life an apprentice stonemason, bricklayer, and woodworker. The acquired skills prepared him for subsequent adept use of all construction materials, including the metals and glass that distinguished great buildings of his design.

Mies, whose mother's surname was van der Rohe, learned to cut stone, and to build with it, in the shop of his father, a master mason. The son attended the Cathedral School at Aachen, or Aix-la-Chapelle, Germany, where he was born in 1886. At thirteen, he entered a trade school and, at fifteen, became an apprentice in the design of stucco ornaments needed by local architects for decoration of their buildings. Although established as a draftsman-designer by 1905, he left Aachen for Berlin. There he learned about woodworking through association with an outstanding cabinet-maker and decorator, Bruno Paul.

Mies was twenty-one when he undertook his first architectural commission, the Riehl house at Neu Babelsberg, Germany, a work conventional at the time. The following year, 1908, he joined the office of Peter Behrens, the Berlin architect and industrial designer who also trained Walter Gropius and, for a shorter time, Le Corbusier. For Behrens, Mies supervised construction of the German Embassy at St. Petersburg and, through that and other responsibilities, gained practical experience in large-scale building techniques.

After World War I, Mies returned to his own office opened shortly before he entered military service. From 1919 to 1924, he designed five major projects that not only made him famous but had far-reaching influence. For nearly two decades, following 1919, Mies was a power in the European revolution of architecture. In addition to completing numerous projects and private commissions, he sponsored a magazine, organized and contributed to expositions, designed furniture, and served as director of the Bauhaus school.

Walter Gropius, 1883–1969, an outstanding teacher of architecture, created the Bauhaus, April 1919, by merging an art academy and a crafts school at Weimar, Germany. The purpose of the Bauhaus was to correlate the arts, architecture, crafts, and modern industrial techniques. Gropius set up the curriculum that required every student to be grounded in classroom theory and in workshop practice. The machine was accepted as "our modern medium of design," and mass-production methods were applied to construction of buildings and manufacture of their decor, including furniture.

Under pressure, the Bauhaus was removed to Dessau, 1925, because reactionaries in politics and the arts were opposed to the school's emphasis on functionalism, a movement that stressed utility, form, and the forthright use of materials, unadorned. The complex of Bauhaus buildings at Dessau was notable among the architectural works of Gropius who, often through his career, happily collaborated with one or more partners, or with a group of associates. His structures designed for Dessau provided exactly the studios, the classrooms, and the workshops needed by his faculty and students.

Gropius, resigning as head of the Bauhaus, in 1928, returned to private practice in Berlin. He moved to the United States following a couple of years of association in London with Maxwell Fry, and in 1938, became the chairman of the School of Architecture, Harvard University, retiring from that post in 1952.

Young architects with whom Gropius planned the graduate center at Harvard were organized, by him, as Architects Collaborative (TAC), 1946. The group designed a number of important buildings, including the American Embassay at Athens, Greece.

On recommendation of Gropius, Mies was appointed head of the Bauhaus, 1930, following a two-year interim director, Johannes Meyer, another architect. A local Nazi group forced the removal of the school from Dessau, 1932, and Mies relocated it in Berlin. Continued official harassment caused the 1933 closing of the Bauhaus which, over a period of fourteen years, had made an irrevocable and immeasurable impact on architecture and industrial design.

Mies continued the practice of architecture in Germany until he, like Gropius, left for the United States. At age fifty-two, he was named director of architecture of Armour Institute that, shortly after, as the result of a merger, became part of the Illinois Institute of Technology. Mies was commissioned to plan the new I.I.T. campus at Chicago, Illinois, 1939. Five years later, he became a naturalized citizen of the country where he was to have a second distinguished career in architecture.

Mies said, late in life, that the one of his projects he would most like to have seen built was the *office building*, Friedrichstrasse, Berlin, 1919. It was the first of consecutive works known to his peers as the *five projects* which, as such, are already recorded in the history of architecture.

The proposed Friedrichstrasse structure marked the first design for a glass office building. It was composed of three towers with a central core containing lobbies and banks of elevators. Mies "used a prismatic form which seemed to me to fit best the irregular site of the building." The skyscraper appeared to be taller than twenty storys because of the division of façades that created an optical illusion. Mies said the walls were slightly angled to "avoid the monotony of over-large glass surfaces." His charcoal sketch of the *First Scheme* of the building is a striking example of his drawing ability, first evidenced at Aachen when he drafted designs for stucco ornaments.

His second famed project, the *glass skyscraper,* 1920–1921, was for an indeterminate site. He made experimental models, installing one outside the window of his office. By daily observation, he learned that, with glass, the important thing is the play of reflections and "not the effect of light and shadow as in ordinary buildings." There was nothing commonplace about the second project, with its self-reflecting curves.

Each of the glass skyscrapers was flat-topped and without cornices. Their straight horizontal rooflines suggested that the buildings might be stacked up and up to infinity. Neither structure had its interior space defined or compartmentalized for practical, specific purpose.

The third of the five projects was the *concrete office building,* 1922, its glass confined to continuous bands of ribbon windows. Under a thin roof-plate and above a ground floor, with entrance, the concrete floor slabs of five storys were cantilevered from columns, and beyond the windowbands, turned up like so many gallery trays.

Mies wrote in reference to the third project: "Reinforced concrete structures are skeletons by nature. No gingerbread. No fortress. Columns and girders eliminate bearing walls. This is skin and bone construction."

His description of the concrete office building was in the periodical *G* (Gesaltung). He was a frequent contributor to the magazine and underwrote its first three issues, 1923–1924. In writing and statement, Mies was concise and lucid, his communication of ideas and theories being analogous to the precision of his architectural design.

Ironically, the 1923 project by Mies was inspired by *Rhythms of a Russian Dance,* a painting by Theo van Doesburg who, critical of the skin-and-bone designation, called Mies an "anatomical architect." Onetime lecturer at the Bauhaus, van Doesburg was founder and, with Piet Mondrian, active promoter of *de Stijl,* a group of Dutch painters, sculptors, and architects. They were dedicated to nonobjective forms and to the limitation of the use of color in art.

The project that showed van Doesburg's influence on Mies was the latter's *brick country house.* Its freestanding walls with pane-glass joints extended from a flat roof, an independent plane, like the individual walls. Interior and exterior were interrelated through extension of those walls.

The *concrete country house,* an experiment in the use of the particular building material for a dwelling, was designed on a zoned plan. Extended groupings of rooms, zoned by function, formed open-sided outdoor areas, giving the structure a modified swastika shape. Philip C. Johnson, in his book on Mies, wrote that the plan "combines the maximum of indoor and outdoor privacy with the minimum of dispersal of architectural units."

Salient features variously associated with the five projects showed Mies to be both artist and innovator. He refined certain designs already known and pioneered with new methods later developed to the ultimate by him and other architects.

Having introduced glass skyscrapers, Mies designed them to the end of his career, making each a work of art with its own distinction. With sure hand, he produced for the concrete office-building project the matchless ideal of the ribbon window which, until then, had been experimental, and afterwards was to become popular and banal. Walls extending beyond the roof and glass corners had been introduced by Frank Lloyd Wright for the purpose of integrating living areas with the landscape, but in the brick country house of Mies, emphasis was on space, inside and out. His archetype zoned house lead to many American adaptations, a number being successfully executed by Marcel Breuer who, as student and teacher, had been associated with the Bauhaus. Concrete, the material Mies chose for the zoned house, his project five, proved later to be practical even for low-cost houses.

* * *

Mies received the commission for the so-called Barcelona Pavilion following his successful management of the International Housing Exposition, Stuttgart, 1927. He was then a vice-president of the sponsoring group, the *Deutsche Werkbund,* founded in 1907 by architects and leaders of industry concerned about the improvement of Germany's industrial design.

The original exposition plan was for a small community made up of numerous public squares, some partially walled, and of hillside houses grouped on streets restricted to pedestrian traffic. Because the city of Stuttgart intended ultimately to sell off the structures of the exposition, the first scheme was scrapped and the second featured freestanding buildings.

Mies designed not only the interesting site plan, but the glass exhibit and a small block of flat-roofed apartments with tiny balconies that had railings of horizontal metal rods. Of the apartments, he wrote: "Skeleton construction is the one best adapted to our needs. It enables us to rationalize the construction and divide up the interior with complete freedom."

As architect-in-charge of the Stuttgart exposition, Mies stated his views on the intent, writing, in part, "be its technical and economic aspects ever so important, the problem of modern housing is first and foremost a problem of architecture. Rationalization and standardization are not the whole problem, they are the means which must on no account be taken as an end to itself. The problem of a new type of housing is a problem of the prevailing state of mind; the battle for new housing is only one aspect of the great fight for new forms of life." The "prevailing state of mind" was a condition that Mies always related to architecture.

The only architectural restrictions he required of contributors to the *Werkbund* exposition was that all structures be flat roofed. Le Corbusier built his first Citrohan house at Stuttgart, and among others with buildings there were Walter Gropius, Peter Behrens, and J. J. P. Oud, city architect of Rotterdam, Holland, a well-known exponent of *de Stijl*.

After Stuttgart, and before the execution of his most famous European work, Mies designed several projects and residences; of the latter, two at Krefeld, Germany, were severely damaged in World War II. Another home, disastrously damaged, was his Tugendhat house, Brnö, Czechoslovakia, 1930, built following the construction of the German Pavilion for the International Exposition at Barcelona, Spain, 1929.

The Barcelona Pavilion, more than a masterpiece by Mies, is hailed and recognized by experts as one of the great buildings of all time. Its significance as an example of modern architecture is incontrovertible. The fame of the Barcelona Pavilion is the more remarkable because it is known primarily from publication throughout the world and from reproduction of extensive photographic studies. The building was demolished after the closing of the exposition.

When, belatedly, it was decided that Germany should be represented at the International Exposition at Barcelona, Mies, commissioned to design a building, was advised that it was to serve no purpose, to house no exhibit. His Barcelona Pavilion was itself to be the German exhibit, and as it turned out, was a work of art.

Mies drew on his experience to produce refinements of design and techniques. There were in the pavilion independent walls and the free-flowing space of the fourth of his five projects, the *brick country house,* an assured handling of several materials, and specially made furniture, precisely placed by the architect.

The interrelation of interior and exterior of the Barcelona Pavilion was achieved by the use of a variety of materials. Some walls and the podium, or base, were travertine. There were green marble walls and a double panel of etched glass, interspaced with artificial lighting. Partitions were of gray or bottle green glass. Black glass lined two reflecting pools, one graced by a female figure sculpted by Georg Kolbe.

Flow of the enclosed space was accentuated by slender steel columns, sheathed in chrome, and by a freestanding onyx partition against which pieces of furniture were set. Mies, who designed tables, stools, and one style of chair, drafted the furniture placement as accurately as that of a major structural component.

The first piece of furniture ever designed by Mies was a tubular steel chair with cantilevered seat and semicircular supports. It was displayed, 1927, at the silk exhibit of a Berlin exposition where the installation by Mies was typical of his artistry. He had few peers in the field of exhibition installations, designing many famous ones, some in collaboration with Lilly Reich, a justly famous associate.

The leather chair for the Barcelona Pavilion is a beautiful piece of furniture, spacious in size, being large enough to seat two, and elegant in design, the smallest detail having been considered by Mies. The armless Barcelona chair with its steel bands in single and reverse curves was most effective when placed with the Tugendhat leather chair, which has delicate metal bands for arms. Groupings of the two chair types were arranged in the Tugendhat living room by Mies who, for that house, also designed all other furniture and such hardware as door handles, curtain tracks, and lighting fixtures.

Entrance to the house, situated on a steep slope, is from the top floor. A glass-enclosed staircase connects the bedroom level with the main living floor below. Division of its free-flowing space, 50 feet by 80 feet, is by a straight wall of onyx at the living room area and by an ebony wall curved at the dining room section. Part of the lower story can be turned into a partial terrace by the automatic lowering of alternate panels of a hundred-foot glass wall. By day, exterior and interior, as in other houses by Mies, are interrelated; by night, the interior is handsomely closed in by floor-to-ceiling curtains of raw silk and velvet.

Twenty years later Mies designed a small but equally spectacular residence in the United States. It was the world's first all-glass house, built at Plano, Illinois, 1950, for Dr. Edith Farnsworth. Here exterior and interior are totally related, the walls being clear plate glass, and only raw silk floor-to-ceiling curtains providing privacy, as needed.

Mies had been in Chicago for little more than a decade when he did the Farnsworth house, and by then his plan for the complex of the Illinois Institute of Technology was well underway. His preliminary scheme for the campus was not approved because it required the elimination of a major street. His second plan, for the same rectangular site, encompassing eight blocks on Chicago's South Side, included an athletic field and twenty-one rectangular buildings, different in size but based on a twenty-four-foot module. The exception was the Library and Administration Building, which was designed to have bays about three times the size of the other buildings.

Structural unity resulting from the standard module is not obvious, because Mies designed buildings of various materials, steel, brick, and glass, often imaginatively combined. He also varied the placement of exterior panels and the breadth, height, and width of structures.

The Architecture and Design Building, 1956, is glass

with exterior steel columns which are at once the decoration and the structural supports. In the vast one-room interior, 120 feet by 210 feet, Mies met his students until his retirement from I.I.T., 1958. As teacher, he was understanding and tolerant even of those who challenged his theories and techniques. Aware that not every student was a genius, Mies taught the fundamentals, beginning with how to "put two bricks together."

By the time the Architecture and Design Building was opened, Mies had completed several off-campus commissions. One was the apartment houses, 860 Lake Shore Drive, Chicago, 1951, which Philip Johnson wrote, "is indeed Mies's first masterpiece in America." The second undoubtedly is the Seagram Building, New York, 1958, designed in collaboration with Philip Johnson. Experts identify as a third tower masterpiece One Charles Center, Baltimore, Maryland, 1962.

The apartment houses are twenty-six stories high, and set at right angles to each other but obliquely to the site's main road. The identical glass and steel towers seem, from certain directions, to be one building, but are connected only by an outdoor covered passageway that follows a section of the continuous travertine platform. From it, both buildings are raised to the height of two stories on exposed columns, like the *pilotis* of Le Corbusier. The glass walls are held in place by steel welded to the floor slabs, and for effect, steel mullions are attached to the structural columns. Plasticity is achieved by the projecting steel mullions that from some angles are unobtrusive and, from others, are predominant, to the point of obscuring the glass.

The Seagram Building is a thirty-eight-story tower of topaz-tinted glass sheathed in bronze which according to Mies, "is a very noble material and lasts forever if it is used in the right way." He was the first architect to dare incorporate bronze in skyscraper construction. To the rear of the Seagram tower are flanking wings and two full-height walls built as protection against high winds.

Approach to the tower is from a plaza, extending for a full block along Park Avenue. Pools with fountains are at either side of the plaza, which is edged with green marble strips and punctuated with a seventy-five-foot bronze flagpole. The building's podium is pink granite, and its lobbies have terrazzo floors and travertine walls. As always with Mies, every detail was planned to the fraction. The module, four-foot, seven and one-half inch, was not varied more than one-sixteenth inch, whether in utility closets or rest rooms, in spacious offices or public hallways. All hardware and such essentials as mail chutes and fire alarm installations were designed to scale harmonious with the building.

The interior was designed by Philip Johnson, distinguished American architect and worthy collaborator of Mies. When director of architecture and design at the Museum of Modern Art, Johnson wrote a book about the work of Mies and also planned the Museum's comprehensive Mies van der Rohe exhibition in 1947.

One Charles Center, designed by Mies, was the first building of a downtown Baltimore complex for which planning was begun in 1958. Thirty-three acres were allotted for nine office buildings, high-rise and medium; for two apartment towers and one hotel; for a theater, a retail store, open plazas, a park and fountains.

Mies's twenty-three-story tower, its tinted glass sheathed in dark brown aluminum, is set on a concrete podium. The interior has the precise and meticulous details typical of Mies. Again, as with the Seagram Building, set back a hundred feet from the sidewalk, for dramatic effect, the placement and shape of One Charles Center was planned by Mies after extensive study of the site.

The building is eight-sided to conform to a preestablished zone. The rectangular area, with its southeast corner sliced off, is along a fourteen-foot northsouth slope. One Charles Center's main entrance is reached by a ramp leading from Charles Street, to the east, to the travertine plaza. At the west, the tower juts past that part of the plaza designated as a park.

None of the great buildings by Mies were universally accepted. Like every other architect of renown, he had his detractors, many of them disagreeing with his long-famous claim that, in architecture, "less is more." Not being contentious, he almost never answered the critics of his theory about elimination of nonessentials from architectural designs. He held to his own early concepts and continued always to produce disciplined structures, but undertaking each new commission with a fresh approach.

Mies was the first American architect to receive the Presidential Medal of Freedom, 1963, and that year also received a gold medal from the National Institute of Arts and Letters.

Those were just two of many honors and awards given to the man who, in 1924, defined architecture as "the will of the epoch translated into space."

*He invented a science for human
settlements and envisions one worldwide city
early in the twenty-first century.*

CONSTANTINOS APOSTOLOS DOXIADIS,

1913–

ANCIENT GREEK temple complexes and modern
Greek communities were the incentives to the career of
Constantinos Doxiadis. The world-renowned spokesman
for *entopias,* or good cities, projected into the twenty-
first century, explored temple sites while a student. In
the line of duty, he later toured Greek towns and villages damaged or razed by fighting during the World
War II years.

Born in Bulgarian Thrace, son of Greek parents,
Doxiadis was brought up in Athens. In 1922 the senior
Doxiadis, a doctor, became Minister of Refugees for
Greece where, post-World War I, refugees totaled one-
quarter of the population. Constantinos, then nine
years old, was taken to refugee camps by his mother, a
volunteer supervisor of the kitchens. At the camps, the
son first became aware of the problems of displaced persons. The experience was to have meaning for Doxiadis
when he planned housing for refugees and relocated
peoples of several countries.

After graduating from the National Metsovion Technical University in Athens, Doxiadis went to Germany for graduate study. In 1936 he received his doctorate in civil engineering from the Berlin-Charlottenburg University. His thesis presented an original theory that temple sites of ancient Greece were designed to exact specifications.

The concept continues to be controversial, although Doxiadis based it on extensive studies of ancient religious communities of the mainland and the islands. He inferred, from observations and measurements, that the complexes extended along radial lines emanating from an entrance gate. Some experts think his conclusions are correct. A number of archaeologists disagree, recognizing at their digs no confirmation of uniform plans for the ancient religious communities.

Doxiadis was appointed chief town-planning officer for the Greater Athens area, in 1937. From 1939 through 1944, he was head of the department of regional and town planning in the Ministry of Public Works. Concurrently, he was acting professor of town planning at the University. Independently, in those years, he accepted commissions in architecture and engineering.

When Italy attacked Greece in the fall of 1940, Doxiadis had been called back to service. A reserve sergeant of artillery, he received the Greek Military Cross for valor on the Albanian front. As observer and coordinator of artillery fire, he served with a battalion that refused to surrender in 1941. The soldiers gave their small arms to peasants, sank major weapons in a lake, and struck out across wild country for Athens.

While crossing mountains with his comrades in arms, Doxiadis resolved earlier thoughts about architecture and planning in the modern world. What developed was his theory of *ekistics,* the science of human settlements.

With Greece in turmoil, he briefly went underground, and then returned to the Ministry of Public Works. With others from the Ministry, he traveled widely in Greece, ostensibly to evaluate war damage and to make recommendations for reconstruction. With Doxiadis as leader, the group gathered information about Germany's military objectives in Greece and forwarded the collected data to allied headquarters in Cairo.

Doxiadis masterminded a coup against Italian intelligence officers in 1943 and for that action was subsequently decorated by the British.

Ten days after the liberation of Athens, in 1944, Doxiadis opened an ekistics exhibition there. He developed ekistics as an exact science that correlates scientific and related disciplines. The multidisciplinary method is used to study human settlements of all types and to provide buildings and services, as required, in particular locations for specific peoples.

In the four years preceding the first ekistics exhibition, 23 percent of the buildings in Greece had been destroyed, a fact well known to Doxiadis, who had thoroughly studied war damage for his Ministry. The exhibition of 1944 highlighted, by maps, charts, and photographs, the ekistics needs in various sections of the country. The presentation attracted international attention, and books about the exhibit were published in French, English, and Russian, as well as in Greek.

Doxiadis, chairman of the United Nations working group on housing policies, was also coordinator of American Aid to Greece under the Marshall Plan. From 1945 to 1948, he was minister and permanent secretary of the Greek Housing Reconstruction Agency; from 1948 to 1951, minister-coordinator of the Greek Recovery Program. Under his supervision, bridges, railroads, and power lines were rebuilt. Three thousand villages were established, and more than two hundred thousand new homes, or half the number of dwellings destroyed, were constructed.

Already experienced as town planner and regional developer, Doxiadis started his own engineering consultancy firm in the early 1950s. From the time of its founding, Doxiadis Associates rapidly expanded. In little more than a decade, the organization had a staff of six hundred, offices in a dozen worldwide metropolises, and commissions under way in thirty countries. New-city plans and development projects, urban and regional, ultimately affected ten million people, living, variously, in North and South America, the Middle East, Egypt, Africa, and India.

In Greece, where Doxiadis had earlier provided essential housing for fellow countrymen, his firm undertook the development of a two-mile stretch of beach bordering the Aegean Sea. The recreation area was designed with facilities for both low-income Greeks and free-spending tourists.

Improvements of the coastal site required the services of about fifty specialists, including a sports consultant who had helped to design the grounds for the 1956 Olympics at Melbourne. For Doxiadis Associates, the Australian advised on a national sports center included in the beach-resort plans. Such specialization in development projects is not today unique, but Doxiadis uses the system to its ultimate.

The system was pioneered by ASCORAL (Assemblée de Constructeurs pour une Renovation Architecturale), founded by Le Corbusier in 1943. The organization was made up of architects, city planners, sociologists, biologists, engineers and even doctors. Since then representatives of other technological and scientific disciplines have been recruited for studies of land settlement, community development, and housing as related to man.

The need for more kinds of experts is due to the increase of population and pollution, of motor and air transportation, and the deterioration of cities that are being supplanted, as residential areas, by suburbs.

Wherever in the world Doxiadis Associates is engaged in site-study, design and execution of a project, its staff includes all, or most, of the following: architects, engineers, economists, sociologists, agriculturists, landscape architects, meteorologists, geologists, and, of course, skilled technicians and expert draftsmen. Other specialists as, for example, aerial photographers, are retained as needed. Doxiadis, as a twentieth-century man, relies on the computer for correlation and projection of information. When personally in the field, he gathers data with his own tapeline and camera.

An understanding of the ills of modern cities and a comprehension of the ekistics needs of new settlements require, according to Doxiadis, consideration of the constituents inherent in all communities. He writes, "The elements are: nature, the container; man who settles in it; society formed by man; the shells (houses and buildings) constructed by man; and the networks (roads, water supply, power, etc.)."

In speeches and in his books, Doxiadis touches on or states in depth his certainty that, unless there is a reversal of present urban patterns and uncontrolled expansion, dystopias, or bad cities, will make a "wasteland" of our earth.

He thinks of himself as a mason who builds or rebuilds "small parts of the earth for man." In fact, the areas of Doxiadis's planning are only relatively small. His Islamabad, the capital of West Pakistan, was designed for a maximum population of two and a half million. The development project for the region of Detroit, Michigan, encompasses thousands of square miles in the United States and neighboring Canada.

Islamabad has self-contained centers for thirty to fifty thousand inhabitants. Doxiadis has said, "each one of its sectors corresponds to a natural city of the past." When Islamabad was first operative in 1964, fifty thousand people could be accommodated. Ultimately the city was planned to extend over an original six-village site.

In certain residential areas, minor roads, almost as narrow as footpaths, were built to preclude speeding by any kind of vehicle. The plan for the capital projected one hundred bridges for foot and vehicular traffic, and one hundred miles of all grades of roads, counting the tiny streets between dwellings. As everywhere, Doxiadis separated heavy traffic thoroughfares from working and living areas.

The planning of a brand-new city, like Islamabad, is much less chancy than redevelopment. Predetermined patterns of expansion are more likely to be realized when there is no hindrance from existing interests. Difficulties arise through interference from political, industrial and/or real-estate groups, and even, as with the Detroit project, from established growth patterns.

Detroit is one of the cities of the Great Lakes Megalopolis where, by the year 2000, an estimated 45 million people will live. In preparation for inevitable growth and expansion, the Urban Detroit Area Research Project, under the direction of Doxiadis Associates, was initiated in 1965.

Three million dollars was the budget for the five-year study of an area 150 miles long and 220 miles wide. Within the boundaries are twenty-five counties of Michigan, nine of northern Ohio, and three of Ontario, Canada. A three-stage report of the project was intended for wide circulation by the sponsor, the Detroit Edison Company, in cooperation with Wayne State University.

Phase One of the research project resulted in the publication of an encyclopedic report on the geologic, climatic, and physical resources of the area, and about the economic and urban developments within it.

Phase Two was concerned with alternatives of the future, and the prediction of probable trends of ongoing urbanization. Phase Three presented specific plans for expansion and development that required mutual agreement and action by city and state governments, planning commissions, industries, utility companies, and transportation authorities.

Recreation areas were specified and green belts recommended for much-needed beautification of the region. Services to cities and towns were assured by industrial redevelopment and by the building of roads, shopping centers, airports, and shipping ports, research facilities, and connecting transit systems, automated and high speed.

More than eleven hundred communities in the Michigan-Ontario-Ohio area were included in the planning, but few proposals were readily accepted. Officials of local governments either refused to collaborate on the

Phase Three master plan or failed to show any interest in it.

The pattern of Detroit's expansion further jeopardized immediate realization of the master plan. Phase Three was predicated on Detroit's growth toward Port Huron to the northeast. As future twin cities, they were blueprinted to be encircled by ten satellite cities, five of them new. However, Detroit's suburbs continued to sprawl in every direction but north, and its industry did not move that way to take advantage of the shipping potential of the St. Lawrence Seaway.

A similar shift from the predicted trend of expansion was partially responsible for the setback of Doxiadis's earlier plan for a dynapolis at Washington, D.C. He defines dynapolis as the "dynamic city or dynamic polis. The ideal dynapolis is the city with the parabolic unidirectional growth which can expand in time and space."

The business district of a dynapolis ideally spreads along a main transportation artery. The central core is flanked, along the axis, by residential neighborhoods, each with its schools, churches, small commercial centers, and recreational areas, interlocking parks being of prime importance to the human settlement.

The Washington dynapolis, designed for the Redevelopment Land Agency, was to be to the south, along the banks of the Potomac River. Entrenched real-estate interests opposed the plans, and the natural growth of the capital was in the opposite direction. Washington and major cities to the north, Baltimore, Philadelphia,

New York, and Boston, make up the 450-mile Eastern Megalopolis.

Doxiadis Associates has designed housing projects for Louisville, Cincinnati, and Miami. The firm's Park Town, Cleveland, Ohio, and Eastwick, Philadelphia, Pennsylvania, are gradual urban developments. The latter is a reordering and rebuilding of industrial and residential districts for ten thousand families, or fifty thousand people. A suburban community for those of middle income, it was begun in 1950, part of a project incorporating designs by various city planners. The master plan depended on radial and circumferential expressways leading to subunits of decreasing size.

Eastwick residences are uniform in design, like those done by Doxiadis Associates at Karachi, West Pakistan. There, the houses, first chiefly occupied by refugees, have prefabricated, mass-produced flat roofs and concrete walls. A single dwelling, one twelve-foot by twelve-foot room with veranda of the same size, was budgeted at four hundred dollar. Expansion potential on the plot was for a maximum twenty-four-foot by forty-two-foot indoor-outdoor home.

Those who decry the lack of architectural invention in Doxiadis's housing for redevelopment areas and for new cities fail to perturb him. He is an exponent of the orderly plan and an expert in the use of the module.

Like Frank Lloyd Wright and Le Corbusier, Doxiadis stresses the human scale in architecture, taking man's stride for measurement. Doxiadis uses thirty inches, the length of the average man's pace, and lays out designs in fractions or multiples of that figure. Even the floor of his own living room in Athens is made of thirty by thirty slabs of Pentelic marble.

Doxiadis makes no apology for the standardization of construction planned by Doxiadis Associates. All is deliberate. Some results from budgetary restrictions and others, especially in underdeveloped countries, from the lack of skilled workers.

He thinks human settlements should be planned and zoned with walkways, service streets, and major roads; with dams, canals, and essential conduits; with power lines, sewers, and other sanitation facilities. The life-support systems once blueprinted or built, respective communities ideally should then be free to construct their own buildings.

Since homes should vary with locale, being consistent with customs, Doxiadis recognizes the necessity for enclosed homes in cold climates and the advantage of open-air enclosures in torrid regions. In countries where Doxiadis Associates develops communities, provision is made for any outdoor activities that are a way of life. In Karachi, for example, there are verandas and court-yards for household chores, principally laundry and cooking, and walled roof terraces for sleeping.

There are imponderables to man's reaction to his housing that Doxiadis illustrates by reference to his Rio de Janeiro redevelopment. When the master plan showed elimination of the *favelas,* the slums, he was asked, "Who, in this case, is going to write the sambas?" In other words, as he expressed it, ". . . is it the slum and the suffering in it that lead to sambas, or the human scale that modern developments do not have?" Only time will supply the answer.

Human values, no less than human scale, concern Doxiadis. Again and again, he enumerates the drawbacks of today's cities. In the typical metropolis, the former "normal, natural person-to-person contact" is impossible. Fear keeps people isolated indoors. Children, held by the hand when crossing streets, are made to feel that "they live in hostile surroundings." Noise, filth, and ugliness adversely affect man. Doxiadis wonders what man will become if he smells only the exhaust of motor cars and never the scent of flowers.

To him, the monster of the modern city is the automobile. Among other things, it destroys the age-old love affairs of man with architecture, with buildings that can be enjoyed only when one walks and observes. Doxiadis wants to forestall the imminence of cities inhabited chiefly by cars and only incidentally by human beings. He sees as the ultimate goal the complete separation of all roads with machines from the paths of men.

He would relieve traffic congestion with deepways, his word for a complete underground system for private cars, trucks, and mass-transportation vehicles. They will move in deepways constructed at different levels, those lowest in the ground being for the highest speeds. In addition to shortening the time spent for long distance trips and daily commutes, the deepways offer other advantages. They would cost less than highways built across expensive real estate and would circumvent the mutilation of the surface of the earth, leaving it "free for man and his human development."

The place for that development should be entopia, which Doxiadis defines as a "practicable place that can exist." He does not suggest doing away with the big city, "because it is already a fact." What must be done is to interlock his dynapolis and its static units that are developed to serve "all the needs of man" and to assure "his happiness." The solution, as he sees it, ". . . is not decentralization but new-centralization."

Entopia is a sweeping concept that for fulfillment draws on dreams and science. "What we need is a place where the dream can meet with reality, the place which can satisfy the dreamer, be accepted by the scientist, and some day be built by the builder, the city which will be in-place—the *entopia*."

As the mason, the builder for man, Doxiadis depends on facts and statistics. As a thinker-philosopher, he draws on his imagination and from prodigious knowledge of related literature. In both roles, he sets forth his ideas with a vocabulary for which he has coined half a dozen words. Not a few critics say Doxiadis simply puts new names to old ideas. He counters by questioning what is original in the world and denies any claim as creator by pointing out that nature, water, and earth are created things.

Doxiadis does insist that the planning of better cities depends on theory. "Personally, I believe in one theory which may or may not be right. It does not matter since we can only make progress by expressing a system of ideas and by challenging society as a whole to respond to it." A sought-after and charismatic speaker, Doxiadis appears on lecture platforms all over the world. He expounds his theory and discusses those of others, past and present, ever attempting to elicit society's response to the challenge of human existence in a changing world.

At the Athens Center of Ekistics which he founded, Doxiadis supervises the staff and makes decisions about curriculum. His *Ekistics, an Introduction to the Science of Human Settlements,* a principal textbook at the Center, is widely distributed elsewhere. Doxiadis enjoys teaching and, when possible, takes on a class at the Center. He says that he himself learns whenever a student questions, "Why?"

In 1963, Doxiadis initiated the annual Delos symposium held on the Greek island of that name. The select group invited to exchange ideas on Delos has variously included philosophers, politicians, industrialists, historians, scientists, and city planners.

A participant at one Delos symposium was R. Buckminster Fuller, architect, engineer, scientist, who said, in 1970, that he no longer thinks of himself as an architect. Even he could not deny his pioneering in architecture with the 4-D house, 1927, the Dymaxion house, 1944–1945, and geodesic structures, spherical, lightweight, and strong. His domes based on the Dymaxion principle of maximum output for minimum input, have established a trend with consequences not yet determined.

Others at the same Delos symposium with Fuller were Fritz Zwicky, astrophysicist, Arnold Toynbee, historian, and Margaret Mead, anthropologist. It was she who read aloud the summation of ideas presented by participants. One sentence stressed the necessity "to design now the material framework for a viable worldwide system of human settlements."

That worldwide system will be what Doxiadis named Ecumenopolis, a composite of the megalopolises now proliferating. It is widely recognized that the era of isolated cities is over, and all too soon there will be a universal city on earth. World population is projected at six billion people by the year 2000 and to twenty-five to thirty-five billion not long after in the twenty-first century.

Doxiadis points out that successful cities of history exceeded no more than about a mile in length, five square miles in area, and fifty thousand inhabitants. In the past, larger communities "were doomed to fail, were short-lived and offer us no solution."

The paradox of growth offers the Ecumenopolis and the "absolute need for man to live in small cities." Doxiadis proposes a "gigantic city of superhuman dimensions, made up of small units." He never fails to mention the importance of the happiness of man, "the happier form of existence." Having already built cities beginning with static cells for thirty thousand to fifty thousand people, Doxiadis hopes his entopia will be a reality of the next century.

Plans for many a megalopolis have failed because of lack of understanding of the problems and lack of co-operation among principal interests. Whether a livable Ecumenopolis is possible depends on human beings.

For Doxiadis, the "goal of the city is to make man happy and safe," a statement made twenty-four-hundred years ago by the Greek philosopher Aristotle.

INDEX

Readings in
Radical Psychiatry

by
CLAUDE STEINER
HOGIE WYCKOFF
JOY MARCUS
PETER LARIVIERE
DANIEL GOLDSTINE
ROBERT SCHWEBEL
and
MEMBERS OF THE
RADICAL PSYCHIATRY CENTER

GROVE PRESS, INC., NEW YORK

Contents

CONTENTS

Section I
Manifesto

Manifesto

by Claude Steiner

1. The practice of psychiatry has been usurped by the medical establishment. Political control of its public aspects has been seized by medicine and the language of soul healing ($\psi\upsilon\chi\eta + \iota\alpha\tau\rho\epsilon\iota\alpha$) has been infiltrated with irrelevant medical concepts and terms.

Psychiatry must return to its non-medical origins since most psychiatric conditions are in no way the province of medicine. All persons competent in soul healing should be known as psychiatrists. Psychiatrists should repudiate the use of medically derived words such as "patient," "illness," "diagnosis," "treatment." Medical psychiatrists' unique contribution to psychiatry is as experts on neurology, and, with much needed additional work, on drugs.

2. Extended individual psychotherapy is an elitist, outmoded, as well as non-productive, form of psychiatric help. It concentrates the talents of a few on

a few. It silently colludes with the notion that people's difficulties have their sources within them while implying that everything is well with the world. It promotes oppression by shrouding its consequences with shame and secrecy. It further mystifies by attempting to pass as an ideal human relationship when it is, in fact, artificial in the extreme.

People's troubles have their source not within them but in their alienated relationships, in their exploitation, in polluted environments, in war, and in the profit motive. Psychiatry must be practiced in groups. One-to-one contacts, of great value in crises, should become the exception rather than the rule. The high ideal of I–Thou loving relations should be pursued in the context of groups rather than in the stilted consulting room situation. Psychiatrists not proficient in group work are deficient in their training and should upgrade it. Psychiatrists should encourage bilateral, open discussion and discourage secrecy and shame in relation to deviant behavior and thoughts.

3. By remaining "neutral" in an oppressive situation psychiatry, especially in the public sector, has become an enforcer of establishment values and laws. Adjustment to prevailing conditions is the avowed goal of most psychiatric treatment. Persons who deviate from the world's madness are given fraudulent diagnostic tests which generate diagnostic labels which lead to "treatment" which is, in fact, a series

4]]]

of graded repressive procedures such as "drug management," hospitalization, shock therapy, perhaps lobotomy. All these forms of "treatment" are perversions of legitimate medical methods which have been put at the service of the establishment by the medical profession. Treatment is forced on persons who would, if let alone, not seek it.

Psychologial tests and the diagnostic labels they generate, especially schizophrenia, must be disavowed as meaningless mystifications, the real function of which is to distance psychiatrists from people and to insult people into conformity. Medicine must cease making available drugs, hospitals, and other legitimate medical procedures for the purpose of overt or subtle law enforcement and must examine how drug companies are dictating treatment procedures through their advertising. Psychiatry must cease playing a part in the oppression of women by refusing to promote adjustment to their oppression. All psychiatric help should be by contract; that is, people should choose when, what, and with whom they want to change. Psychiatrists should become advocates of the people, should refuse to participate in the pacification of the oppressed, and should encourage people's struggles for liberation.

PSYCHIATRIC DISTURBANCE IS EQUIVALENT WITH ALIENATION WHICH IS THE RESULT OF MYSTIFIED OPPRESSION.

5]]]

READINGS IN RADICAL PSYCHIATRY

PARANOIA IS A STATE OF HEIGHTENED AWARENESS. MOST PEOPLE ARE PERSECUTED BEYOND THEIR WILDEST DELUSIONS. THOSE WHO ARE AT EASE ARE INSENSITIVE.

PSYCHIATRIC MYSTIFICATION IS A POWERFUL INFLUENCE IN THE MAINTENANCE OF PEOPLE'S OPPRESSION.

PERSONAL LIBERATION IS ONLY POSSIBLE ALONG WITH RADICAL SOCIAL REFORMS.

PSYCHIATRY MUST STOP ITS MYSTIFICATION OF THE PEOPLE AND GET DOWN TO WORK!

—Claude Steiner

(*Note:* The first Radical Psychiatry Manifesto was written in the summer of 1969 on the occasion of the annual American Psychiatric Association Conference in San Francisco, which was widely disrupted by members of the Women's Liberation, Gay Liberation, and Radical Therapy movements.)

Section II
Theory

1. PRINCIPLES by Claude Steiner[1]

Psychiatry is the art of soul healing. Anyone who practices the art is a psychiatrist. The practice of psychiatry, usurped by the medical profession, is in a sad state of disarray. Medicine has done nothing to improve it; as practiced today, medical psychiatry is a step sideways, into pseudo-scientism, from the state of the art in the Middle Ages when it was the province of elders and priests as well as physicians.

Psychiatry as it is predominantly practiced today needs to be changed radically, that is, "at the root."

Psychiatry is a political activity. Persons who avail themselves of psychiatric aid are invariably in the midst of power-structured relationships with one or more other human beings. The psychiatrist has an influence in the power arrangements of these relationships. Psychiatrists pride themselves on being "neutral" in their professional dealings. However, when one person dominates or oppresses another, a neutral participant, especially when he is seen as an authority, becomes an

---

[1] All of the articles in this book are reprints with minor changes of articles which first appeared in *The Radical Therapist* in 1970–1971.

enforcer of the domination and his lack of activity becomes essentially political and oppressive.[2]

The classic and prime example of this fact is found in psychiatry's usual role in relation to women where, at worst, psychiatrists promote oppressive sex roles and at best remain neutral, therefore supportive of them. The same is true of psychiatry's traditional role in relation to the young, black, and poor; in every case psychiatry's "neutrality" represents tacit support of the oppressive status quo.

There are four types of psychiatrists:

Alpha psychiatrists are conservative or liberal in their political consciousness and in their practice and methods of psychiatry; the largest majority of medical psychiatrists fall into this category.

Beta psychiatrists are conservative or liberal in their politics and radical in their methods. Examples of this type are men like Fritz Perls and Eric Berne and the human potentialities psychiatrists, usually not physicians, who expand the boundaries of psychiatric practice, but tend to be unaware of the manner in which oppression is a factor in psychic suffering and thus ignore the political nature of their work.

Gamma psychiatrists are radical in their politics but conservative in their practice. Examples of this are Laing and others (as a special case, Szasz whose awareness of the politics of psychiatry is quite heightened) who practice old, out-moded methods of therapy based on Freudian or neo-Freudian theory with emphasis on individual psychotherapy, "depth," and "insight."

The fourth kind of psychiatrist is the radical psychiatrist, who is radical both politically and in his psychiatric methods.

The first principle of radical psychiatry is that in the

---

[2] For an argument demonstrating the political nature of neutrality, liberalism, or tolerance read "Repressive Tolerance" by H. Marcuse, in *A Critique of Pure Tolerance* (Boston: Beacon Press, 1969).

absence of oppression, human beings will, due to their basic nature or soul, which is preservative of themselves and their species, live in harmony with nature and each other. Oppression is the coercion of human beings by force or threats of force, and is the source of all human alienation.

The condition of the human soul which makes soul healing necessary is alienation.[3] Alienation is a feeling within a person that he is not part of the human species, that she[4] is dead or that everyone is dead, that he does not deserve to live, or that someone wishes her to die. It may be helpful, in this connection, to remember that psychiatrists were originally known as alienists, a fact that seems to validate the notion that our forefathers knew more about psychiatry than we. *Alienation is the essence of all psychiatric conditions. This is the second principle of radical psychiatry.* Every psychiatric diagnosis except for those that are *clearly* organic in origin is a form of alienation.

The third principle of radical psychiatry is that all alienation is the result of oppression about which the oppressed has been mystified or deceived.

By deception is meant the mystification of the oppressed into believing that she is not oppressed or that there are good reasons for her oppression. The result is that the person, instead of sensing his oppression and being angered by it, decides that his ill feelings are his own fault, and his own responsibility. The result of the acceptance of deception is that the person will feel alienated.

The difference between alienation and anger about one's oppression is unawareness of deception. Psychi-

---

[3] The view that man's alienation is the result of mystified oppression stems from Marx.

[4] In order to avoid the sexist connotations implicit in the use of solely masculine pronouns such as "he" and "his," we have throughout this book deliberately included "she" and "her" as well.

atry has a great deal to do with the deception of human beings about their oppression.

$$\text{Oppression} + \text{Deception} = \text{Alienation}[5]$$

$$\text{Oppression} + \text{Awareness} = \text{Anger}$$

EXAMPLES

Consider a seventeen-year-old American youngster during the Vietnam war. He is told that he must offer his life to destroy the enemy in Asia. He is told that this is good for him, for his brothers and sisters, for his country, and even for the enemy. He is taught that a man will defend his country without question, and that a man who hesitates or questions this principle is a coward who does not deserve to be called a human being. If he fails to understand that he is being oppressed and if he believes these lies, he will eventually come to think of himself as less than human for not wanting to defend his country. He will doubt his own opinions and experiences concerning the war. He will come to consider himself a coward; he will become disgusted with himself; he will cut himself off from his peers and will become depressed. He may lose interest in everyday activities; he may begin to speak about hopelessness and meaninglessness; he may start using drugs to give himself a temporary reprieve from his despair. If his shame and despair reach large enough proportions, he may attempt to destroy himself. He will see himself as no good and will believe himself in need of psychiatric attention.

If he were to consult a "neutral" therapist, he might be asked, "What is wrong with you? Why are you de-

---

[5] Thanks are due to Hogie Wyckoff for her contribution to the development of Radical Psychiatry's basic formula.

pressed? Why do you hate your father? Why do you rebel against authority? Let's talk about it, and you'll feel better. Tell me about your childhood. Maybe the bad things that happened then make you sad now. Other boys your age aren't depressed about the war and killing. These are troubled times, but others are able to adjust to them. Why don't you? Tell me your dreams. Maybe we can find what is wrong with you. The army is bad, I know, but it has its good points. It might make a man out of you."

This young man may eventually feel better because of the friendly and warm attitude of the therapist, thus mystifying his true feelings about the war. He may "pull himself together," his personality-trait disturbance (passive-aggressive, aggressive type) may improve, and he may wind up in a flag-wrapped box. His therapist will feel and will contend that he was neutral throughout the therapeutic intervention and that he did not attempt to influence the young man. But in truth he acted as a recruiting officer for the army, all the more effective for his disarming smile.

It is awareness of the oppressive quality of "neutral" psychiatric intervention that keeps most of the oppressed young, black, and poor away from psychiatrists who, they know, will behave as if no oppression were occurring. Neutrality in an oppressive situation is equivalent to oppression; scientific detachment in a concentration camp is support for the murderers who run it.

A radical psychiatrist will take sides. He will advocate the side of those whom he is helping. The radical psychiatrist will not look for the wrongness within the person seeking psychiatric attention; rather, he will look for the way in which this person is being oppressed and how the person is going along with the oppression. The only problem that radical psychiatry looks for inside someone's head is how he empowers and enforces the lies of the oppressor and thereby enforces his own oppression.

The classic and prime example of the oppressive role of psychiatry is found in its usual relation to women, where at worst psychiatrists promote oppressive sex roles and at best remain neutral, therefore supportive of them.

Take, for example, a woman who lives with a man who dominates her in every way, including treating her as a sexual object. The assumption of their sexual relationship is that she will have intercourse with him any time *he* wants it, while he has no particular responsibilities or concern for her pleasure. If she achieves orgasm, fine; if she does not, they agree that orgasm is not a necessary ingredient of female sexual pleasure. If this woman becomes "frigid" and talks to a radical psychiatrist, she will say to her, "You have as much right to sexual pleasure as he. If you do not achieve orgasm, it isn't because you are frigid but because he is selfish. Don't make love unless you want to, and demand to achieve orgasm at least as often as he does. There is nothing wrong with you except that you're accepting his domination and that you are justifying it; so that instead of seeing that you're quite right in not enjoying sex, you have come to the conclusion that you are 'frigid.' "

METHODS

What, then, are the methods of radical psychiatry? *The radical psychiatrist sees anyone who presents himself with a psychiatric problem as being alienated; that is, as being oppressed and deceived about his oppression, for otherwise he would not seek psychiatric succor.* All other theoretical considerations are secondary to this one.

The basic formula of radical psychiatry is:

$$\text{Awareness} + \text{Contact} = \text{Action} \rightarrow \text{Liberation}$$

The formula implies that for liberation two factors are necessary: On the one hand, *awareness*. That is, awareness of oppression and the sources of it. This type of awareness is amply illustrated by the writings of Laing and the writings by radical feminists and blacks, and gays. However, this formula also implies that pure awareness of oppression does not lead to liberation. Awareness of oppression leads to anger and a wish to do something about one's oppression; so that a person who becomes so aware changes from one who is alienated to one who is angry in the manner in which some black people and women have become angry. Anger, therefore, is a healthy first step in the process of liberation rather than an "irrational," "neurotic," or otherwise undesirable reaction. But liberation requires *contact* as well as awareness. That is to say, contact with other human beings who, united, will move against the oppression. This is why it is not possible to practice radical psychiatry in an individual psychotherapy context. An individual cannot move against his oppression as an individual; he can only do so with the support of a group of other human beings.

Still, awareness and contact cannot yield liberation except through some form of *action*. Only action by groups of people who have become aware of how they are oppressed will lead to *liberation*.[6]

Thus it appears *radical psychiatry is best practiced in groups* because contact is necessary. Because people seeking psychiatric help are alienated and therefore in need of awareness, *a radical psychiatry group seems to require a leader or leaders* who will undertake to guide the liberation process. To avoid the leader's oppression of group members *each individual member should propose a contract with the group* that indicates his wish to

---

[6] The element of *action* was added to the formula by collective decision of the members of the Radical Psychiatry Center.

work on a specific problem. Liberation from the leader's guidance is the ultimate goal of radical psychiatry and is indicated by the person's exit from the group.

Contact occurs between people in a number of different forms. Basically, contact is human touch, or strokes, as defined by Berne. But contact includes also when people become aware of their oppression, as well as permission, and protection.

Permission is just what the word implies, a safe-conduct for a person to move against his oppressor and to "take care of business." This permission needs to come from a person or persons who at the moment feel stronger than the one who is oppressed, usually the leader. Along with the permission, the person who is to move against the oppression also needs to know that he will be protected against the likely retaliation of the oppressor.

This, then, is the vital combination of elements in radical psychiatry: awareness to *act* against deception, and contact to *act* against alienation. It should be reemphasized that *neither awareness by itself nor contact by itself will produce liberation.* As an example, it is very clear that contact without awareness is the essence of the therapeutic encounters of the "human potentialities" movement. The potency of human contact and its immediate production of well-being, such as found at Esalen and within the "human potentialities movement," is rightfully eyed with suspicion by therapists in the Movement because, without awareness, human contact has a capacity to pacify and reinforce the mystification of the oppressed. It is equally clear that pure awareness, whether it be psychoanalytic or political, does not aid the individual in overcoming oppression, since the overcoming of oppression requires the banding together of the oppressed.

2. ALIENATION by Claude Steiner and Hogie Wyckoff

Alienation is a term that is commonly found in psychiatric writings, especially in relation to youth, the poor, and minorities. The word "alienation" in this context is referred to in the sense of "being apart from the main group, out of the mainstream, a state of estrangement; of being far removed or inconsistent with. . . ."

We believe that this is the shallow meaning of the word. For a more meaningful interpretation of alienation one must refer to Marx and his *1844 Manuscripts;* an interpretation which has as its indispensable elements oppression and mystification.

ALIENATED LABOR AND NEEDS

Marx believed that as people produce objects in their labor they are producing themselves; that is, people come to know themselves as producers of objects. This is also the way in which people master their world. They find their meaning in their labors, and when their labor becomes fragmented and meaningless or when the means of production and decision lie in the hands of others (e.g. capitalists), labor becomes alienated, and the person loses his sense of mastery and meaning; that is, the person becomes alienated.

In the Marxian sense, alienation is not just being separate from others as it is being separated from oneself, one's human potentialities, one's labor, one's intelligence, one's capacity to love, or one's body—and it is always seen as the result of the mystified acceptance of oppression.

One of the most meaningful human needs is the need to be creative and effective in mastering one's environment. Yet, today, people are alienated from the satisfaction of this need and instead are isolated and stunted by doing labor for wages which is largely meaningless to them and over which they have no real control. People sell their time and energy at a job which requires them to expend themselves and to forgo effective control over the total process of production. People are required to be passive in crucial ways while they are allowed to be active in meaningless ways. People work on parts of a whole, never getting closure, and are intentionally kept as cogs in the corporate wheel, made to feel ineffectual—and ultimately powerless. Workers find little satisfaction or joy in their labor and are told such meaning must be sought in leisure, a passive non-work where they attempt to gain satisfaction as consumers of things and services, rather than as doers.

When people are alienated from meaningful labor, fragmented, cut off from each other and forced to be competitive, they also become alienated from other people. Having been cut off from the meaning in communal social relations, they are forced by the bleak alternatives made available to them into developing a false need to try to escape, to buy the means of forgetting the pain and emptiness of their working lives, to dream of being human through fantasies created by the media's seduction, and to struggle for attainment of objects that are imitations which approximate and create a caricature of real humanness and human happiness.

People's needs, above and beyond the most basic needs for food, shelter, and clothing, are not permitted to spring forth naturally from them, but are manipulated by external powers over which they have no control, like the media, advertising, and fashion.

As an example, a worker on an automobile assembly line who works eight hours a day and spends two hours commuting to her place of work has a real need for transportation. Communal public transportation is made unavailable, so that this real need for transportation which was created by her work becomes her own individual responsibility. She can only fulfill this need through the expensive personal purchase of one of the automobiles she has had a meaningless and alienated, and yet essential, part in producing. She now finds herself in a place where she creates a part of a part of an object and is later seduced (if not actually forced) into purchasing it. This car which she has helped build and which is totally alien from her will, turns on her in the form of exorbitant monthly payments, repairs, taxes, etc., so that it becomes necessary to deal with it on its own terms, to be passive in relation to it rather than active as would be the case if she had built the whole machine and could fix it herself, in which case she could have some pride of craftswomanship for her labor as well.

When our labor is not alienated, the power of the object becomes an extension of our power. The object we create does not turn against us or deplete us, but rather adds to us. Thus, our labor becomes a positive force rather than a potential enemy.

In order to combat alienation it is necessary that we get back in touch with our underlying or truly felt needs and that we break the strangle hold of advertising and fashion upon our appetites. Human needs cannot just be accounted for in terms of material things, although this is a value the capitalist system desires to instill in us, since making money is its only motive. We are manipulated and corrupted in our desires because they are created by others for their benefit rather than for our own. We must break the bonds of the consumer culture on us and expose the false promise of individul liberation through the acquisition of commodities for the empty lie that it is.

Our real, felt needs can only be clearly identified once we begin to fulfill them because we are so detached from them now. Through a growth process beginning with partial solutions, a gradual rediscovery of them can develop. We must remember the social character of human needs—needs for cooperation, contact, support, love that cannot be bought and sold.

Marx saw thought as alienated when it is merely abstract, speculative theory, not grounded in action or practice: that is to say, when it is separated from being actually tried out in the world.

People can separate thoughts from action and not test them in reality. But any thought which keeps us from action is alienated. The psychiatrically disturbed or behaviorally incapable who are not able to be effective in the world are extreme examples of the alienation of thought. But we are *all* being taught in different, subtle ways to be behaviorally incapable.

In the midst of the severe alienation from our human potentiality, we are being tricked into believing that we have real choices because as consumers we can supposedly choose between the kinds of goods that we purchase or the politicians that we elect to office. These choices are, of course, not providing us with real freedom, but are rather diversions that keep us pacified and prevent us from actively seeking actual liberation.

ALIENATION AND RADICAL PSYCHIATRY

In radical psychiatry we see all psychic difficulties as forms of alienation. People at this historical moment are to one degree or another alienated from their real needs and potential. Most people are oppressed (coerced through force or threats of force) away from autonomy and wholeness as human beings, and are mystified about their oppression. This oppression is based on keeping people incomplete and not fully satisfied so that they will be willing and highly motivated consumers and exploitable workers. We believe it is necessary for psychiatry to make people aware of this oppression; to demystify it and to create sensibilities against it in people so that they will recognize it and refuse to continue to suffer it.

In the same period in which Marx was speaking about alienation in relation to labor, the word "alienation" was used in relation to the "mentally ill or deranged," and those who were their caretakers were called "alienists." The word "alienist" eventually became the word "psychiatrist," as the medical profession put its imprint on it as one of the medical specialties.

The sense that we (based on Marx) ascribe to alienation is intimately connected with mystification: that is to say, a sense that something is wrong and that there is no understanding of what is wrong; that the process that has caused the alienation has become opaque and not understandable to the person. This sense of alienation is especially apt in the case of so-called paranoid schizophrenia. The paranoid's experience is that there is something wrong in the world, something that he does not necessarily know or understand; that she is in some way persecuted and that she feels alienated from reason, from herself, and from others. His alienation includes ineffectual alienated thoughts, e.g. delusions which are impotent attempts to break through the mystifications that surround his oppression, in an effort to make that which is opaque more understandable. One of the tenets of radical psychiatry is that paranoia is the result of heightened awareness, an attempt by the mystified oppressed to explicate or make clear the mystified oppression under which they labor. The paranoid's experience of being persecuted is oppressed and the oppression of her experience is mystified.

The sense that we (again based on Marx) ascribe to alienation is also intimately connected with oppression, as in the case of the assembly-line worker who is pressed into unsatisfying labor, the product of which is taken away from him, and deceived into believing that rather than being oppressed he is truly fortunate in being able to use his earnings by purchasing a late model automobile, the colors, accessories, and horsepower rating of which he has *complete* freedom to choose. When this worker's automobile breaks down in the midst of heavy traffic on his way to work, he will not see himself as a victim of oppressions designed to satisfy the greed of certain privileged persons in society, but he will in all probability be mystified into seeing himself as the cause of his quandary. He will blame himself for not knowing how to repair his car, or for not having taken his car to a mechanic before it broke down, or for not having been able to afford a more expensive model, and so on. He will feel isolated from the thousands of others in similar circumstances and see them as competitors and enemies. He will feel depressed or angry, and he will vent his mood on his family, thereby transmitting the oppression downward in the hierarchy and away from its source.

The oppression of human beings begins early in their lives. The capacities of loving, thinking, enjoyment, and production are systematically attacked by parents and schools. Children, the most oppressed within each class of human beings, are enjoined against the expression of the need to "make" things, against the free exchange of strokes, against the full enjoyment of their bodies, and most significantly because of the need to mystify these injunctions, against the use of their capacity to understand and experience the world as it is. Parental and societal injunctions are eventually incorporated by the person in the form of the "Pig Parent" which, like a chronic implant in the brain, controls people's behavior according to an oppressive scheme. The acceptance of these injunctions is the only thing that is wrong with persons seeking psychiatric aid. The rest of the difficulties must be found in the person's external world.

OUR BODY

We are separated and oppressed away from our bodies, especially from our capacity to enjoy bodily pleasure. As Marcuse points out, Freud's oral/anal/genital scheme of erotic development is really an imposition upon a much more natural development which leaves the body capable of enjoying erogenous pleasure. According to Marcuse, we are forced to concentrate our pleasures in the genitals in order to free the rest of our body so that it may be readily oppressed in labor. Separated from our bodily sensations we are capable of suffering the abuse of alienated labor. We cease to feel either pleasure or pain. Our musculature becomes cramped as it is increasingly devoted to defensiveness rather than action or pleasure. We are told from childhood that things that are pleasurable are bad for us and that something that is unpleasurable is likely to be good for us, and we come not to expect pleasure from our work. By the time we have grown up we cannot enjoy the rhythm of our functions, the movement of our muscles, the sensations in our skin—we are, in short, alienated from our bodies. Separated from our bodies we engage in alienated sex and drug abuse in an effort to regain some semblance of bodily pleasure and experiences.

Drug abuses, from cigarettes to heroin, are attempts to re-establish contact with our bodies; the man who is sitting at a bar reminds one of a person who puts a dollar in the slot of a machine in an amusement park and receives in exchange for that dollar fifteen minutes of communion with his body. A shot of whiskey makes the cold, stony body feel, briefly, like a newborn baby's. Cigarettes do the same thing on a lesser level, and heroin is the ultimate drug for re-establishing touch. Heroin is, as most addicts will attest, unsurpassed in its capacity to produce feelings of well-being for its users. Unfortunately, drug use for the purpose of regaining touch with the alienated body becomes complicated by the fact that most drugs of this sort, except perhaps marijuana, are addictive, so that a larger and larger dose must be taken which has an increasingly lower effect; so that, in time, they become ineffective in breaking down alienation as they become increasingly lethal to the body.

Based on this point of view, radical psychiatry's approach to the abuse of drugs is focused on breaking down body alienation. This process is basically one of permission to *feel*. One of the great factors in drug abuse, naturally, is the promotion by the media of tobacco, alcohol, and other drugs. The main incentive for the oppression of people away from their bodily pleasure is to create a labor force which will submit to alienated work conditions, but drug companies constitute the supporting cast in this situation, providing as they do pacifying doses of de-alienation, for a price. Eventually, the drug companies have become as powerful an influence in the maintenance of bodily alienation as are those who wish to exploit human labor. In any case, these forces conspire heavily against any person's chance of growing up in our culture without being alienated from her or his own body.

OUR MIND

Alienation from our mind is a state of affairs commonly called schizophrenia. The schizophrenic was the alienist's principal customer. Ronald Laing, in his writings, covers this form of alienation quite thoroughly. In brief, he observes that it seems necessary for groups of people, especially families, to prevent individuals within them from expressing or being in touch with their own experiences of the world; and that this process is one which invalidates or makes invalids out of people so that those who insist on maintaining their point of view are tagged as schizophrenic or deviant and driven mad in a systematic conspiracy. Laing sees psychiatrists as acting in a naive collusion with the powers that be in policing individuals who show any sign of not relinquishing their experiences of the world in favor of the official version of it.

An extreme example of this type of alienation is paranoid schizophrenia. Varying degrees of being crazy, feeling crazy, or acting crazy are lesser manifestations of mind-alienation. The radical psychiatrist's approach to this difficulty is to align herself squarely with whatever the person experiences, and to teach people how to recognize and deal with discounts which are the transactional operation whereby people are invalidated. In the most extreme situation of paranoid schizophrenia the approach is to accept as a given truth that the person who is paranoid is being persecuted in approximately the way in which she claims to be, and to investigate the exact dimensions of the persecution. Validation of a person's experience of being persecuted, combined with protection from the persecution, results in a reinstatement of the valid connection between people's experiences and thoughts and what *in fact* is going on around them.

OUR LOVE

Human beings are not only separated from their bodies and their capacities to think, but also from their capacity to love others. Human love and warmth are essential for the survival of human beings. Berne has restated that fact in terms of the concept of strokes. Steiner's paper, "The Stroke Economy" (Chapter 3), describes in detail the manner in which human loving is alienated away from human beings. Briefly, our capacity to love is enjoined against and regulated and then turned against us in order to exploit us. People who are stroke-starved will do anything: work, buy, tolerate pain, in order to obtain strokes.

Increasing levels of stroke starvation leads from the commonplace "cruising" of the lonely young and the agitation which is observable in most people to the withdrawal commonly called clinical depression and, finally, to catatonic withdrawal in which strokes are not accepted even when offered. This continuum of stroke deprivation is related to by radical psychiatrists through making strokes available to the deprived by creating free stroke economies in groups and by teaching people in them to ask for, give, accept, and reject strokes freely.

The above three forms of alienation, plus alienated labor, are not seen by radical psychiatrists to be all-inclusive. They are arbitrary categories chosen at this point in time as being the most understandable and reasonable; and while they cover the gamut of psychiatric "psychopathology," they are obviously not complete and are capable of being improved.[1] In any case, the notion is that all psychiatric disturbance represents some form of alienation which in every case is the result of the oppression of a human capacity which is then mystified.

---

[1] For an exhaustive description of these three forms of alienation and their therapy, see *Scripts People Live*, by Claude Steiner (New York: Grove Press, 1974).

3. THE STROKE ECONOMY
by Claude Steiner

In *Games People Play*,[1] Eric Berne says: "Liberation is only possible at all because the individual starts off in an autonomous state: that is, capable of awareness, spontaneity, and intimacy." Colloquially, this statement reads: "Children are born princes and princesses and their parents turn them into frogs."

The theses of this chapter are:

1. That the method used by parents to turn children into frogs derives its potency from the control of strokes, so that a situation in which strokes could be available in a limitless supply is transformed into a situation in which the supply is low and the price parents can extract for them is high.

2. That the re-claiming of awareness, spontaneity, and intimacy requires a rejection of the parental teachings or "basic training" regarding the exchange of strokes.

3. That people's submission to their early basic training in relation to the exchange of strokes produces a population of stroke-hungry persons who spend most of their waking hours procuring strokes; they are therefore

---

[1] Eric Berne, *Games People Play* (New York: Grove Press, 1964).

easily manipulated by persons who control the supply of strokes through a monopoly of them.

In *Games People Play,* speaking about stimulus hunger, Berne says: "A biological chain may be postulated leading from emotional and sensory deprivation through apathy to degenerative changes and death. In this sense stimulus hunger has the same relationship to survival of the human organism as food hunger." The notion that strokes are, throughout a person's life, as indispensable as food is a notion that has not been sufficiently emphasized. Therefore, I wish to restate the fact: *strokes are as necessary to human life as are other primary biological needs such as the need for food, water, and shelter—needs which, if not satisfied, will lead to death.*

As Berne pointed out in the chapter on strokes in *Transactional Analysis in Psychotherapy,*[2] control of stimulation is far more effective in manipulating human behavior than brutality or punishment. Thus, while a few families still use brutality in an attempt to control their offspring, most injunctions are enforced in young persons through the manipulation of strokes rather than through physical punishment.

Previous writers have linked the control of vital human processes with broader economical and political points of view. Two such will be reviewed here: Wilhelm Reich and Herbert Marcuse.

Reich, as Berne, saw man at his deepest level to be of "*natural* sociality and sexuality, *spontaneous* enjoyment of work and capacity for love."[3] He felt that the repression of this deepest and benign layer of the human being brought forth the "Freudian unconscious" in which sadism, greediness, lasciviousness, envy, and

---

[2] Eric Berne, *Transactional Analysis in Psychotherapy* (New York: Grove Press, 1961).

[3] Wilhelm Reich, *The Function of the Orgasm* (New York: Farrar Straus and Giroux, Inc., 1961).

perversion of all kinds were regnant. Wilhelm Reich invented the term "sex economy" since he was interested in the economic analysis of the neuroses; according to this theory, sexual energy is manipulated for political reasons. The orgasm, the release of sexual energy, liberates a human system whose sexuality has been oppressed.

"The connection between sexual repression and the authoritarian social order was simple and direct: the child who experienced the suppression of his natural sexuality was permanently maimed in his character development; inevitably he became submissive, apprehensive of all authority and completely incapable of rebellion."[4] In other words, he developed exactly that character structure which would prevent him from seeking liberation. The first act of suppression prepared the way for every subsequent tyranny. Reich concluded that repression existed not for the sake of moral edification (as tradition religions would have it), nor for the sake of cultural development (as Freud claimed), but simply in order to create the character structure necessary for the preservation of a repressive society.

A great deal of Reich's writings were an attack against the patriarchal family which he saw as "a factory for authoritarian ideologies and conservative structures."[5] Reich felt that the authoritarian government and economic exploitation of the people were being maintained by the family and that the family was an indispensable part of it, which fulfilled its function as a supporter of exploitation by the oppression of sexuality in the young.

Herbert Marcuse is another writer who ties an economic point of view to the difficulties of mankind.

---

[4] P. A. Robinson, *The Freudian Left* (New York: Harper Colophon Books, 1969).

[5] Wilhelm Reich, *The Sexual Revolution* (New York: Noonday Press, 1962).

According to him, human beings are suffering alienation from themselves, their fellow human beings, and
nature. This alienation is the result of a surplus repression superimposed on the repression that Freud
postulated as necessary for the development of civilization. This surplus repression forces human beings to
live according to the performance principle.

The performance principle is a way of life imposed
on human beings which causes the desexualization of
the body and the concentration of eroticism in certain
bodily organs such as the mouth, the anus, and the
genitals. This progression is not a healthy, biologically
logical sequence, as Freudian theory sees it, but one that
results in a reduction of human potential for pleasure.
Concentrating pleasure into narrow erogenous zones
leads to the production of a shallow, dehumanized, one-
dimensional person. Marcuse feels that the concentration of sexual pleasure in the genitals is accomplished
in order to free the rest of the body for the use by an
oppressive establishment as an instrument of labor
which can be exploited. "The normal progress to geni-
tality has been organized in such a way that the partial
impulses and their 'zones' were all but desexualized in
order to conform to the requirements of a specific social
organization of the human existence."[6]

Thus Marcuse and Wilhelm Reich connect the social
and psychological manipulation of human beings by
human beings surrounding them—including the family—with an oppressive social order. The following theory about the stroke economy is a similar effort in which
it will be proposed that the free exchange of strokes,
which is at one and the same time a human capacity, a
human need, and a human right, has been artifi-
cally controlled for the purpose of rearing human beings
who will behave in a way which is desirable to a larger

---

[6] Herbert Marcuse, *Eros and Civilization* (New York: Vin-
tage Books, 1962).

social order. This manipulation of the stroke economy, unwittingly engaged in by the largest proportion of human beings, has never been understood as being a service to the established order, so that human beings have not had an opportunity to evaluate the extent to which such control of the stroke economy is to their own advantage and to what extent it is not.

In order to make this point more vivid, allow me to ask you to imagine that every human being was at birth fitted with a mask which controlled the amount of air that was available to him. This mask would at first be left wide open, allowing the child to breathe freely; but at the point at which the child was able to perform certain desired acts the mask would be gradually closed down and only opened at such times at which the child did whatever the grownups around it wanted it to do. Imagine, for instance, that a child was prohibited from manipulating his own air valve and that only other people would have control over it, and that the people allowed to control it would be rigorously specified. A situation of this sort could cause human beings to be quite responsive to the wishes and desires of those who had control over their air supply. If sanctions were made severe enough, people would not remove their masks even though the mask was quite easily removable, but would instead follow the prescriptions that regulated breathing of air.

Occasionally, some people would grow tired of their masks and take them off; but these people would be considered character disorder criminals, foolish, or reckless. People would be quite willing to do considerable work and expend much effort to guarantee a continuous flow of air. Those who did not work and expend such effort would be cut off, would not be permitted to breathe freely, and would not be given enough air to live in an adequate way.

People who openly advocated taking off the masks

would justifiably be accused of undermining the very fiber of the society which constructed these masks; for it would be very clear that as people removed them they would no longer work or be responsive to many of the demands that were placed upon them. Instead, these people would seek self-satisfying modes of life and relationships which could easily exclude a great deal of activity previously valued by a society based on the wearing of such masks. "Mask removers" would be seen as a threat to the society, and would probably be viciously dealt with. In an air-hungry society, air substitutes could be sold at high prices and individuals could, for a fee, sell clever circumventions of the anti-breathing rules.

Absurd as this situation may seem, I believe that it is a close analogy to the situation which exists presently among human beings in the area of strokes. Instead of a mask that controls the air, we have very strict regulations as to how strokes are exchanged. Children are controlled by regulating their stroke input, and grown-ups work and respond to societal demands to get strokes. The population is generally stroke-hungry and a large number of enterprises, such as massage parlors, Esalen, the American Tobacco Company, and General Motors, are engaged in selling strokes, or implying that their product will obtain strokes for their consumers ("ginger ale tastes like love").

Persons who defy the stroke-economy regulations are seen as social deviants, and if enough of them band together they are regarded as a threat to the National Security.

Most human beings live in a state of stroke deficit; that is, a situation in which they survive on a less-than-ideal diet of strokes. This stroke deficit can vary from mild to severe. An extreme example of a person's stroke starvation diet is the case of an alcoholic, by no means unique, who lived in a skid-row hotel. By his own account he received two strokes daily from the clerk at the hotel desk from Tuesday to Sunday and approximately thirty strokes on Monday when he appeared at the alcoholic clinic and exchanged strokes with the receptionist and the nurse administering medication. Once a month, he was treated to a dozen extra super-strokes from the physician who renewed his prescription. His vitality was almost completely sapped; he reminded me of human beings who live on starvation diets of rice. Eventually, his stroke-starved state of apathy prevented him from coming to the clinic and soon afterward he was found dead in his room.

Experiences of a person in such food- and stroke-starved circumstances are of a completely different order than the experiences of one who is properly fed. This man was little more than an automaton and certainly had nothing that could be interpreted as autonomy or self-determination. Most people, however, live in a less severe form of starvation leading to varying degrees of depression and agitation. People in these circumstances exhibit, instead of the apathy of the severely starved, a form of agitation or "search behavior," which is also found in the mildly food-starved person or animal.

Because people are forced to live in a state of stroke scarcity, the procurement of strokes fills every moment of their waking hours. This is the cause for structure hunger—that need to optimally structure time in social situations for the procurement of a maximum number of strokes. Just as in the case of money, certain people are able to obtain large numbers of strokes in return for little effort; that is, they have established a stroke monopoly in which they are able to accumulate others' strokes. In the stroke economy, just as is the case elsewhere, the rich get richer and the poor get poorer while the majority have to struggle daily to make ends meet.

The notion of stroke monopoly became clearly evident to me in connection with therapeutic marathons. A marathon, as I would conduct it, is in essence a temporary subculture with an anomalous stroke economy in which an attempt is made to disarm the injunctions that exist in people against stroking: "Don't give strokes." "Don't ask for strokes." "Don't accept strokes." "Don't reject strokes." Thus, a marathon is organized around the permission to ask and give as well as reject and accept strokes, so that the stroke economy can be said to be "free" and strokes are available in unlimited numbers. Such manipulation of the stroke economy profoundly affects the transactions between people. The group leader may remain outside the economy, not participating in the exchange of strokes, or he can participate in the stroke economy. If he does the latter, he will quickly find that he has an inordinate and unwitting control over the flow of strokes; he will be given strokes without having to ask and he will be able to give without being rejected. A therapist who enters into the economy and is unaware of this inordinate, monopolizing control which he has over the flow of strokes can be a disruptive factor nullifying his attempts at therapy.

Therapists, especially group therapists, are in a position to become stroke monopolists. Wyckoff (see Chapter 4) points out how men monopolize women's strokes. Parents are often interested in monopolizing their children's strokes. In every case, the stroke monopolist profits by the monopoly and at the same time perpetuates the general rules of the controlled stroke economy.

The free exchange of strokes between Child and Child is severely controlled by the Parent ego state on the basis of Parental tapes. These Parental tapes are easily demonstrable by a very simple technique called "bragging." If a person is asked to stand up in the middle of the room and brag—that is, make a number of self-praising statements—there would be an immediate response of reaction within that person's head. The person might feel that it would be immodest or improper to say good things about himself, or that to say good things about oneself might be seen as an insult to the others in the room.

Persons who accept the validity of bragging may find that they are not aware of good things about themselves, that they are incapable of using words which imply goodness or worth applied to themselves. If, at this point, other members of the group are asked to provide honest strokes, it often happens that the recipient of the strokes will systematically reject everything that is said with a Parental discount.

If someone says, "You have beautiful skin," the Parent says, internally, "They haven't seen you up close." If someone says, "You have a lovely smile," the Parent says, "But they haven't seen you cry." If someone says, "You have beautiful breasts," the Parent says, "That's all they think of you—you're just a sex object." If a person says, "You're very intelligent," then the Parent says, "Yes, but you're ugly." Other devices to avoid the acceptance of strokes will be observed, such as: giving token acceptance of the stroke, followed by a shrug so that the stroke will roll off the shoulders instead of soaking in; or an immediate reciprocation with a counter-stroke which essentially says, "I don't deserve the stroke so I must give one in return."

These Parental reactions to stroking are just those that occur in a situation of being given strokes, which is the simplest. In the situation of asking for strokes, it becomes even more complicated. There are all sorts of taboos operating which prevent the free exchange of strokes: the homosexual taboo that prevents stroking between men and men, and women and women; the heterosexual taboo that prevents stroking between men and women unless they are in a prescribed relationship, either engaged to be married or married; and the taboos against physical touch between grownups and children unless they are in a nuclear family, and then only under certain circumstances. In short, the free exchange of strokes is a managed activity, a situation in which the means for the satisfaction of people's needs are unavailable to them. The end result is that the most human of capacities, the capacity to love, is taken away from people, and then turned against them by using it as a means to bring about certain desired behavior.

It can be seen from this that a person or group of persons who free themselves from the strictures of the stroke economy will regain control of the means for the satisfaction of a most important need; consequently, they tend to disengage themselves from the larger society. It is because of this that there is such great panic among lawmakers and government officials in relation to the youth, drug, and sex culture. The notion that human beings will no longer work or be responsible when they liberate the stroke economy may be quite accurate if work and responsibility is seen as defined by others. However, it is quite another thing to assume that human beings in a free stroke economy will be as inert or vegetable-like as Freudian theory and the Judaeo-Christian view of humankind would predict. The notion that satisfied human beings will not work and will not be responsible has been a basic assumption of child-rearing. The facts may be quite different, however. It is my assumption that as they are satisfied in their stroke needs, human beings will be better able actually to pursue the achievement of harmony with themselves, others, and nature.

In my group work, the above stroke-economical understanding has caused me to shift some of my attention and emphasis to the issue of strokes. For instance, marital disharmony can be seen as part of a script, a game, or a pastime; but I have found that the key to its therapy is the freeing and equalizing of the exchange of strokes.

One couple's ten years of "Uproar," "Kick Me," and "Now I've Got You, You SOB" (NIGYSOB) came to a halt when a sharp focus on the exchange of strokes revealed that the husband was simply not interested in an equitable arrangement; he was neither willing to give more nor to ask less. This couple knew the games they played, but had only been capable of achieving social control for short periods. With this new understanding, the woman pressed for a separation.

Another couple found that their love for each other was being eroded by a combination of factors; the wife craved—but had no permission to ask for—certain nurturing strokes and resented her husband for not giving them without being asked. The husband, on the other hand, did not understand the kinds of strokes she needed and had no permission to give them. They clashed repeatedly with accusations of "You don't *really* love me" from her, and stubborn defensiveness from him ("You are too demanding"), ending in despair for both. Therapy centered on a minute transactional analysis of their struggle over this issue and finally focused on giving permission through role-playing: to the wife for asking directly for nurturing strokes, and to the husband for giving them.

One of the functions of games is the extortion of recognition or strokes when they are not freely given. A husbandless mother of four was able to halt a hellish daily stroke rip-off involving "Kick Me" and "NIGYSOB" with her children by establishing a systematic stroke-feeding schedule which satisfied all her children and even left her some time for herself.

Freeing up the stroke economy is most effective the more people that are involved. A therapy group provides a good context in which the free exchange of strokes can be practiced. But persons who are free of stroke injunctions need social contexts which have free stroke economies or they will be under pressure to conform to the societal stroke-economical rules.

In my experience, persons who, in group, free themselves in their stroking tend to form social subgroupings (e.g. couples, families, communes, etc.) which are unresponsive to the larger societal stroke-economic demands. In these groupings, knowledge of the theory of the stroke economy and of the Fuzzy Tale are useful in understanding and coping with the problems of maintaining a free stroke economy.

A FUZZY TALE[7]

Once upon a time, a long time ago, there lived two very happy people called Tim and Maggie with two children called John and Lucy. To understand how happy they were, you have to understand how things were in those days. You see, in those days, everyone was given at birth a small, soft, Fuzzy Bag. Anytime a person reached into this bag he was able to pull out a Warm Fuzzy. Warm Fuzzies were very much in demand because whenever somebody was given a Warm Fuzzy it made him feel warm and fuzzy all over. People who didn't get Warm Fuzzies regularly were in danger of developing a sickness in their back which caused them to shrivel up and die.

In those days it was very easy to get Warm Fuzzies. Anytime that somebody felt like it, he might walk up to you and say, "I'd like to have a Warm Fuzzy." You would then reach into your bag and pull out a Fuzzy the size of a little girl's hand. As soon as the Fuzzy saw the light of day it would smile and blossom into a large, shaggy,

---

[7] Copyright © 1969 by Claude Steiner. *Transactional Analysis Bulletin*, 9:36, October, 1969.

Warm Fuzzy. You then would lay it on the person's shoulder or head or lap and it would snuggle up and melt right against their skin and make them feel good all over. People were always asking each other for Warm Fuzzies, and since they were always given freely, getting enough of them was never a problem. There were always plenty to go around and as a consequence everyone was happy and felt warm and fuzzy most of the time.

One day a bad witch became angry because everyone was so happy and no one was buying her potions and salves. The witch was very clever and so she devised a very wicked plan. One beautiful morning she crept up to Tim while Maggie was playing with their daughter and whispered in his ear, "See here, Tim, look at all the Fuzzies that Maggie is giving to Lucy. You know, if she keeps it up, eventually she is going to run out and then there won't be any left for you."

Tim was astonished. He turned to the witch and said, "Do you mean to tell me that there isn't a Warm Fuzzy in our bag every time we reach into it?"

And the witch said, "No, absolutely not, and once you run out, that's it. You don't have any more." With this she flew away on her broom, laughing and cackling hysterically.

Tim took this to heart and began to notice every time Maggie gave up a Warm Fuzzy to somebody else. Eventually he got very worried and upset because he liked Maggie's Warm Fuzzies very much and did not want to give them up. He certainly did not think it was right for Maggie to be spending all her Warm Fuzzies on the children and on other people. He began to complain every time he saw Maggie giving a Warm Fuzzy to somebody else, and because Maggie liked him very much, she stopped giving Warm Fuzzies to other people as often, and reserved them for him.

The children watched this and soon began to get the

idea that it was wrong to give up Warm Fuzzies any time you were asked or felt like it. They too became very careful. They would watch their parents closely, and whenever they felt that one of their parents was giving too many Fuzzies to others, they also began to object. They began to feel worried whenever they gave away too many Warm Fuzzies. Even though they found a Warm Fuzzy every time they reached into their bag, they reached in less and less and became more and more stingy. Soon people began to notice the lack of Warm Fuzzies, and they began to feel less and less fuzzy. They began to shrivel up and occasionally, people would die from lack of Warm Fuzzies. More and more people went to the witch to buy her potions and salves even though they didn't seem to work.

Well, the situation was getting very serious indeed. The bad witch who had been watching all of this didn't really want the people to die so she devised a new plan. She gave everyone a bag that was very similar to the Fuzzy Bag except that this one was cold while the Fuzzy Bag was warm. Inside of the witch's bag were Cold Pricklies. These Cold Pricklies did not make people feel warm and fuzzy, but made them feel cold and prickly instead. But, they did prevent people's backs from shriveling up. So, from then on, every time somebody said, "I want a Warm Fuzzy," people who were worried about depleting their supply would say, "I can't give you a Warm Fuzzy, but would you like a Cold Prickly?" Sometimes, two people would walk up to each other, thinking they could get a Warm Fuzzy, but one or the other of them would change his mind and they would wind up giving each other Cold Pricklies. So, the end result was that while very few people were dying, a lot of people were still unhappy and feeling very cold and prickly.

The situation got very complicated because, since the coming of the witch, there were less and less Warm

Fuzzies around; so Warm Fuzzies, which used to be thought of as free as air, became extremely valuable. This caused people to do all sorts of things in order to obtain them. Before the witch had appeared, people used to gather in groups of three or four or five, never caring too much who was giving Warm Fuzzies to whom. After the coming of the witch, people began to pair off and to reserve all their Warm Fuzzies for each other exclusively. If ever one of the two persons forgot himself and gave a Warm Fuzzy to someone else, he would immediately feel guilty about it because he knew that his partner would probably resent the loss of a Warm Fuzzy. People who could not find a generous partner had to buy their Warm Fuzzies and had to work long hours to earn the money. Another thing which happened was that some people would take Cold Pricklies (which were limitless and freely available), coat them white and fluffy, and pass them on as Warm Fuzzies. These counterfeit Warm Fuzzies were really Plastic Fuzzies, and they caused additional difficulties. For instance, two people would get together and freely exchange Plastic Fuzzies, which presumably should make them feel good, but they came away feeling bad instead. Since they thought they had been exchanging Warm Fuzzies, people grew very confused about this, never realizing that their cold prickly feelings were really the result of the fact they had been given a lot of Plastic Fuzzies.

So the situation was very, very dismal and it all started because of the coming of the witch who made people believe that some day, when least expected, they might reach into their Warm Fuzzy Bag and find no more.

Not long ago, a young woman with big hips and born under the sign of Aquarius came to this unhappy land. She had not heard about the bad witch and was not worried about running out of Warm Fuzzies. She gave them out freely, even when not asked. They called her the Hip Woman and disapproved of her because she was giving the children the idea that they should not worry about running out of Warm Fuzzies. The children liked her very much because they felt good around her, and they began to give out Warm Fuzzies whenever they felt like it. The grownups became concerned and decided to pass a law to protect the children from depleting their supplies of Warm Fuzzies. The law made it a criminal offense to give out Warm Fuzzies in a reckless manner. The children, however, seemed not to care, and in spite of the law they continued to give each other Warm Fuzzies whenever they felt like it and always when asked. Because there were many many children, almost as many as grownups, it began to look as if maybe they would have their way.

As of now, it is hard to say what will happen. Will the grownup forces of law and order stop the recklessness of the children? Are the grownups going to join with the Hip Woman and the children in taking a chance that there will always be as many Warm Fuzzies as needed? Will they remember the days their children are trying to bring back when Warm Fuzzies were abundant because people gave them away freely?

4. WOMEN'S SCRIPTS AND THE STROKE ECONOMY by Hogie Wyckoff

Many of the women in group with me experience themselves as being in a stroke deficit. Strokes are positive human recognition which can be in the form of compliments, lovemaking, etc. There are several reasons for this, but I believe the primary one to be that women tend to give out more strokes than they receive. They are enjoined to do this by the dictates of their roles as women. The instruction to give more strokes than they receive and to be willing to settle for this disparity are essential aspects of women's life scripts.

A script is a life-plan decided upon at an early age. It is induced by certain powerful messages—injunctions (Don't) and attributes (Do)—which are transmitted by parents and society. In this chapter I am concerned with the everyday, garden variety of scripts known as banal scripts.[1] These do not necessarily lead to a tragic ending as do hamartic scripts but, rather, result in restrictions of autonomy and, in the case of women, allow exploitation of their stroking capacities.

Stroke exploitation is necessary because of the deficiencies created in men and women as a result of sex

---

[1] Claude Steiner, *Scripts People Live* (New York: Grove Press, 1974).

roles. Speaking in generalities, men are encouraged to develop their Adult capacities and function well as producers and performers. Women, on the other hand, are encouraged to develop their Nurturing Parent to use on others, to be loving wives and mothers, and function well as nurturers and supporters. Dot Vance[2] points out that the worst thing a man can be is impotent, unable to perform; and the worst thing a woman can be is frigid, unable to be warm.

Because of their role expectations, men often lose touch with their feelings and their warmth. They tend to be tuned out to other people's emotional needs, and thus lack the ability to be tuned in and to respond. Women are more in touch with their feelings and also have more permission to respond to the feelings of others. It is thus that sex roles turn human beings into one-dimensional specialists incapable of functioning autonomously. Because of this incompleteness, men and women tend to fit together much like halves of a whole; and, like puzzle pieces, mesh to fill each others' empty spaces. This is why a woman will often agree to enter into a relationship in which she provides most of the loving Nurturing Parent and strokes in return for monetary and security considerations. She and others consider her incapable in certain areas of Adult functioning and believe that safety and fulfillment can only be provided by someone else, specifically a man. This incompleteness has forced women and men to barter with strokes. Traditionally, women have been forced to use their capacity as stroke givers as a means of enticing a man into a marriage. They can thus barter with a man for emotional and economic security. Classically: "I won't sleep with you unless you marry me."

This bartering is also promoted by the stroke econ-

---

[2] Dot Vance, "Reclaiming Our Birthright—Getting It Together with Warmth and Potency," *Radical Therapist,* II, 3 (October, 1971).

omy, an artificial limit placed on strokes. It makes strokes into a commodity with object value rather than the free, unlimited expression of human affection that they can be. When being indoctrinated in our culture, we are told: "You may only stroke certain people at certain times under certain conditions." So people come to think of their stroking in terms of cultural limitations, making the situation one of artificial scarcity. Stroking tends to be seen as sexual, and people are cut off from each other's strokes unless they relate on this basis. Thus, men mustn't touch other men or they may be thought homosexual. Women have a little more permission to touch each other and this can easily be encouraged in women's groups, a very important first step in helping them to free themselves from their stroke hunger and disadvantageous barter agreements.

I am going to present some women's scripts in an effort to explicate how women are trained to accept the mystification that they are incomplete, inadequate, and dependent, and how this promotes them to embrace a situation of stroke exploitation. The fantasies women have about themselves as they grow up, life-plan expectations of being mothers and attractive sex objects, begin to be instilled into their every fiber the moment they are wrapped in pink rather than in blue, and are continually reinforced from that moment on by parents, schools, and peers. The media impinge upon women in constant, subtle ways, seductively backing all these messages. The sex-role stereotypes are not only urged on women by the media but are age-old, and are reflected, for instance, by goddesses in Greek mythology: Athene as a prototype of Woman Behind the Man; Hera as a Mother Hubbard; Aphrodite as Plastic Woman; and also by reifications in psychotherapy, such as the Anima and Animus archetypes in Jung.

The scripts I will describe are chosen for recognition value. They differ in many aspects but they all share one thing in common: they promote stroke exploitation of women. They illustrate how some women are programmed to blindly accept their role as stroke sources, giving more than they receive, often like stroke cows, bred to be "stupid" and willing to be consumed as members of an exploited and violated herd.

Women engage in stroke barter according to the guidelines of their scripts. In presenting them I will indicate the thesis or life plan and how it permits stroke usury, the injunctions and permissions or attributes, the counter-oppression, the therapist's role, and finally, the antithesis.

The therapist's role is that which supports the script and which the "patient" expects the therapist to play when she applies for treatment. The counter-oppression is included because it often is mistakenly pointed to as proof of women's oppression of men. Clearly, however, these two categories—men's oppression of women and women's oppression of men—are not comparable; the script specifies that women are to be secondary to men and/or their subjects, and the counter-oppression is an attempt at righting this inequity which, however, never completely succeeds. In this sense it is like the guerrilla warfare of the oppressed who may be quite successful in draining the energies of the oppressor but who are not able to get out from under.

MOTHER HUBBARD (OR WOMAN BEHIND THE FAMILY)

THESIS: She takes care of everyone but herself. She gives twenty strokes for every one that she gets and accepts this inequity because she feels she is the least important member of the family and that her worth is only as a source of supplies. This inequity is constantly made legitimate by the media's promotion of the role of "housewife and mother" as capable of providing women with meaning and fulfillment. She feels worthless because strokes and meaning in life do not come to her for herself and her labors, but for her "family"—husband and children. When her task and usefulness to others in life ends, often with menopause, she undergoes psychic death (involutional melancholia) and may be dealt a rude shock (ECT) in return for her life's labor.

INJUNCTIONS AND ATTRIBUTIONS:
Sacrifice for others
Be nice
Be a good: housewife/cook/mother

COUNTER-OPPRESSION: She refuses to make love to her husband, saying she's too busy or too tired, or by having a headache, with the hope that he will finally give her nurturing strokes in return.

THERAPIST'S ROLE: The therapist tells her not to get angry, gives her tranquilizers to keep her comfortable, and eventually finishes her off with electroshock therapy (ECT).

ANTITHESIS: She begins listening to and respecting her own inner desires; she starts getting strokes *for who she is* and *not for what she can give*. She starts demanding that people ask for what they want from her, and does not give more than she receives in return. It's essential that she begin to put herself and her needs before those of others.

Once it is under way, this script is difficult to overcome because of the bleakness of the alternatives available to, say, an unskilled mother of four. But women who really want to change can take power over their lives—they can fight to create their lives *the way they want them to be* and to cooperate with and get support from other women to do it. They can work and cooperate in raising their children together and in exchanging child care. Eventually, they can also fight together in action groups for improved day care and welfare rights.

WOMAN BEHIND THE MAN

THESIS: She puts all her talent and drive into supporting her husband who is often less talented than she is, but is "supposed" to be the successful one. She has no children, looks "smart" at cocktail parties, is a good hostess and campaign manager. She is a female Cyrano de Bergerac: the grey eminence who cannot shine because of a congenital defect (her sex) that makes her socially unacceptable in a position of leadership.

She gives her husband many strokes in an effort to be supportive and allows him to receive ones she's actually earned. For example, she ghost-writes most of her husband's book and *he* takes all the credit. She must be satisfied to glow in applause for *him*. She must not get upset or jealous when other women want to give him strokes because he's such a success.

This script can be the least exploitative when it provides some real recognition for the woman as "the woman behind the man."

INJUNCTIONS AND ATTRIBUTIONS:
Be helpful
Don't take credit
Stand behind your man

COUNTER-OPPRESSION: She might have an affair with a political opponent or sporadically break down in her role as "Girl Friday" in order to highlight her importance in his work.

THERAPIST'S ROLE: He reminds her of her limitations as a woman and of her duty to support her husband.

ANTITHESIS: The way out is for her to start taking credit for her talent and to use it in her own behalf. She must take the necessary risks and responsibility to be a success in her own right, on her own terms, and not cop out by being behind "him." She should be angry about past inequity and refuse to go along with it any longer. She can tell her husband to hire secretarial and editorial services and start doing her own work and taking credit for it.

PLASTIC WOMAN

THESIS: In an effort to obtain strokes, she encases herself in plastic: bright jewelry, platform heels, foxy clothes, intriguing perfumes, and dramatic make-up. She tries to buy beauty and O.K.-ness, but never really succeeds. When she loses her looks, she feels she's lost everything. After a certain point, superficial beauty can't be bought and pasted on, so she ends up depressed with no strokes that she values. She may then try to fill the void with alcohol, tranquilizers, or other chemicals.

She gives sexual strokes in return for money, but these don't satisfy her because she doesn't reach orgasm.

INJUNCTIONS AND ATTRIBUTIONS:
Money will get you what you want in life
Don't get old
Don't be yourself

COUNTER-OPPRESSION: She begins "beating" him to death with a plastic charge plate. (He has a heart attack keeping up with her charge accounts.) No return orgasm in sexual intercourse makes him doubt his ability as a lover. She uses her husband's money to buy strokes from an analyst.

THERAPIST'S ROLE: He prescribes drugs and engages her in an extended course of individual psychotherapy sessions. He decides that group psychotherapy is "not indicated" and sees her three or four times a week.

ANTITHESIS: She starts to like her natural self and decides not to settle for an unsatisfactory sex life. She concludes that her "power" as a consumer is an illusion and decides to reclaim power over her life by taking responsibility for creating it. She no longer takes drugs to blur out what's unsatisfactory about her life but, rather, joins a problem-solving group and learns how to make real changes. She works on developing aspects of herself other than her appearance that both she and others can appreciate. She begins to enjoy exercising and gets herself into a hiking club to meet new people. She commits herself to being concerned with how she feels on the inside rather than how she looks from the outside. She discards cosmetics and other plastic, unnatural junk.

POOR LITTLE ME

THESIS: Her parents do everything for her because she is a girl, thus debilitating her and making her completely dependent upon them and under their control. After she tries fighting against this she finally gives up and becomes a Victim looking for a Rescuer. She succeeds in this by marrying a "prominent man," often a doctor or psychiatrist who plays a rescuing Daddy to "his" helpless little girl. She gets no strokes for being an O.K. person and is kept not O.K. because she only gets supportive strokes when she's really down. The strokes she does get are thus bittersweet to her. He, on the other hand, gets strokes for being a good Daddy to a loser, sexual strokes in appreciation from her and, finally, strokes as a martyred husband when she totally falls apart.

INJUNCTIONS AND ATTRIBUTIONS:
Don't grow up
Do what your parents say
Don't think

COUNTER-OPPRESSION: She goes crazy, makes public scenes to embarrass him, and generally creates doubt in the community as to his competence as a man or therapist.

THERAPIST'S ROLE: He plays Rescuer, and when she relapses after a brief period of progress, he calls her "unmotivated" or schizophrenic and switches to Persecutor.

ANTITHESIS: She decides to be a responsible adult and take care of business for herself. She begins to get strokes for being O.K. and refuses to accept strokes for being a Victim. She knows those strokes collude with the self-destructive Pig in her to make her feel powerless. She starts developing her own physical and mental powers. She feels high on her own strength and health. She makes a commitment to herself to keep it that way.

CREEPING BEAUTY

THESIS: She has the standard attributes of "media beauty," yet she doesn't feel very good about herself as a human being and really doesn't believe that she's lovely. Rather, she thinks of herself as being shallow and ugly. When she looks in the mirror she does not see her beauty but only sees her blemishes and imperfections. People only seem to respond to her as a pretty face; and, because she's not treated as an equal or respected as an intelligent person, she decides to give up fighting and to "sell" herself as a sex object in order to get what she wants from others. However, she believes she's deceiving everyone who thinks she's beautiful and believes people who buy that deception are fools, anyway.

She gets strokes for being beautiful but discounts them. She really wants to be liked as a person but no one is willing to see past her exterior beauty. She ends up giving sexual strokes, but not receiving any acceptable strokes in return. Any man with her gets strokes for having such a lovely "possession."

INJUNCTIONS AND ATTRIBUTIONS:
    Be lovely on the outside
    You're not O.K.
    Don't be close to people

COUNTER-OPPRESSION: Getting men to come across with as much as they will and then not delivering the goods (herself).

THERAPIST'S ROLE: He becomes sexually aroused by her and propositions her. She then concludes he is just like all the rest.

ANTITHESIS: She must demand strokes for qualities people appreciate in her other than her beauty and refuse to accept strokes for only her physical appearance. She can then begin to like herself and begin to enjoy her true inner and outer beauty. She can do things that are meaningful to her and learn how to cooperate in a women's problem-solving group to get what she wants.

Strokes are essential to human life, and adequate stroking is essential to well-being. Women's scripts, by promoting a constant stroke deficit in women, are the sources of much difficulty and unhappiness.

One way for women to overcome these inhibiting and self-defeating scripts is to work on their problems in a women's problem-solving group. There women discuss problems and develop a subtle awareness of how various forms of oppression, particularly sex role definitions and expectations, affect them. While gaining this awareness a woman is given permission to transact with others in new ways and learn to assert her equality to men. The group provides her with protection and support as she makes the changes she desires, as well as supplying her honest strokes, thus decreasing her chronic stroke-hunger and making her less likely to accept inequitable barter agreements.

Ultimately, however, the way to eliminate sex role scripting is by telling children that they are complete, whole human beings and not indoctrinating them into the sex role ideology.

A woman who frees herself of a banal script would be free not to accept unequal situations. She wouldn't be an incomplete person bartering for safety. She would be able to avoid being stuck in unhappy relationships. She would be open to a greater variety of stroking relationships and be able to choose freely what's best for herself.

5. TEACHING RADICAL PSYCHIATRY
by Claude Steiner

Radical psychiatry has as one of its goals the demystification of human activities. The growing awareness that the process of schooling is the most fundamental and thoroughgoing means of mystification and therefore ultimately of oppression of people in our society and that schools are fundamentally low-security, correctional institutions has compelled many to completely reject the official forms of professional education and set out to search for reasonable alternatives to it.

Radical psychiatry was first taught at the Free University in Berkeley, one such alternative project of education. The Free University is an enormously successful institution which is practically indestructible and which serves large numbers of people through the simplest skeleton operation. The theoretical principles guiding the Free University are vague, primarily counter-instituional, and its functioning mostly pragmatic. The purpose of this chapter is to outline a similar educational system expressly for the purpose of teaching psychiatry.

In the development of this system I am greatly indebted to Ivan Illich whose ideas on de-schooling are the foundation on this paper.[1]

---

[1] Ivan Illich, "Schools Must Be Abolished," *The New York Review of Books*, XV, 1 (July 2, 1970). Also, Ivan Illich, "A

Psychiatry is probably the most vivid modern-day example of the manner in which ordinary schooling mystifies and makes unavailable to people their own most important resources. "Rich and poor alike depend on schools and hospitals which guide their lives, form their world view, and define for them what is legitimate and what is not. Both view doctoring oneself as irresponsible, learning on one's own as unreliable, and community organization, when not paid by those in authority, as a form of aggression or subversion."[2]

The "knowledge" which is part of psychiatric training is without a doubt the most complex, mystified system of half-truths and irrelevancies ever taught as a body of knowledge, approached in its absurdity only by its cousin, phrenology. No one in the field of psychiatry takes more than a small segment of it seriously, and every part of what is taught in psychiatry is fundamentally questioned by some sector of the profession. No parallel to this type of a situation exists in any other form of professional training, although it closely parallels the situation existing in medicine when medicine usurped the practice of psychiatry during the nineteenth century.

For instance, in psychiatry the student is taught psychoanalytic theory on the one hand, and psychopharmacology on the other. Yet, in almost every case, those who believe in psychoanalytic theory will reject psychopharmacological knowledge, and vice versa. The same is true concerning any number of other subcategories: individual psychotherapy versus group psychotherapy, Freudian theory versus neo-Freudian theory, and so on. Practicing psychiatrists are forced to reject as useless the majority of what they are taught as psychiatric knowledge in their schooling, even though they

New System of Education Without Schools," *The New York Review of Books,* XV, 12 (January 7, 1971).

[2] *Ibid.,* "Schools Must Be Abolished."

may continue to teach it to others. As psychiatrists are produced by the high institutions of learning they are all represented as being equally competent and equally knowledgeable in what is thought to be an accurate, valid, and reliable science by those who practice it, and the few who are its consumers. The fact that the largest majority of the public rejects psychiatry as having no validity for themselves, and that the largest portion of the medical profession is quite skeptical of it, on the other hand, is seen as a form of perversion of thinking or understanding rather than as a valid criticism of the profession.

This situation finds no parallel in any other science. Imagine, for instance, a physicist questioning in her thinking half of what she learned in her training, so that no group of physicists could be found to agree on more than a minute portion of their theoretical beliefs. Such a state of affairs would truly invalidate them as scientists or as useful, pragmatic professionals. Yet, psychiatry, through the mystification of the complexity and useful- ness of psychiatric knowledge, continues to maintain incredibly powerful holds on the well-being of people; psychiatrists are seen as experts on human behavior even though it is impossible to get any agreement between them except that which comes from propin- quity (schoolmates, officemates, businessmates); and psychiatry continues to be taught, at incredibly high expense, to a few chosen ones who can master the hurdles of "higher education" who then will, in the tradition of the medical profession in the United States, see themselves as justified in extracting high incomes from its practice.

TEACHING RADICAL PSYCHIATRY

Experiences of teaching radical psychiatry at the Berkeley Rap Center have brought to light certain problems which have their roots in the assumptions inherent in the schooling of persons wishing training as well as those providing training. People seeking training had a passive, somewhat resentful, and consumer-like attitude about what they were learning; they approached the teachings in radical psychiatry much in the same way as the student approaches courses at the university. Because these courses are forced on them and because they have no control over their destiny in the institution, students are generally resentful of being students and express their resentment through garrulousness about what is being taught and through an attitude of passive consumerism much like that of a person who sits in front of a television set, turns it on, complains about the quality of the programming throughout the viewing, and then shuts the television off and forgets everything except the vaguest outlines of what he has viewed. This attitude is matched by the teachers who, because they are not generally teaching what they know best or what they are most interested in, and because they realize that what they are teaching is being forced on the students, are willing to take a rather benign, liberal attitude about their teaching which allows for the expression of hostility in the form of theoretical debate. This attitude is similar to the attitude of a parent feeding a child spinach or some other "good" but bad-tasting food and indulgently allowing the child to complain and make a minor mess while doing so.

These attitudes were found to be a great problem at the Berkeley Rap Center. People would hear that there was a training program in radical psychiatry; they would attend; they would sit and listen to what teachers had to say; they would argue some small point and/or eventually discount or criticize all of the teachings. Teachers, on the other hand, would make themselves responsible for a curriculum and were willing to engage in interminable arguments, many of which were perverse forms of discounting on the part of the students, and generally wear themselves out in what seemed a fruitless attempt to train competent psychiatrists. In time the training program was filled with an excess of people, many of whom were resentful of the teachers whom they saw as withholding information from them, and expressed their resentment by constant questioning of basic principles and tenets, while at the same time withdrawing the work or individual effort which was required to maintain the operation of the Rap Center. The teachers, on the other hand, saw themselves as beleaguered, not appreciated, resentful of the trainees, and guilty about withholding from individuals the loving and devoted teaching which they felt a teacher should offer students.

At the new Radical Psychiatry Center (1970):

1. Persons wishing to be trained as radical psychiatrists should be made aware of the fact that what we are offering is a situation where people can learn to do what we are doing. As a consequence, our principal activity will be to teach and demonstrate our skills, rather than to debate or demonstrate their validity. Thus, a person entering the training program will stay in the program as long as she feels that what we're doing is something that she wants to participate in. The purpose of the program is not to proselytize or to convince people who do not believe what we believe in; therefore the discussions in the training situation will primarily be discussions of what we are doing, and what we believe will be explained rather than justified. This could be misinterpreted to mean that we don't welcome criticism. In fact, we feel criticism is essential, about *how* we teach from our trainees, but about *what* we teach only from those we feel have understood and used it.

People entering the program will be given some of the basic readings which, together with what they may have observed in the way of psychiatric activity in the contact rap and otherwise, will give them an idea of whether they want to participate in the program. If, as they get deeper into the material, they find that it is antithetical to their point of view, or that they do not want to participate in it, they should not try to stay in it. This model is similar to the craftsman-apprentice training situation where the apprentice is allowed to work in close proximity with the craftsman. In a situation of this sort, an apprentice will be able to make observations and suggestions which a good craftswoman will take into consideration and accept or reject as she sees fit. However, the apprentice is at no point under the illusion that he can change the craft fundamentally until he himself has become a craftsman. Teaching is a labor of love, and a person should not have to teach or learn from one with whom she does not have positive rapport any more than she would make love to such a person.

2. The training at the Radical Psychiatry Center will be given for and in the context of work at the Radical Psychiatry Center. Radical psychiatry depends for its functioning on people who are not learning simply for the purpose of acquiring knowledge that can be catalogued alongside other forms of knowledge. Such people are not acceptable in a program of this sort because they will not produce work for the community. People who want to learn radical psychiatry for use in other communities may do so, but must demonstrate their interest in work by working at the Radical Psychiatry Center during their apprenticeship. Work, or the performance in the service of psychiatry, will be the only criterion whereby a person's advancement in the training program should be judged. Neither professional degrees nor any other mystified performances such as utterances at meetings or promises of services to be performed in the future should be allowed to have any decision-making power in the running or the adminis-

tration of the Radical Psychiatry Center's activities; and the extent of a person's influence in the workings of the Radical Psychiatry Center should depend only on the extent of their work.

Work can be of two basic forms: direct service to the incoming public at the Contact rap or Heavy rap groups; and the training of radical psychiatrists. The responsibility of training is assumed not only by teaching one's skills but also by being an active participant in the peer groups; that is to say, by replacing the usual student's passivity with an active commitment and interest in the subject matter and its understanding so that a person's training responsibilities begin on their first day of training.

According to Ivan Illich, an educational system or network which adequately replaces the present schooling situation includes the following three purposes: "It should provide all who want to learn with access to available resources at any time in their lives; empower all who want to share what they know to find those who want to learn it from them; and, finally, furnish all who want to present an issue to the public with an opportunity to make their challenge known. . . . I believe that no more than four, possibly even three, distinct 'channels' or learning exchanges could contain all the resources needed for real learning."[3]

Illich's concern is primarily with the education of children, but what he says about children can be applied almost in its entirety to the education of radical psychiatrists. "The child grows up in a world of things, surrounded by people who serve as models for skills and values. He finds peers who challenge him to argue, to compete, to cooperate, and to understand; and if the child is lucky he is exposed to confrontation or criticism by an experienced elder who really cares. Things, models, peers, and elders are four resources each of

---

[3] *Ibid.*, "A New System of Education Without Schools."

which requires a different type of arrangement to insure that everybody has ample access to them."

These four resources—things, models, peers, and elders—are of great relevance in the training of psychiatrists, and I will postulate a training program which is based on them. Illich uses the word "network" to designate specific ways to provide access to each of the four sets of resources. The radical psychiatry training program should provide four such networks: a network of educational objects; a network of skill exchange; a network of peers; and a network of elders.

EDUCATIONAL OBJECTS

The principal educational objects of radical psychiatry are freely available and accessible to the student; namely, other human beings.

One of the mystifications of psychiatry is that human beings are not easily observable or understandable, and that it takes a greatly trained eye to understand their behavior. Illich points out how "industry has surrounded people with artifacts whose inner works only specialists are allowed to understand. The non-specialist is discouraged from figuring out what makes a watch tick or a telephone ring or an electric typewriter work by being warned that it will break if he tries. He can be told what makes a transistor radio work, but he cannot find out for himself. This type of design tends to reinforce a non-inventive society in which the experts find it progressively easier to hide behind their expertise and beyond evaluation."

The problem presented by Illich in regard to the way in which industry mystifies the working of its products can be extended to psychiatry, which mystifies the workings of its materials so as to make it impossible for people to feel that they are able to manipulate and work with other people and so as to cause them to be afraid that if they do they will cause irreparable harm. This also makes it possible for psychiatrists to hide behind their expertise so as to remain beyond questioning. Remaining beyond questioning is especially important to the psychiatrist because of his sense that his knowledge is not really scientific or valid.

While the objects of study in radical psychiatry are freely available in the streets and where everyone goes, certain settings are more conducive to understanding the basic structure of human beings. The Contact rap, as an instance, is such a place in which human beings are more likely to expose themselves openly to the scrutiny of other human beings for the purpose of being understood and understanding others. People who come to the Contact rap may, if they are in dire psychiatric distress, expose themselves freely. Others may wish to engage in psychiatric games or exercises which make the inner workings of the human being more readily available and open to scrutiny by others. Games such as "Bragging," "Trashing the Stroke Economy," or "Offing the Pig," games specifically designed for the study of radical psychiatry, are good mediums for making the objects of study available to the student in the Contact rap.

The most fundamental phenomenon to be observed in the study of radical psychiatry is alienation. Alienation can be observed under many guises: the alienation of a person who is listening to a conversation without participating; or the alienation of a person who has become the focus of a whole group's attention; or the alienation of a teacher who finds himself unable to satisfy his class; or the alienation of a man from his body in the form of drug abuse; or the alienation of women and men due to male chauvinism; or the alienation of persons from their own experiences are all readily observable phenomena of interest to the student of radical psychiatry. The deductions about the mystifications that veil the oppression that causes the alienation are, of course, of encompassing interest to the radical psychiatrist. Materials for the study of this data are readily available and at the disposal of anyone at any time he wishes to study them.

Writings are the other class of educational objects essential in radical psychiatry, and can be roughly divided into principles and techniques.

Radical psychiatry includes certain principles which are seen as essential to it and which are therefore accepted by radical psychiatrists a priori. They are:

1. *That psychiatry is a political activity.*

2. *That psychiatric difficulties are forms of alienation which is the result of mystified oppression, so that the activity of psychiatry is to seek liberation which is achieved through contact and awareness.* The rest of the writings in radical psychiatry are descriptions of techniques which define the state of the art at this point in time in the context of the Berkeley Radical Psychiatry Center. They involve group leadership skills, transactional analysis theory, gestalt techniques, and a series of other tools, gleaned from other modern psychiatric technology and developed by radical psychiatrists. This body of technique is highly flexible, and it is expected that it will change as contexts change and as better tools are developed.

The above description excludes as *essential* educational objects all other writings in psychiatry. This exclusion is a deliberate attempt to demystify the knowledge in a field which is overwhelmed with irrelevant writings.

The demystification of educational objects becomes more difficult as one teaches persons with "higher" levels of education. Postgraduates tend to see lectures, turgid writings, and persons with "higher" degrees as the most desirable sources of education. High school dropouts, on the other hand, know that neither lectures, degrees, nor most writings have much relevance to their lives and have a healthy disrespect for them. As a consequence, it is much easier to train a talented high school dropout of a certain age than it is to train an equally talented graduate of the same age. The rule of thumb in this respect is: "It takes five years to train a radical psychiatrist, except that it takes an extra year for every year of graduate training the person has had." This is because much of what is involved in training radical psychiatrists is deschooling or unlearning of mystifications.

The perversion of people's capacities due to "higher" education finds specific manifestations in reading and writing. A good college student is likely to have been severely damaged as a writer; graduate students especially are trained to write about things that interest no one in a way that no one would want to read—which is understandable since professors have a vested interest in not allowing any writing that is more readable than their own. Reading is likewise damaged: college students are burdened by a sense of guilt about all that they have not read, so that pleasurable reading is prohibited until the "required" reading is done. The result is that a reading phobia develops and no reading at all takes place. This is the desired end result of our educational system; namely, that no meaningful writing or reading be done by the educated. One of the tasks of radical psychiatry is to reunite people with their alienated capacities for communicating through the written word; we accomplish it through demystification of writings and through a writers' group in which writings in radical psychiatry are discussed and encouraged.

SKILL EXCHANGES

The practice of radical psychiatry requires certain undeniable skills. These skills, while quite definite and quite important, are, on the other hand, relatively easy to transmit to most people who are inclined to learn them. The skills of psychiatry have been widely mystified to such a point that most people feel incapable of performing or learning them.

"A 'skill model' is a person who possesses a skill and is willing to demonstrate its practice. A demonstration of this kind is frequently a necessary resource for a potential learner. . . . For most widely shared skills a person who demonstrates the skill is the only human resource we ever need or get. . . . A well motivated student who does not labor under a specific handicap often needs no further human assistance than can be provided by someone who can demonstrate on demand how to do what the learner wants to do. . . . What makes skills scarce on the present educational market is the institutional requirement that those who can demonstrate them may not do so unless they are given public trust through its certificate. . . . Converging self-interests now conspire to stop man from sharing his skills. The man who has the skill profits from its scarcity and not from its reproduction. The teacher who specializes in transmitting the skill profits from the artisan's unwillingness to launch his own apprentice into the field."[4]

These quotes from Ivan Illich concerning the nature of skill exchanges suggest how the radical psychiatry "skill models" should be made available to students. These skill models need only be individuals who have demonstrated a certain level of skill. They need not be in any way diagnosticians of learning difficulties or motivators, but simply individuals who know how to do a certain thing. When students convene with these skill teachers it should be made clear to them that the skill teachers'

---

[4] *Ibid.*

only responsibility is to demonstrate their skill and not to be good teachers, inspiring lecturers, or brilliant demonstrators. This can be explained in terms of an anti-consumerism stance which places in the student as much burden for learning as it does on the skill model. The only "teaching skill" needed by the skill model outside of his skill as a radical psychiatrist is the ability to convey to the learner the above participatory attitude which has often been squelched in people. Skills should be taught in small groups of no more than ten to make a participatory attitude possible.

PEER MATCHING

The concept of peer matching is perhaps the most revolutionary concept of Ivan Illich's. It involves getting together two or more people who have simply identified themselves by name and address and have described the activity in which they seek a peer. This approach, unpretentious and simple-minded as it may seem, has the great advantage of creating groups of people around their self-chosen and motivated interest. The only possible disadvantage or drawback of such a coalition of people is that their stated interest may not match their real interest, as is often the case when people appear to coalesce around a certain subject matter when in fact they are coalescing around interest in stroking or human contact. This difficulty can be dealt with by making human contact groups one of the possible categories for peer matching. In any case, this type of peer matching should be a part of radical psychiatry training. It dovetails with the skill exchange level in that a certain peer-matched group may choose to coalesce around a certain skill model to learn certain skills.

ELDERS

After having been liberated from the authoritarian structure and the consumer attitudes of the university setting, people's willingness to seek leadership will tend to increase. The same effect will be observed with respect to people's willingness to return to reading relevant writings. "We may expect that they will experience more deeply both their own independence and the need for guidance. . . . As they are liberated from manipulation by others they learn to profit from the discipline others have acquired in a lifetime. . . . As teachers abandon their claim to be superior informants or skill models, their claim to superior wisdom will begin to ring true."[5]

This is essentially an argument for the validity and value of the expertise of elders. The relationship of an elder to a student is that of a skilled craftsman to an apprentice. "What is common to all true master-pupil relationships is the awareness both share that the relationship is literally priceless—and in very different ways a privilege for both. . . . Aristotle speaks of it as a 'moral type of relationship, which is not on fixed terms; it makes a gift or does whatever it does as to a friend.' . . . Thomas Aquinas says of this kind of teaching that inevitably it is an act of love and mercy. This kind of teaching is always a luxury for the teacher and a form of leisure for him and his pupil: an activity meaningful for both having no ulterior purpose."[6]

Ivan Illich here vividly describes the sense that has become so urgent in radical psychiatry about the leveling of leadership and hierarchies. One of the difficulties encountered in teaching radical psychiatry is the criti-

---

[5] *Ibid.*

[6] *Ibid.*

cism encountered by "levelers" or "prison guards" in the Movement.[7] The criticism runs roughly as follows: "One of the greatest evils of all are oppressive hierarchies. All hierarchical structures must be abolished. Anyone pretending to have an expertise or presenting himself as a teacher is allowing the germ of an ultimately oppressive hierarchy to take root. This must be avoided and hierarchies must be uprooted as they begin developing." The result of this attitude when it takes hold in any kind of a training situation is to invalidate the knowledge and expertise of elders, and it is a mystified form of oppression where people are prevented from engaging in the transmission of knowledge. Elders are not designated or appointed, but simply are people whom others recognize as being especially knowledgeable or skillful. The elder-student coalitions can't be planned or pre-designed—they simply develop in any close working situation. They should, however, be encouraged by recognizing them for what they are; namely, one of the most rewarding and worthwhile of human relationships.

PRACTICE

On the basis of these principles a radical psychiatry training program would include:

1. An orientation to the materials.
   a. Contact rap.
   b. A guidebook describing contexts in which alienation can be studied.
2. A list of skill teachers who will make themselves available to groups of ten or less to demonstrate their skills.

---

[7] See Chapter 15, "Radical Psychiatry and Movement Groups," for a description of leveling and "Lefter Than Thou."

3. Written skill descriptions as skills are developed and made specific.

4. A mechanism (bulletin board with suggestions) for peer-group matching.

5. Working *elders* who are willing to establish learning relationships.

Section III
Therapy

6. CONTRACTUAL PROBLEM-SOLVING GROUPS by Claude Steiner

The bulk of the work of radical psychiatry goes on in contractual problem-solving groups. Such a group is composed of between eight and twelve persons who see themselves as having a problem, one or two trained radical psychiatrists who are capable of being helpful in solving such problems, and one or two observers who are trainees in the process of becoming radical psychiatrists. The group meets between two and three hours so as to provide each person with at least fifteen minutes of time at least once weekly. The group may be a men's group or a women's group or a mixed group, but there is no further attempt to select the persons who might be "suitable" for such a group; anyone stating that he or she has a problem and who seems willing to work on her or his problem in the context of the group is acceptable.

THE CONTRACT

All the persons in a group are bound by a contract. Drawing up a contract is the indispensable first step of the work in group.

73]]]

A working contract is an agreement between the person seeking help and the group, including (especially) the group leader. The person seeking help should state what problem he or she has and how they desire the problem to be improved, in specific, behavioral, observable terms. This may include such wishes as finding a loved one, not being depressed, getting along with people, stopping drug abuse, or getting over being crazy. On the other hand, such wishes as self-understanding, emotional maturity, responsibility, or other such vague achievements sometimes expressed as the desired effect of group cannot be used in a contract because these terms aren't clear enough and are non-specific. It is not possible to enter into a contract on the basis of such vague goals; and, generally speaking, the best contracts are phrased in short sentences made up of short words understandable to an eight-year-old. In order for a contract to satisfy the requirements of mutual consent, it is necessary that all parties are able to specify to what they are consenting. The contract should therefore contain a clear description of what the person wants, what the group will offer, and the conditions which we consider to constitute the fulfillment of the contract.

The basic transactions of mutual consent are: 1) a request for help; 2) an offer of help; and 3) an acceptance of help. It is not unusual for a person to enter a therapeutic group without having achieved one or more of the above conditions. When a person enters group without requesting help, it is very unlikely that any work will be achieved. On the other hand, if a person requests help but the group leader or group members do not commit themselves to helping, it is likely that the person will be discounted. Finally, a group will usually include certain conditions to be fulfilled by the person seeking help, such as regular attendance, doing homework, and any number of other requests that imply acquiescence to the group culture; and a person requesting help who does not accept these conditions will also probably not get any work done. Thus, a clear acceptance of the offer to help is needed.

A person may, at the initial group meeting, not be able to precisely state what it is they want help with. However, this is usually because of people's reluctance, due to psychiatric mystification, to examine their situation in a simple-minded and straightforward way. When the question, "What are you unhappy with?" is asked, it is almost always possible to get a simple, straightforward answer which will ordinarily reveal some form of alienation, such as "I feel I am no good," "I am very depressed," "I can't make friends," "I cannot meet a lover," "I am addicted to drugs," "I can't think," "I am afraid all the time," "I can't get an erection," and so on. When problems are stated in this simple manner, it is equally simple to formulate a state of affairs which implies that the problem is solved and to enter into a mutual agreement to work on the problem.

A contract protects both the person who has a problem and the persons who want to help. The person who has the problem is able to delineate precisely where she or he wants help, and what needs to be changed, thereby avoiding having other people's value judgments as to what changes are needed or how they should live, imposed on him. On the other hand, the helpers are not drawn into a vague and nondescript plea for a Rescue.

THE GROUP WORK

The proceedings of a group can take two major divergent courses. On the one hand, the group can engage in work; or on the other it can engage in games.

Work

A group that engages in work follows approximately the following pattern: either by his own choosing or by being singled out by someone else, one group member will become the center of attention. This does not necessarily mean that he will be placed on the "hot seat" where he will become the *focus* of all interaction, but simply that he tends to be at the center of it. The first phase of this process is one of *clarification*. The person presents a problem, or someone else suggests that a problem exists, and some exploration is needed to ascertain whether there is in reality something to work on. The problem suggested by the person may be a "red herring" or a "bone" thrown at the group to distract it from a more serious problem. Or the problem, if suggested by another group member, may represent a projection or misperception. In any case, the process of clarification continues until the feeling develops that the group is working on a real problem area in which some change can or should occur. At this point the clarification gives way to *challenge*, and someone will ask overtly or covertly, "Now that we know the problem, what are you going to do about it?" The person ordinarily is at a loss for a solution or unwilling to use those which are suggested. A cherished old pattern of behavior is being examined and the person is expected to balk. This is the *impasse*. The group leader or someone else in the group proposes a certain course of action. This course of action is ordinarily one which the person has not used because of fear or uncertainty, and therefore the group and leader may have to apply some pressure. This pressure is consistent with the terms of the contract, and at this point the process shifts from *impasse* to *climax* if the person accepts the group's proposal, or to *anti-climax* if he deflects it. If the proposal is accepted, the group members will ordinarily have an experience of satisfaction and closure, and a silence will follow, after which the process starts over with another person as the focus of attention. If the person deflects the proposal, the leader is faced with a question of strategy. Should the work continue on the person or should the group give up and go on to someone else? This is probably the most crucial decision that a group leader must make. The leader who is under time pressure has the dual responsibility of not allowing time to be wasted and of pursuing matters to their completion. Skillful decisions along these lines distinguish the experienced group leader from the novice who will either pursue matters endlessly to no avail or drop them just as the impasse is ready to be broken.

Games

It takes a skillful leader to maintain the work orientation of a group. When a group loses its work orientation it will fall into game playing. Game playing can take several forms. The group can play Rescue in a situation where one of the persons presents himself as a Victim and the rest of the group scramble madly in their attempt to rescue. A group of this sort will be taken up by games such as "Why Don't You?—Yes, But," "Do Me Something," "If It Weren't For Them (or Him) (or Her)." The general outcome of such groups is that the Victim and Rescuers all end up in a state of heightened frustration and anger. Very often when a group has played a Rescue game the Rescuers will switch to Persecutors and now mercilessly attack the Victim. Now the games will be "Uproar," "Kick Me," "Now I've Got You, You Son Of A Bitch," "Stupid," and so on. Or the Victim becomes Persecutor and plays "Nobody Loves Me" or "See What You Made Me Do." The game roles of Victim, Rescuer, and Persecutor will switch around in the group with different people taking different roles so that everyone eventually plays every role in an endless merry-go-round.

The role of Rescuer is the natural game role that group leaders tend to fall into; and it is believed in radical psychiatry that for every long minute that a leader plays Rescuer, she or he will eventually have to play an equally long minute as Persecutor. The playing of Rescue is basically a situation in which the person is no longer honestly asking for the leader's help or is no longer willing to work in order to improve her situation. Another way of stating this is to say that when the leader or the group members are doing more than 50% of the work on a person's problem, a game of Rescue is taking place.

A group leader must be alerted to the possibility that a group member may no longer be holding to the contract, and when noticing that this is the case must call for the proceedings to come to a halt. The tendency for group leaders to engage in rescuing usually comes out of a sense of guilt or exaggerated responsibility for the group member. When a group leader maintains a position of "I'll help you as long as you are willing to work on your problem as hard as I do and not one second longer," she will avoid the dangers of the Rescue role. Needless to say, Persecuting any one person in a group is even less desirable than playing Rescue. In radical psychiatry we have concluded that problem-solving can be achieved without any necessity of "pigging" or the use of the Critical Parent. Yelling, screaming, attacking, goading, and other "therapeutic" maneuvers introduced into group work by Synanon are found to be unnecessary when a leader learns how to confront people in a human and loving way. Therefore, persecution is not allowed in radical psychiatry groups, especially not under the guise of "I'm Only Trying To Help You."

The view in radical psychiatry is that people who need psychiatric help are alienated and therefore the victims of mystified oppression. Thus, the correct response to a person who presents himself as a Victim is one of unconditional protection, understanding, and support. Given this support, the process of clarification

in group will deal with what the person can do to remove the oppression and/or the mystifications that
cause his alienation. It is at this point that a person may
prefer to continue to be a Victim to moving against her
oppression, at which time she is clearly in violation of
her contract. The person who insists on being a Victim
is not rejected or ostracized, but is simply made to see
that his participation in a contractual problem-solving
group is contradictory with his behavior, and that, for
the moment at least, work on his problem can no longer
continue.

7. PROBLEM-SOLVING GROUPS FOR WOMEN by Hogie Wyckoff

Because women as a class are grossly and subtly oppressed, while being mystified about this oppression, the majority of people who seek psychiatric help are women. Women are denied full access to their power as human beings; and, rather than expressing righteous anger about this violation, they regretfully come to view themselves and each other as being somehow deficient. Under the stress of this robbery and mind-rape, women break down more often than men. Due to sex role progamming, women have more permission than men do to be in touch with and admit their need for psychiatric help. The problem with this is that most of the "help" women receive is from psychiatrists whose values are ultimately anti-liberal and anti-women's liberation. At this point in history we as radical feminist psychiatrists believe that men, particularly professional, elitist, and sexist men, cannot help free women.

We *can* and *must* free ourselves. We can effectively take care of our own heads and souls. We can have the means of producing and preserving our own mental health. As oppressed people accustomed to adapting and compromising ourselves to the desires of others, scrupulously trained to tune in to other people's feelings, to second-guess, and to take care of their unspoken needs, we have already well-developed skills in intuition and insight. When these skills are coupled with permission and training to be strong, to take care of business, to think rationally, and to talk straight, the result is a skillful and powerful people's psychiatrist. For some time now, women in Berkeley have taken possession of the means of reclaiming their own mental well-being. Women who have themselves worked in women's problem-solving groups are learning to facilitate women's groups in training collectives.

The problem-solving group model has been developed, based on a synthesis of psychiatric theories taken from Eric Berne, R. D. Laing, and Claude Steiner, among others. Radical psychiatry's practice incorporates some basic tools of Eric Berne's transactional analysis.[1]

HOW THE GROUPS WORK

The basic structure is a group of eight women with one or two leaders which meets once a week for two hours. To facilitate the work a *contract* is used. This is a work agreement with the whole group, and in it each group member states simply and clearly what she would like to work on. The desired goal must involve some observable behavioral change. This is a vital element of a contract, since if there is no overt behavioral change desired there is no way for the group to be certain that the contract has been fulfilled. The contract guards the facilitator against imposing her values on the group member and allows them to decide if they can work with each other. If they can't both agree on a contract, they won't be able to work productively together. The contract keeps the emphasis on work in the "here and

[1] Eric Berne, *Principles of Group Treatment* (New York: Oxford University Press, 1966).

now" and provides a means for stimulating a person to work on her problem. It protects the group member from being manipulated by the facilitator or other group members and gives her a sense of her own potency in being able to act effectively as an agent producing changes she decides to make in her own life.

Another tool used to promote problem-solving efficiency is *homework*. After a woman has a contract, she can be assigned or assign herself homework which she works on during the week. Homework is used to work on the long-range goal of the contract on a step-by-step basis. People are able to feel safe enough to make real changes in their lives by moving in stages and using a timing they feel they can handle rather than moving too fast in frightening leaps.

A blackboard can be used to diagram and explain the social transactions between people and is also used for women to "sign up" to work at the beginning of group. Signing up facilitates the work: it lets the members of the group know who wants to work, so that the entire group can take cooperative responsibility for everyone having enough time.

Another valuable tool has been Eric Berne's definitions of the three observable ego states. Berne proposed a system based on the observation that people act in three definitely different ways or modes, called *ego states*. They act like parents—people who *know* without questioning what's right and wrong and how things should be done. They act like adults—that is, they process information and make predictions from that data about the future like a computer without feelings. And they act like children—they can be creative, open, and direct; play; be in touch with exactly what they want and what their feelings are. Using these three ego states—*the Parent, the Adult,* and *the Child*—we can explain in group what's going on with people, help them demystify what's happening within themselves and what's happening in their transactions with others. For example, with the aid of ego states, it's possible to explain to a woman why she feels resentment when her husband repeatedly tells her how to do things. The transaction is supposedly Adult-Adult, but because of the repetition, she experiences it as his Parent giving orders to and dominating her Child (Figure 1). We in radical psychiatry feel that it is vital to be able to explain in easily understood language what goes on between people.

Our main goal in using language tools such as the ego states is to make it simple and easy for people to understand themselves and others in ways that have mystified them before.

It has been evident in women's groups that women have a lot of permission to use their Nurturing Parent;

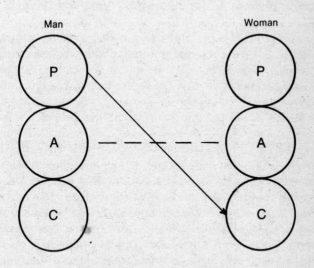

A Man Speaking to a Woman

that is, being loving and caring for other people. They also have permission to act in their Child, to be dependent, playful, intuitive, and needy. But it has also become obvious that women have little permission to use their Adult; that is, to be able to figure things out logically, to be intellectually potent and "take care of business." Women are enjoined from their earliest days *not* to use these powers. They are pressured not to develop skills that give them control over their lives, their bodies, or the means of production in society. They are encouraged to take care of and service the needs of others. They are taught to be good cooks or good housekeepers or good secretaries, but definitely not to know how to fix the car or how to figure things out. One of the main efforts we make in women's groups is to give women permission to use their Adult, to develop their rational power to get what their Child wants in life. Unfortunately, while women have a lot of permission to be nurturing to others, they have very little permission to love and take care of themselves *first*. Often in group it's necessary to teach women to love themselves, be their own best friend, and stop giving away *all* their loving and caring.

POLITICS OF THE PROBLEM-SOLVING GROUP

In radical psychiatry we approach problems from a radical political perspective. From this perspective we make certain assumptions about human beings. We assume that people are O.K.; that they are basically good and in their inner core wish to and are capable of living in peace and harmony with themselves, with each other, and with the earth. We believe that alienation is the result of mystified oppression: i.e., Alienation = Oppression + Mystification.

By *alienation* we mean a sense of not being right with

the rest of the world or humankind, a feeling of being not O.K. because something is wrong with you that makes you incapable of being happy and in tune with your world. The alienation that most women experience daily is enormous. It is shocking, for instance, to consider how many women are alienated from their own sexuality. Sound data isn't readily available, but a survey in *Psychology Today* which reported on a very select, relatively enlightened, and sexually free audience related that 20% of the women in the group said that during intercourse they reached orgasm never or almost never, and an additional 10% only one-fourth of the time. That is, 30% of these women achieve orgasm every four times they make love at the most.

Women have the right to have orgasm at least as often as men, but this won't come about if shrinks continue to listen to sexist theories like Freud's which cast women's sexuality in a demeaning light with accusations of penis envy and inadequacy. A woman's alienation from her sexuality causes her to feel that she is not O.K. Usually, she assumes she is "frigid" when, in actuality, if the oppressiveness of her situation was made apparent to her, she would view herself compassionately as a victim of the prejudices concerning women's sexuality.

Another form of alienation can be found in older women who are slandered as being bitchy or menopausally depressed when, in actuality, they are reaping the full thrust of an oppressive role in life. Because they have not pursued careers or been "producers" within the system, they receive little in the way of recognition for Adult work. Due to ageist and media prejudices about sexual beauty they are no longer considered viable love objects. And as for their roles as homemakers and mothers, they receive scant thanks for spending their lives sacrificing and caring for their families. Yet, when they become depressed about this unjust payoff, they often receive the outrageous punishment of electric shock therapy and/or stupefying drugs.

Further examples of alienation in women are: those who never decide to love themselves but are full of self-hate and contempt for themselves and other women; and women who see themselves as ugly and torture their minds and bodies, eternally vacillating between over-eating and disgust with their overweight bodies and going on torturous and ineffective diets, all the while mistaking their physical selves for their enemy.

The other vital element in this equation is the idea of *mystification*, which simply means deception. Women are deceived into colluding with their oppression; they are deceived into believing there is something wrong with them rather than understanding that they are being exploited, as in the case of the woman who considers herself frigid. Once mystification is removed, a woman can realize that she actually is being oppressed, and she will then no longer feel that *she* is not O.K. Once she can clearly see and taste this injury she can become angry and finally begin to move against the real culprit. We believe that Oppression + Awareness = Anger. The anger that comes from awareness is very useful to motivate women to use their Adult and focus their energy on fighting for and reclaiming their power.

The antithesis to Alienation or Mystified Oppression is Liberation—that is, Awareness + Contact = Action → Liberation. By *awareness* we mean the opposite of deception: consciousness. Consciousness must incorporate an understanding of the necessity for action. To be able to make your life better, you must seize control over it; thus you must *act*. Consciousness alone is not enough. Thought, when it excludes the necessity for action, is alienated. For thought not to become an alienated and disconnected headtrip, it must be grounded in practice; that is, based on real life experience. A psychiatric example of a headtrip without necessary action would be psychoanalysis, in which most people experience themselves as growing in understanding about themselves through dream analysis, etc., but still are not able to understand how to make real changes in their behavior.

We also believe that to overcome our oppression and gain liberation we need support and impetus from others. This is called contact. Women working in group need strokes and support from other women. Strokes are positive human recognition, examples of which would be a warm smile, a sincere compliment, a hug, a caress, or credit for hard work.

HOW RESCUE OPPRESSES WOMEN

We feel that it is vital that members of groups understand the sources of their oppression. We constantly work on awareness of how sex roles and capitalist society oppress people. But the idea we view as crucial is that, for people to feel better, for people to get what they want and "take care of business," they must act, they must move. People have to act to get what they want; they have to work for themselves in group and between meetings. To facilitate this work, women make a contract with the group to accomplish some definite goal. An example would be: "I want to ask for and accept strokes." No one can do this work for her; we can only help her work on it, and protect her when she gets scared. The ultimate responsibility for the decision to do it and the actual work to get there, lies with her.

We can't *Rescue* people who are oppressed. Rescue in this case means something very particular. It is an attempt to save someone whom you view and who views herself as helpless and powerless. To Rescue someone is oppressive and presumptuous, since it colludes with people's apathy and sense of impotence. Rather than demanding that people take power and ask for what they want, it reinforces people's passivity. The image it evokes is a world full of helpless consumers, powerless victims aching for visitation from powerful rescuers.

When two people play this game, they each take on one of three roles which they then constantly change. The three roles are Victim, Rescuer, and Persecutor (Figure 2), and are capitalized here to distinguish them from the true states of being a victim, rescuer, or persecutor.[2]

Here's an example from group:

Frances felt very sorry for her roommate, Sarah, whose lover was killed in an accident. She had a lot of sympathy for her and wanted very much to console her. But Sarah never seemed to feel better. For months she continued to feel bad and constantly wanted to tell Frances how hard it was not to have a man. After a while, Frances began to dread talking to Sarah, but she would listen (play the Rescuer role) because she felt guilty since her own relationships with her lovers were fine.

Frances couldn't see her way clear to tell her friend Sarah she didn't want to hear her complaints anymore. Finally, Frances began to get angry and think about moving out. She felt her friend was persecuting *her* because Sarah didn't work to make things better for herself. The group advised Frances to stop being angry (get out of the Persecutor role) and get into her Adult and have her Nurturing Parent available for her friend. The group told Frances to talk straight to Sarah, tell her how she felt about her playing the Victim role, and let her know she wanted her to start taking care of herself. As it turned out, it was hard for Sarah to take this feedback from Frances, but after she began working on it, she felt a lot better and let Frances know how much

---

[2] See Steven Karpman, "Script Drama Analysis," *Transactional Analysis Bulletin*, 7, 26 (1968).

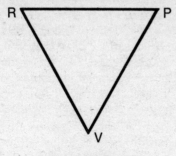

Drama Triangle

she appreciated her stopping the Rescue that might have destroyed their friendship and prolonged Sarah's period of mourning and self-pity.

I think in political terms we do people a great disservice when we attempt to Rescue them or to provide them with a consumable, feel-better therapy. We can help people by showing them new options they had been previously blinded to and teaching them problem-solving skills, but it's up to them to make the leap of faith to work through their fears about changing and taking power over their own lives. It's also up to them to do the struggling to learn to work cooperatively together in a group so that everyone can get what they want.

WOMEN'S OPPRESSION

There appear to be at least three realms in which women are oppressed. Women are oppressed in relation to themselves, that is, "within their own heads." They are oppressed in their intimate relationships with other individuals; and, finally, they are oppressed as members of society. In women's groups women can become familiar with what insidiously keeps them down—not only the obvious, overt male supremacy of which many of us are already aware and struggling against, but also oppression which has been internalized, which turns women against themselves, causing them to be their own worst enemy rather than their own loving best friend. This internalized oppression I have called the Pig Parent. It is the incorporation of all the values which keep women subordinate—messages saying, for example, that she mustn't outdo a man, she must be humble (i.e. not love herself), she must take care of others first, she must not be angry or bitchy; messages which also terrorize the Child part in her when it tries to be fine.

We see people acting in three different ways when they are behaving in their Child. They act as the *Natural Child,* that is, like a free child that is in touch with its feelings, acts spontaneously in behalf of them, and is creative and knows what it wants. They act as child-like Adults or like *Little Professors* whose intellect is intuitive rather than rational and logical. They act as the *Pig Parent,* which is the Parent in the Child. This is an immature, Child-like parent whose nurturing is conditional and not reliable. The Pig Parent only loves and cares for the Child as long as the Child adapts to what it wants. If the Child doesn't adapt, the Pig Parent withdraws its protection and support (Figure 3).

Women are oppressed in *all* their ego states. As I mentioned earlier, they are oppressed in their Nurturing Parent because in their roles as women they are enjoined to give all their nurturing away, to Rescue others, especially their husbands and children, but not to nurture themselves. In fact, if a woman is a loving, nurturing parent to herself she's seen as selfish, cold, and uncaring because she won't be self-sacrificing. Our goal in women's groups is to stop this absurd altruism and have all women love themselves *first.*

Women's groups are an excellent place for women to

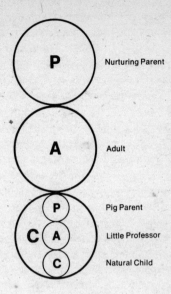

Ego States

feel safe enough to begin to use their Adult in a powerful way. They get support to use their intelligence, to think about things they have never thought about before, and to take the power to make decisions based on knowledge they hadn't previously given themselves credit for having. They are given an opportunity to experience and respect the intelligence of other women.

Women are made to feel crazy when men refuse to validate the intuitive perceptions of their Little Professor. Because men are often tuned out in this ego state, they often discount—that is, they refuse to account for many of the things women pick up on or are aware of intuitively. For instance, a woman who senses that her husband is loving her less and less each day is often discounted by him because when she asks him if he loves her he feels so guilty and scared that he has to lie to himself and her about his true feelings. Women also discount their own intuitive feelings and the feelings of others in the service of Rescuing them from the truth. They're afraid they'll have to deal with someone's anger or dislike of them.

Women are oppressed in their Natural Child; they don't feel safe enough in the world to do whatever they feel like doing. They tend to be what Maslow called "other directed"; that is, they look to others to see if it's O.K. to do certain things rather than just trusting their guts and doing what feels good.

When women nurture themselves, use their intelligence, trust their intuitions, and don't listen to their Pig Parent, they can act purely in behalf of what their Natural Child wants, which is their core—their center. We women can be truly powerful when we are in touch with this part of ourselves. Then can we know the truth of what feels right and what doesn't, what hurts and oppresses us, what causes us joy, fulfillment, or righteous anger.

The Nurturing Parent, Adult, Professor, and Natural Child are oppressed from the outside as well as within the Person. The Pig Parent is the enforcer of internal oppression.

The oppression by the Pig Parent can be easily illustrated by using a technique we call *bragging*. Children who feel O.K. about themselves love to tell how fine and wonderful they are until their parents and other grown-ups teach them that it is really bad (conceited, narcissistic) to truly like yourself and even worse to tell other people about it. Children believe this lie and often grow up unable to really love themselves. It is regretfully easy for a person to get in touch with their Pig. They merely need to get up in front of friends and tell them what they like about themselves, especially forbidden subjects, such as that they take delight in their body, or the way they look, or the way they make love. They will often experience anxiety and begin to qualify what they want to say. The Pig in their head wants them to be humble, and its messages are like these: "You'll make a fool of yourself because nobody believes that about you" or "Shut up, you're boring them."

When women are acting in their Pig Parent ego state they are constantly comparing and measuring their performance and productiveness. Their attitude toward themselves is demanding, not accepting. Things are never good enough. This internalized form of oppression can be devastating. In women's groups we are very interested in helping women "off" (destroy) their Pigs. In group it is important for women to become aware of the Pig and its messages as a powerful element of their oppression. To overcome it, women should be sensitized to when it makes them feel bad or actually says negative things about them. It's helpful to anticipate when the Pig may become active. It usually comes down heaviest when the Child wants to be out doing what she really wants (ignoring the dictates of the Pig), or when she has been feeling fine. It is often helpful to get in touch with what the Pig says and become familiar with its language. It often uses words like "must, should, ought, better, best, bad, stupid, ugly, crazy, or sick." Pigs also have *programs* which are ways of operating and carrying out its plans. It's important to figure the Pig's program. An example of a Pig program might be for someone to be so scared all the time that she can't get in touch with her real feelings and what she really wants in life. The way in which the Pig Parent would enforce this program would be by making threats to the person about frightening things that were supposedly going to happen. Pig messages are literally heard as voices speaking within the head, like a repetitive tape recording.

Sometimes Pig Programs operate like a vicious circle; certain patterns of behavior or thoughts get set up that are difficult to escape once the cycle begins. An example of this might be a woman who never asks for what she wants. She only asks for what she thinks people have for her. She wants to avoid putting anyone on the spot or being turned down. In other words, she Rescues people from how she actually feels and what she actually wants. When she does finally ask for something, she *really* wants it. So she applies a lot of pressure to get it. If she doesn't get it, she feels very bad and ripped off. Her Pig then gets a victory, because it can then say, "See, it doesn't pay to ask for what you want!" So then she asks even less for what she wants and feels even worse when she doesn't get it. The only way out of this cycle is for her to make a decision that radically changes her behavior—to ask for 100% of what she wants 100% of the time. She thus stops Rescuing people from her desires, and lets them take care of themselves by accepting a "no" answer from them without playing on their guilt by being a Victim. Because she'll be getting a lot more of what she wants, she won't be so disappointed about things she doesn't get; and, overall, she'll be having more of what she wants when she wants it.

To be sure, some people will sometimes do things for her which they don't want to do; that is, they'll Rescue her. And since Rescuers inevitably become Persecutors, she will have to absorb some anger from some people. But the benefits of asking for what she wants far outweigh the problems that accompany it, since they defeat the Pig Parent that says: "You don't deserve anything; there is no use in asking." She also can let them know she resents their Rescue and not relate to people who won't stop doing it.

OFFING THE PIG PARENT

It is vital to work out good, solid responses to the Pig Parent when offing the oppression within and replacing it with a humane and tolerant view of oneself. This tolerant view is the Nurturing Parent's. It is important to create a Nurturing Parent for oneself which is free of contaminated statements. That is, to be sure that the nurturing is complete and straight, not an inverted Pig message saying "You're not ugly" rather than something completely positive like "You are beautiful." Along with making a decision not to listen to or empower their Pig Parent, it is vital that women decide to become their own best friend and stop working against themselves. I want to emphasize that most women must strengthen their Adult since it is crucial for making decisions. The ability to think rationally and make decisions is necessary to attain a solid sense of identity as an effective human being.

Two valuable inter-related techniques developed by Steiner[3] are *Permission* and *Protection*.

Permission is given to the Child to do things she wants to do, but which the Pig won't allow. Following the giving of permission, the leader and other group members must provide protection in the form of strokes and support. The facilitator must be potent when giving permission that goes against the original parental injunctions. She must be strong and sure of what she says and back up her permission with protection by being available together with the group to give support with her presence in group or over the telephone. In giving permission and protection she uses her own Nurturing Parent ego state to reassure the person against the Pig, whereas ordinarily she uses her Adult in most of the group interactions.

The notion of permission and protection is vital also in helping women to stop following *banal scripts*.[4]

[3] Claude Steiner, *Games Alcoholics Play: The Analysis of Life Scripts* (New York: Grove Press, 1971).

[4] *Ibid.* See also: Claude Steiner, *Scripts People Live* (New York: Grove Press, 1974).

Banal scripts are life styles or ways of being that are chosen early in life, decisions to live one's life by a certain plan that fits in with the Pig's program.

Women are enjoined to live their lives following sex-role scripts. Commonly, at an early age, a woman is given a doll and a dollhouse and told she should be a good mommy and housekeeper. Such messages are incorporated, and women are often acting in behalf of these sorts of parental messages rather than living their lives autonomously and for themselves, guided by their own true desires. In group we give women permission to get in touch with what they really want and then to go after it and get it.

THE GROUP IN ACTION

It's crucial that women be turned on to what's good about changing. They have to be able to taste what's yummy about it; what's in it for them. To get people to take risks it's often necessary to entice them, seduce them to make the leap of faith that is going to get them there. This often happens through testimonials by group members who have already done this, by exciting Child descriptions in group of what the payoff is like, and also by object lessons. For example, a woman who has a contract to ask for what she wants will be much more motivated if she practices it in group and gets an opportunity to enjoy the reward for her efforts in that safe situation.

I'd like to give some sense of how a successful group feels in action. A good group might look as follows: Attendance is high and prompt. Members who are interested in working sign up. Anyone in crisis puts a circle around her name.

An example of a group interaction might be: Jane wants to work. Her contract has been established as "I want to be able to know what I want, and be myself with others." She wants to work on this contract because all her life she has adapted to other people. She acts on the basis of what others want her to be, rather than on her own standards and desires. Today she reports that she's having trouble at work. She feels that she's lost touch with her co-workers. Her job is very oppressive and working conditions are dehumanizing. The group sympathizes with her oppression and advises her not to take action alone, but to try to organize her co-workers so that they can all make demands and get satisfaction as a group. Jane works hard giving and getting feedback from the group on this problem. She talks about how to take power in this situation, and the group gives her strokes for her hard work. She asks for homework, and the group recommends that she work at talking straight to people at work and getting their support to take care of business there. This woman is well-liked. The members of the group care deeply about her, and she gets the strokes that she wants. Jane has worked well in group and done much to transform herself and her life. She has struggled against things that were inhibiting her and done much to make her political awareness a part of her everyday personal life.

A recurrent discussion in women's groups is the issue of women Rescuing their children. In the stereotypic program of the nuclear family it's Mom's job to take care of everyone. The assumption is that she's supposed to do things for her kids for gratis. In return, they should obey her, love her, etc. This sets up a Rescue triangle. Mom is the Rescuer doing good things for the kids. They are helpless Victims who supposedly can't take care of themselves. (It's my paranoid belief that this is a conspiracy to teach children that they are powerless in the world.) Thus her children are kept dependent and basically experience themselves as not having power. But as they fail to do what they are told to do, Mom eventually feels unloved and Victimized by them because she's already over-extended and she comes to view them as Persecuting her.

Once she's accumulated enough held resentments, she can cash them in by "pigging" the children. She then becomes the Persecutor to their Victim until she feels guilty. And once again the roles switch—and on and on it goes. The only way out is for her to completely reappraise her living situation in her Adult. She has to decide to give up the fairy tale of the happy nuclear family and decide to begin living collectively; that is, act as if she were living in a commune, where everyone is expected to work cooperatively and take responsibility for making the collective work by contributing all they can to the situation. This gives children an opportunity to use their power, to ask for what they want, and for parents to give only what they want to give and to also get things back from their children.

Here's an example of how this problem was worked on in group by one woman who has two adolescent children. Her contract is: "I want to know what I want and get it." She complained to the group that after working her boring and badly paid job all week, she has to spend all day Saturday cleaning her house, with little or no help from her kids or the man she lives with. Because she feels bad she Persecutes everybody on Saturday and by Sunday everyone's feeling bad and her weekend is shot. The group gave her feedback about how she plays Rescue and gave her homework to take care of herself and ask her family clearly and strongly for what she wants. They pointed out to her that her family may not understand what she wants from them or what's in it for them if they cooperate. The group's feedback sunk in, and soon she announced to the group that things were much better. During the week she had come home from work and found a sink full of dishes. She refused to cook dinner until the dishes were done and sat in the living room just taking care of herself. This sit-down strike was a really good object lesson for her lover and children. They let her know the next day that they wanted to have a house meeting and figure out how to work together better.

The women in the group were really pleased she had taken care of herself and gave her lots of strokes. The following week she told us that, working together, they had gotten the house clean Saturday morning and had the afternoon open to go play and enjoy each other for a change.

The following is an example of a history of a woman who has been in group for a little over a year. When she came into group she was frightened and felt helpless about being able to take care of herself and get what she wanted in life. She was constantly playing the role of a Victim and looking for a Rescuer. She would engage in playing "Ain't it Awful?" (which is a futile game of complaining about oppression but not working to change anything and which co-opts a person's energy and keeps her passive). She would describe how much of a Victim she was; and when group members would make suggestions about what she could do about it, she would make excuses and play "Yes, But. . . ." A year ago she had been "diagnosed" at a clinic as "agitated depression." Her general stance in group was that she wanted other people to do something for her and take care of her rather than to do something for herself and take responsibility over her own life.

I'd like to describe briefly the dialectical process of this woman's contracts with the group; that is, the different stages by which her work in group proceeded.

First, she started with a contract to get her Pig off her back. This contract was vague and served only to help us get a sense of what her Pig Program was. This evolved into a contract to talk straight. For the first time in her life she told people how she really felt about them and began getting in touch with her true feelings. The contract changed then into being able to say what she thought or felt at a given time. This helped her to be spontaneously in touch with herself. Her final contract is to be powerful for herself. In the first six months of her work in group this woman would repeatedly make phone calls to me which she attempted to stretch to twenty or thirty minutes. She would be very frightened and looking for a Rescue and showed little interest in taking care of business for herself. With the awareness that she has gotten in group, plus support from group members, she has slowly learned to take care of herself and assume responsibility for her own life. Now, if she calls, she asks for something specific which can usually be given in five minutes, like: information, reassurance, or strokes. She no longer looks for people to Rescue her and resents it when people do. She is interested in getting support from others and information as to what she can do to take care of things for herself. She comes to group and works hard and prefers to assign herself homework rather than having it assigned to her.

I believe that she will soon be leaving group; and, as has been the case with other women, she will then have completed her contract and have a sense of closure. She will feel that she has gotten what she wanted and will take away with her skills and ability to solve her own and others' problems and be able to take power over her own life. It will also be evident to her that she cannot get everything she wants in life on her own as an individual, that solutions will have to come through working with others. She knows if she gets in trouble in her head she can ask some friend who has been in group and knows how to problem-solve to get together with her and help her. If she gets into hassles with another person she can ask a friend to meet with her and the other person to mediate their difficulties.

She understands that the game of Rescue is vicious

and debilitating, and it robs people of their power. It keeps them from talking straight to each other and having the power to get what they want. She is now keenly aware that there are definite forces in society that keep her from having a full and happy life, that there are power structures invested in robbing her of her full humanity. For example, she is clearly aware of sexism and how it affects her possibilities of getting needed strokes.

RELATING TO MEN

A constant source of problems for women in group are their loving relationships with men. The Pig Program seems to be for women to fall in love with men, not get what they want, and then be very hurt and go into a "depression." Women consistently refuse to use their Adults in their loving relationships; they follow their Child feelings and are rudely surprised and hurt when they come up against the reality of where the men they are relating to are really at. When relationships fail, women think there's something wrong with *them*. But, for the most part, the trouble lies in the fact that men and women have very different attitudes about how to be in life. Often, men are not as interested in struggling as women are. They're either happy where they are at, or are too scared to change; or, due to the comfort of their privileged position, they are changing very slowly. Women in group, on the other hand, are for the most part eager to change. But their old scripting about loving relationships sets them up to be hurt. They are so desirous of being loved and finding someone to love that they often fall in love with their own Child fantasies rather than the actual person. They seem to be out of control, and they experience their loving feelings as dominating them: "I can't help myself. I know he doesn't love me the way I love him, but I can't stop feeling the way I do." Their feelings have *them* rather than *they* having their feelings.

The way out of this powerlessness and exploitation is for women to take a long, hard look, with their Adults, at the men whom they have empowered. They need to decide not to love anyone who doesn't love them back, and keep their loving feelings equal with those of whomever they're relating to, and decide *first* to be in love with themselves, and then exchange love with others.

Many women who feel disappointed in their relationships with men have decided to give up struggling with them completely. They've found they can get a lot more satisfaction and appreciation in loving relationships with other women. They can develop strong friendships and enjoy the richness of other women's nurturing, intuition, intelligence, strength, and sexuality.

GROUP COLLUSIONS

One of the pitfalls of women's groups is that there may develop group collusions. There might be subtle agreements between group members not to talk straight about certain things, or not to press each other about certain problems. This *keeping of secrets* can become part of the group culture, its "Karma." An example of this might be a group that encourages its members to look for a Rescue. Women are pressed to feel like Victims, to be powerless, to feel sorry for themselves and each other; but they have little permission to be Adults, to talk straight, to be potent, to take their power and take care of business, and to get what they want. Women in group may make a covert deal to give each other strokes and protection in order not to have to talk straight. In a group like this the facilitator can demystify what her Professor is sensing and what she sees going on. The facilitator can ask that people talk about solutions and what can be done about problems, rather than have them talk in detail about how bad things are or how heavy the problem is. She also should give people strokes for working and not going with their Pig and encourage others to give strokes for being powerful and taking care of business.

A useful tool for demystifying what's going on in a group is the process of letting go of *held resentments*, or "stamps."[5] The process, as worked out in radical psychiatry, is done in the following manner.

It may be decided, usually at the beginning of a group, to "do stamps." People will say to each other, "I have a stamp for you, do you want it?" The other person says "yes" or "no" depending on whether or not she feels strong enough to accept critical feedback. It is understood that a stamp may be quite paranoid, that it can be "off the wall," and that it is often generated by a misunderstanding; that is why no discussion or disagreement is allowed to follow stamp-giving. This is how it's done: "I was angry at you when you didn't talk to me at the party on Saturday." The person receiving this may say nothing, or "I hear you," and it is let go at that. The resentment is given some time to sink in; and if further discussion is needed, it can be taken care of at a later time. No one is given more than one in a row.

At the same time that held resentments are let go, so are *paranoid fantasies*. An example might be: "I think you've got a secret you're not telling the group." The person given the paranoid fantasy will then answer; and often there is at least a grain of truth in the paranoia.

I want to make it clear that people are urged to talk straight in the here and now and encouraged not to hold resentments or paranoid fantasies. But people don't

---

[5] See "Trading Stamps" in Eric Berne's *Principles of Group Treatment* (New York: Oxford University Press, 1966).

always do that, so this is an efficient way to keep things clean between people in groups.

After all the stamps and paranoias have been given out, people then give strokes; often, when people are holding stamps, they are also holding strokes they haven't felt free to give. Stamps, paranoias, and strokes are powerful antidotes against collusions in groups.

CONCLUSION

I think one of the most important aspects of group work is to stress teaching people to work cooperatively together. All of our Pig programming teaches us to compete and consume each other, not cooperate and create each other. In group, women can cooperate on making sure they share the time, work hard on each other's contracts, talk straight, keep no secrets, and not Rescue each other.

One of the most important jobs of a facilitator is to teach people to take back their power. While turning people on to new options in life and skills in problem-solving, it is necessary that she demand that people take as much responsibility as they can for what happens in group. The goal isn't to build dependency relationships or admiration for the facilitator, but rather to work on a constant transferral of power and expertise. I encourage women to challenge my work in group. I welcome criticism and feedback and work hard to respond to it. I don't work on my own problems in group, but I do mention relevant experiences I've had, so women know I'm fighting the same oppression that they are coming up against. I answer any questions they have about my own life and strive to be absolutely transparent in group about how I feel while I'm there. I work in my Adult to give information, with my Nurturing Parent available to give support and strokes, and with my Child ready for a good laugh or joyous smile at someone's latest victory.

In closing, I want to stress that we in radical psychiatry begin with a definite radical political perspective. We are not interested in being "hip" shrinks who service counter-culture people. We are community organizers; we want to teach people problem-solving skills, political awareness; and we want to provide protection to people while they make changes they want to make in their lives. But the ultimate responsibility for this happening rests equally in the hands of the group members—not just with the facilitators. We desire to put people in touch with their power. Our aim is to impart problem-solving skills and teach people to take power over their own lives. We are interested in having people reclaim themselves as full and potent human beings. We believe that the group situation is the most auspicious for women, since the group process obviously indicates that there are no individual solutions for oppressed people and that to have strength we must band together.

It is especially valuable for women to interact with other women and develop a keen sense of sisterhood. The group structure is also very efficient for problem-solving work since it provides much diversified feedback. Still, I also feel it is important to make clear here that complete human liberation is not possible in our present capitalist society. Individuals cannot be free from sex-role oppression in a society where such oppression is built-in as an integral part of how the economy maintains itself. For individuals to be free, society must be free. Women cannot overcome social oppression as individuals. Only by working cooperatively together can we become powerful enough to make the substantive changes that we want in our world.

8. PERMISSION by Hogie Wyckoff

Permission work acts is complimentary to work done in a problem-solving group. It provides the necessary time, room, and equipment that is not available in a regular radical psychiatry group. Permission is done when specifically needed, whereas problem-solving is ongoing.

Permission exercises are designed to help people do things they want to do, but can't, because they have internalized prohibitive and inhibitive parental messages. For example, a person's real desire and need may be to be able to ask for the strokes (a hug, a kiss, etc.) she or he wants, but their Pig Parent says, "NO! Don't you dare!"

A useful means for understanding people (which I shall explain here because it is integral to understanding permission) is to observe that they behave in three distinctive modes, or ego states: the *Parent, Adult,* and *Child.* In the Parent ego state the person may be Nurturing or Critical. The Nurturing Parent is the part of them that is unconditionally loving and accepting. The Pig Parent is critical and unaccepting, always demanding a performance, perfection, and saying: "Not good enough." The Child is the part of a person that plays, is creative and free, and does what it likes to do.

In order to help a person be able to ask for strokes, the person leading the exercise must provide *three P's:* Permission, Protection, and Potency.[1] Permission is approval given to the Child to do what she wants. Protection is safety provided by the leader's Nurturing Parent. It is absolutely necessary that the person leading the exercise be nurturing to the people doing it. Potency is the strength to back up what you say, carry through on it, and deal head-on with someone else's Pig Parent. In the above example I would say: "Okay, I want you to ask someone here for a stroke." I would *insist* that the person did this (assuming we had a *contract* between us specifying what she wanted to work on). If she got frightened, I would reassure her; if someone else pigged her, I would protect her; and if her own Pig came in on her, I'd help her get rid of it. I wouldn't back down or "chicken out"; yet I would be very sensitive to where the person was at and be as supportive and responsive to her individual needs as I could while teaching her a new way to be.

As I said, it is necessary to have an agreement, a contract arrived at ahead of time in their problem-solving group (Chapter 6). The contract should state simply and clearly what the Child wants. It is necessary that the contract be capable of being fulfilled here and now in the permission class situation. Thus a contract for a woman to have orgasm during intercourse is not valid for permission class because this couldn't be accomplished in that setting. It is very helpful to write the contracts up on a wall with large crayons where everyone can see them. It should be understood that no one has to do anything that they don't want to do. People who change their minds are free to terminate the contract.

Permission exercises are not a pacification of people's

---

[1] Claude Steiner, *Scripts People Live* (New York: Grove Press, 1974).

alienation as many touchy–feely–good–vibe therapy techniques are. This is because Permission in radical psychiatry is not just giving people contact but involves awareness as well; therefore, we talk about what happens and provide the necessary consciousness raising for true liberation. We don't want to co-opt the potential of people to discover for themselves how they are oppressed and to become angry enough to do something about it. We don't have angry women just beat on pillows so as to pacify themselves temporarily. We help them learn new ways of being and help them learn how to get what they want. So, in keeping with our example, I would explain how the stroke economy (see Chapter 3) exploits us in our lovings, and not just do a magic trick for someone.

It is important to ask people how they are feeling when doing exercises. Keep communication open. Let people talk about their experiences and get and give feedback.

In doing permission exercises, no one is giving anyone anything they didn't originally have. People are born O.K., but oppressed away from their full human potential.

It is often very useful, although not necessary, to use appropriate music when doing different exercises. This helps bring out the Free Child and set the mood. Throughout this chapter I will give examples of various types of applicable music.

When starting a class I tell people that this is a safe situation—and I mean it. They can do whatever they want to do except hit each other without fear of implied promises, especially sexual, to others in what they do. This allows people to be spontaneous and free without the usual social prohibitions and fears of unwanted commitments.

There are generally five types of exercises, and I will present them in the order in which they should be used:

*Introduction and Trust; Stroking; Getting O.K.; Being
O.K.;* and *Fantasy.* I also will give examples of each
and explain how they are done.

Four aspects of each exercise will be discussed. First,
how the exercise is being done and how contact between
people is made. Second, what the purpose of the exercise is and what it means. Third, how the exercise looks
when it is done correctly and provides a liberating experience. Fourth, how in some cases the exercise can
go wrong and make people feel even more alienated.

Some exercises marked with an asterisk I will only
refer to briefly.

I. INTRODUCTION AND TRUST

Say Your Name

Standing in a large circle, have people say their name
to the rest of the group. Tell them to say it loud and
clear; let it resonate. Have them walk into the center of
the circle when they say it and/or have them say it
three times, in different ways.

The purpose is for people to present themselves to
others and to make a first step in learning to "brag"
(more on this later); that is, to be able to say good
things about themselves.

People should make their names heard and give each
name time to "soak in." It should be similar to a mini
show-and-tell about the person doing it.

Introduce Each Other

Have people choose a partner and find out their name
and the most important things about them. Then have
the partners take turns introducing and telling about
each other to the rest of the group.

The purpose is to have people quickly and intuitively learn about each other. Also, to drop trivial conversation and really find out about other people; that is, make intimate contact.

People should be able to discover what's important about each other in human terms. If there are too many people, it's O.K. to limit what they say to two or three things they were told and something they saw but were not told. The introductions should be honest and some feeling of intimacy achieved.

Large Trust Circle

Have everyone take off their shoes and stand in a circle. (You need at least eight to ten people to do this.) Each person will then take a turn going into the center of the circle, closing their eyes, turning around to disorient themselves, then walking as fast as they feel it is safe to do, moving out to the edge of the circle. They should keep their hands at their sides, have their chins out, and walk straight on, not sideways or with their heads down. People at the edge will catch them with their hands, which are held out ready, while they are well balanced with their feet braced securely. The "catchers" will lean forward slightly to avoid stubbed toes, catch the person, and gently turn her around, pointing her in a new direction. If the person gets frightened, be nurturing with them.

Be sure that the situation *is* really safe. Make sure people can't trip on a rug or hurt themselves.

The purpose of this is for people to learn they can count on others in the group. Also, it's a good chance to practice being trustworthy and a Nurturing Parent to others when they are frightened and need reassurance.

The leader must be tuned in to the person working. Keep in close communication with her; find out what she is feeling and help her feel safe enough to trust.

This may involve telling people to go slower when they are pushing themselves to go faster than feels safe to them, or telling them to take a peek when it's obvious they're having a hard time keeping their eyes shut, or, if they get really scared, taking their hand and walking with them until they feel safe. People will usually start out slowly and a little afraid and build trust and then be able to take chances. They may even be able to run or at least really get off-balance and trust the group. People who are the most afraid will often be the last to try it. Let them do what feels good. This is not a performance. People should learn something, not get their minds blown. People should eventually look comfortable while doing this exercise.

It's important that people don't pull tricks on each other, such as backing off and making the circle larger that it was to begin with. It's also not good for the "catchers" to push the other person off in another direction; they should only be pointed.

People who are afraid may have a counter-phobic response and just jump in, as into a cold pool of water. Don't let them frighten their Child too badly by staying out of touch with their fear and by pushing themselves.

If someone is very afraid, they shouldn't do it; perhaps they should try a Small Trust Circle (see later exercise).

Blind Walk*

Have people choose partners and take turns leading each other around on a walk with eyes closed. It's best if done outside and people turn each other on to things that smell and feel good like flowers, people's hair and skin, etc.

People learn to trust and be nurturing to each other.

People should take good care of each other and have fun and get in touch with their senses. When feeling really trusting, people can get into doing a blind run with their partner.

The Small Trust Circle

Have about eight people stand in a tight, close circle and gently pass back and forth a person standing in the center who should stand straight, knees stiff, feet together, eyes closed, and body relaxed.

People learn to trust the whole group in close contact. It's easier than the Large Trust Circle for some people.

It works if the person relaxes and relinquishes control. The head should hang and the body should be off-balance.

II. STROKES

Group Massage

Have a person needing strokes lie down on their stomach or back as they choose on a mat. Have the group kneel around the person and ask one of the group to lead the massage. This leader can tap, pat, slap, etc., while everyone else follows what she is doing. If a person is particularly needy of loving strokes, it is best to give them just that: loving, tender stroking. People who are scared of getting strokes are most able to accept being touched on their back. If the person receiving is rigid, unable to accept strokes, talk to them in a nurturing and reassuring way and ask them to relax.

The purpose is to give strokes to people who want them but have little permission either to accept them or ask for them. It's a good way to give a lot of strokes to a needy person in a short amount of time.

The person being stroked should have her eyes closed and let the strokes "soak in." People giving strokes should not get into small talk with each other, but rather concentrate on giving. When it's over, time should be taken while the person gets up, opens her eyes, and *sees* everyone caring about her.

Music: anything quiet and soothing (not necessary).

Stroke Mill

Everyone closes their eyes and walks around the room touching other people. Have them explore each other's hands, hair, faces, etc. Guide the mill with instructions geared to the group's tolerance for accepting physical strokes.

The purpose is to let people touch and be touched freely in a safe situation without the usual emphasis on touching necessarily meaning a sexual advance.

People maintain awareness of their Child's innermost desires about what's happening and go with them either to touch or to move away from someone according to what feels good, without forcing themselves to do anything that feels unpleasant.

It is alienated when people adapt to what other people want, not staying in touch with and taking care of their own desires.

Music: "Spirit in the Dark"; "What the World Needs Now."

Trash the Stroke Economy*

After explaining the basic rules of the stroke economy (i.e., don't ask for strokes you want; don't give strokes you have; don't accept the strokes you get; don't reject strokes you don't want; and don't stroke yourself), have everyone stand in a circle, taking turns being in the center. Whoever is in the center does something to break down the imposed scarcity of strokes between people. They can ask for, receive, give, or reject strokes, or stroke themselves. An example would be to ask a particular person for a hug and to accept it if she gave it, or accept her declining the invitation if she refused, not as a put-down, but merely move on to ask someone else.

People can commit revolutionary actions in a limited way in this safe situation by breaking oppressive rules and seeing that it can feel good to do so when there is protection.

People undermine the usual shortage of strokes, and give and take strokes freely.

It is alienated if people adapt; that is, they give or accept strokes when they don't want to or when they adapt to other people's wants.

III. TO GET O.K.

Use the Nurturing Parent (in Three Steps)

STEP ONE: THE WORDS

Using your "other hand" (your left if you're right-handed, or vice versa), with large crayons on big sheets of paper write words or phrases on one side of the paper that describe what your Child would like its N.P. (Nurturing Parent) to be like. The words should be Child-type words, such as: "loves me," "is big and gentle," "holds me," etc.

On the other side of the paper, write what your Child would like your N.P. to say to you: "I love you"; "You're beautiful"; etc. Have everyone share the descriptions of their N.P. and after that read aloud the things they would like to hear from their N.P.

This is a good way for people to get in touch with the quality of their N.P. They can learn what other people's N.P.s are like and also not to be embarrassed to use nurturing, loving words. Let people take their words home with them to use on themselves whenever they need them.

When sharing their lists, people should say the words they want to hear, in the way they want to hear them (warmly, lovingly, etc.), and let them soak in. Everyone will feel warm and good when they are said. Some people may even get homesick and cry.

It is alienated when the words are said in the Adult, or, if the words are subtle reversals of Pig Parent words, such as: "You're not ugly." If this happens, the leader (or other people in the group) should intervene and help to elicit a straight N.P. stroke, like: "You're beautiful."

STEP TWO: SAY THE WORDS TO EACH OTHER

Have people give their words to someone they like; then have that person say the words to her partner while she holds that person on her lap or cuddles him in some way.

It gives people practice in being N.P. to others who need it, and to learn to accept the N.P. that they want from others. It also gets people in touch with their basic goodness and their caring for one another.

People should touch each other and not be afraid to be comforting. They should let the words soak in and not go too fast. People can ask to hear their words repeated as much as they want.

STEP THREE: NURTURING PARENT MILL

Have people close their eyes and mill around the room. When people come in contact with each other, have them be nurturing and loving to the Child in the other person, touching them in a nurturing way and saying N.P. words.

After being N.P. to each other, have them be N.P. to

themselves (e.g. give themselves a hug and say good things to themselves).

This teaches people to be nurturing to others and themselves and to be able to accept nurturing. It also helps break down the stroke economy between people and their own failure to stroke themselves. It gets in touch with the basic O.K.-ness of the group.

This is similar to the regular stroking mill. It works if people do only what feels good.

People should feel free to give and accept nurturing strokes. People should feel that they are really O.K.

It is alienated when people adapt; that is, go through the motions because they think they "should"—but they really don't want to. It's also alienated if it's done in the Adult, not in a warm, loving way.

Music: "Bridge Over Troubled Water"; "You've Got a Friend"; "Let It Be"; "Once There Was a Way."

Off the Pig

This is a powerful exercise requiring skill and great care. Expertise in working with people is definitely necessary to do it right. You must have a contract, an agreement with the person to "off their Pig." It should come after the N.P. exercise and in some ways is similar to it. Only two or three people should do it at any one period of time; the rest of the group (composed preferably of more people) should remain in their N.P. for support. It's a struggle to off the Pig Parent; and when a leader agrees to do it she has to be potent, aware of what's going on, and persistent enough to carry it through.

With the "other hand" and using crayons on large paper have people write on one side Child words or phrases to describe what their Pig is like: "mean, stupid, sneaky, etc."; and on the other side what the Pig tells them: "You're crazy, no one likes you, etc." On a smaller sheet have them draw a face mask depicting their Pig. Then they should read the descriptions and the words of their Pig aloud. Have people act out their Pig non-verbally, using their body and sounds, always with their mask held up to their face. Have them use the words their Pig uses on them. Have them give you their words (for your reference) while they work through destroying their Pig (in the form of the mask).

This teaches people how to get their Pig off their backs. They learn what it is like; what words it uses; how it acts; and the emotions it uses to oppress. People can learn a strategy for fighting their Pig by knowing how it functions as the enemy. This shows them that they can do it, and that other people will back them up. They should get encouragement from others while they're doing it. They thus learn how to answer it, how to stop it, and a means of neutralizing it in the future.

To be effective in this exercise, the person must combine into one forceful act three all-important elements: the right *words, emotion,* and *action*. All three must be present at the same time; otherwise, the Pig won't leave. Without all three present, it would be like trying to get rid of a tricky person just by being angry, or trying to get rid of a bully through words alone. You need a clever strategy to deal with a tricky person and some sort of force or anger to get rid of a bully. Trust your guts while leading this to know if the Pig has really been "offed." It should feel obvious and definite when it happens and end with a flourish of finality.

Others in the room can give all the nurturing needed by the other people to do something scary.

After people "off" their Pig, they should get all the strokes they want from whomever they want. A celebration usually happens because this exercise is scary and feels like a real victory when done well.

It won't work if people don't really want to do it. If someone realizes she doesn't want to go on, let her out of her contract. It's definitely not done right unless *all* three parts of the offing are there. The right emotion and action without the right words won't do it. People have to be able to answer their Pigs to shut them up. Words and emotion without action, or any other combination of merely two elements, will be ineffectual. The leader should allow no Pig Parent behavior during this exercise. Do not let anyone "pig" the person working to try to goad them into action or anger. People feel good after they successfully "off" the Pig, not sad or afraid or doubtful.

IV. I'M O.K.

Bragging

Have the person who wants to brag stand where everyone can see her and say all the good things she can think of to say about herself. Not just things she does, but also things she is. Have her say things she likes about her body and how she looks. Be sure to explain that it's not competitive, and therefore not proper to use comparisons like "better," etc.

This teaches people that although the word "bragging" has a bad connotation in our society it's not a bad thing to do so long as it's not competitive. It trashes the stroke economy and allows people to publicly dig on themselves and see that others like them when they do.

They should use positive words that describe themselves, not comparative words or inverted Pig messages, like "I look good for someone who is so fat." People should cheer each other on and generally be supportive to and appreciative of someone who brags.

It is alienated when people use sentences with negative or relative words, like "I'm not bad" or "I'm better than." It's alienated also if they only talk about *what* they do, not *who* they are; or if they qualify the good things they say about themselves; or if they don't say anything good about their physical selves.

Move to Music as Free Child*

Have everyone close their eyes and listen to music. Ask them to start moving slowly and let the music move them. Ask them not to do familiar dance patterns.

This helps people to move freely and to experience new motions in their bodies.

This should be free and open, with movements loose and spontaneous.

Music: "I Wish I Knew How It Would Feel To Be Free."

Be In the Center: Follow the Leader*

Have people take turns being in the center, moving to music while people follow them in a "follow the leader" game.

This shows people that it's O.K. to be in the center of attention, and frees people to lead.

Music: "Working Together."

V. FANTASY

Trips for Discovery

People can take fantasy trips for growth and discovery. Have people lie back, close their eyes, breathe deeply, and relax while you take them on a trip. An example would be: taking people on a long hike to the top of a mountain where they can ask a wise person only one question. What do they ask? Or: "You have died. It's your funeral. You're in the coffin. Who's there at your funeral? What do they say to you? What do you want to say to them? Say goodbye to people until there is only one person left. Who is it?" The leader should go slowly and permit fantasy to develop.

This helps get people in touch with things they may not be in touch with.

It's useful when people are relaxed and get into it. They should be able to talk about it later.

Music: Soft and airy mood music.

Role-Play Opposite Sex

Have people be the opposite sex. Men can pretend they're in short skirts and high heels while women can see themselves in men's trousers, etc. Have the "men" ask the "women" for a date, for strokes, etc.

A sex-role inversion can be very useful to highlight oppression and mystification. Role-playing is generally very enlightening.

It's right if people are sincere about learning about sex roles. It's O.K. to have fun doing this exercise.

Section IV
Community Organizing

9. RADICAL PSYCHIATRY AND COMMUNITY ORGANIZING by Joy Marcus, Peter LaRiviere, and Daniel Goldstine

INTRODUCTION (by Joy Marcus)

Our emotional life is entwined with our political life. The muscle and blood of political life is the distribution of power. As long as there exists in our society an inequitable distribution of power based on economic wealth in tandem with racial, sexual, and class prejudices no one (no one I know, anyway) will be able to fully realize their human possibilities. But it also seems true that a healthy society would be made up of healthy people. For these reasons we are concerned with the problem of simultaneously changing how we are as individual organisms and radically changing society.

During a class session in radical psychiatry given at the Free University in Berkeley, we talked about doing a form of community organizing as a solution to some of these problems; in that session we described our efforts to organize a psychiatric day-care program. Most of this chapter will consist of the transcript of that class, which I've left intact for the most part. Before presenting it, however, I'd like to place things a bit more in context.

For some time now, radicals in the mental health field have been using their skills to provide "movement people" with direct services. Also, at least in Berkeley, we've been teaching others—mostly non-professionals —how to provide psychiatric help to each other and our allies. These services are increasingly being provided through "counter institutions"—rap centers, psychiatric emergency centers, free clinics, and so forth.

However, while our counter-institutions are important and must be nurtured, I do not see that they alone will insure the kind of thoroughgoing change needed for the health of this country. Nor is it economically possible or even necessarily attractive for most people to "drop out." In order to build the massive base which will be the ultimate guarantee of radical change in our society many people will have to create counter-movements within establishment institutions and agencies to gain control over them, thus taking power over the working conditions of their chosen occupation, which is one of the most basic needs of human life. The transcript of our discussion at the Free University shows how we tackled some of the many problems of self-determination and community control posed by establishment institutions—in this case, Contra Costa County Hospital in Martinez, California.

For example: a therapist whom everyone in the day-care program valued greatly had been told he would be fired because he hadn't met a certain civil service requirement. The requirement had to do with a technicality about credentials. Some of the patients brought up the subject in a community meeting; the possibility of losing one of the most effective and loved workers in the program made many people feel unhappy and helpless. Then one of us said, "Wait a sec. Maybe we don't have to take this flat on our backs." This bit of dynamite produced an avalanche of talk and determination in the patients to "take care of business." More community meetings were held, during which the politics of the situation, as well as people's experiences in it, were discussed.

These meetings encouraged a group of five or six patients plus a few staff people to make an intense argument at the civil service commission hearing. Most of the commission members were astonished to hear the community assert its right to keep the therapist on the staff. But they listened and we won.

If it's possible to separate the two notions, we won in political terms and also in therapeutic terms. Politically, what we won—and "we" means the patient-staff coalition—was not controlling power over the institution but a certain amount of influence, a veto power that would make it possible for us to determine the people we would work with. The therapeutic results were that the patients gained a heightened awareness of some of the forces that oppress them and valuable experience in working cooperatively to change an oppressive condition. Not only were they learning about external oppressive conditions, such as the ancient and totally useless civil service system, but in order to be effective at the civil service hearing these patients—who up until then had had precious little sense of their own potency—also had to fight against their internalized oppression (their images of themselves as crazy, impotent, invisible, unworthy). If acquiring the skills and strength to control the internal oppressor isn't a measure of growth or psychiatric success, I don't know what is.

It was an opening. We don't yet have a particularly clear image of what "the compleat take-over" of a hospital will look like. I only know that if one must work in an establishment institution, doing it with allies—with people who share the same visions—to gain power and control over our own lives is a more satisfying, more integrative experience than the one we've been taught to expect and accept.

THE TRANSCRIPT: A SUNDAY NIGHT IN BERKELEY, 1971

J.M.: If you were all here a couple of weeks ago, then you know that Claude [Steiner] announced that I'd be doing a rap on radical psychiatry and community organizing, with reference to my activity at Contra Costa County Hospital in Martinez. Well, I didn't do it alone out there. With me tonight are Danny Goldstine and Peter LaRiviere. Danny's a clinical psychologist at the hospital; Peter is a physician and also works out there. I'd like to point out that although Peter's an M.D., he's not a certified shrink. He's a good ole down-home radical psychiatrist, as is Danny. Now that I've introduced them, I'd like to outline for you some of the ideas we came up with working at the hospital, and then we can talk about how our ideas were applied.

One thing we've discovered is that, in certain situations, radical psychiatry might be construed as community organizing. We've discovered that the terms "radical psychiatry" and "community organizing" can be interchangeable; often (perhaps not often enough) the two functions intertwine. The only factor which would differentiate the two is the size of the groups. Let me explain. We begin with certain givens. You probably all know by now the formulas we use:

(1) Oppression + Mystification = Alienation

(2) Awareness + Contact = Liberation.[1]

---

[1] The second part of this formulation was later changed by members of the Radical Psychiatry Center. It now reads: Awareness + Contact = Action → Liberation.

STUDENT: Would you mind reviewing that? This is my first time here.

J.M.: Sure. O.K. The biggest problem that psychiatry must solve is alienation. Alienation is the sum of oppression plus mystification—not only are we oppressed, but we empower our oppression by lying to ourselves or believing the lies of others who deny we're oppressed or who say, "That's life, kid, you've just got to accept it." In the absence of oppression, people get along harmoniously with each other and with their environment. In order to achieve that harmonious state, to become free, we need awareness, contact, and action. Awareness alone isn't enough. Contact alone isn't enough. Action not supported by both is bound to be ineffective. Once we see we're oppressed—whether by the internalized oppressor (an often amorphous but insidious "It" which some of us call the Pig Parent) or by an external situation—we need each other, groups of each other, to confront and struggle against whatever oppresses us.

But these concepts, these formulas that I just mentioned, were initially conceived in the context of our problem-solving groups, which are generally limited to eight members and where the most intense focus is on internalized piggery. So we kept asking ourselves, "What new agonies will we perpetrate when our advocacy helps people overthrow internalized oppression if we don't also advocate fighting external oppression?"

Another way of stating the question is: "When people respond to a crazy world by going crazy, what are we really doing for those who seek our help when we elicit in them ways of seeing and acting which are 'different' from (if not entirely counter to) the established modes, when all of us (including me) must return to a world which is stark raving mad?"

Well, my answer is: "Unless we advocate and support radical social-political and economic change wherever and whenever possible we will not be doing much better than traditional psychiatry, we will be oppressors in support of the status quo." But in order to radically change our world we've got to do lots of organizing—in our case, that would mean creating alliances between health-care workers and the people they serve—and get other people excited about organizing. But instead of talking to you about the concepts, I think it would be a good idea to tell you what we actually did. I'm not quite sure how to proceed right now. I feel your attentiveness, and that really feels good to me, but I wonder if you have any questions.

STUDENT: Could you give me a historical perspective on this concept of radical psychiatry as community organizing?

P.L.: I got interested in the possibility of doing something specific with radical psychiatry when I was working as the guy who does the histories and physicals on the acute ward out there at the hospital. I found for the first time in my experience in medicine that though I was doing interesting work, I was feeling really oppressed; I was feeling just as oppressed as when I had been a medical student, and that was plenty oppressed. I knew something was wrong. I didn't know what the hell was wrong. I went to see the program chief in psychiatry. He's very sympathetic toward community psychiatry, but I think it's fair to say that he really hadn't found a way to effectuate his ideals. So when I talked to him and said I'd just had enough of J Ward, that I wasn't able to make any progress there, we were being opposed at every point in doing any therapy, much less radical therapy, he and I agreed that probably the best way to begin to do anything which would allow mental patients to determine things about their own lives, including their own therapy, was to work with what was then called the day-care program. This was then defined as a "day hospital" for people who, while they weren't locked up on J Ward or the other in-patient psychiatric ward, were really deeply alienated.

At that time, day-care was run by a woman, a social worker who did the usual traditional things with a group of say fifteen or sixteen people—outings, stringing beads, a little bit of therapy, stuff like that. And I began then to work with the program, alone at first, but quickly—as we began to discuss this in our radical psychiatry affinity group—other people got interested in what was happening. They began to come out and join in the effort, which has now resulted—not to get too much ahead of myself—in the formation of a psychiatric community which is partially self-determining and which is beginning to spread the practice of radical psychiatry into the general community.

STUDENT: You, Peter, mentioned that your feeling of being oppressed acting as a psychiatrist felt similar to your feelings of oppression as a medical student. Could you elaborate on that?

P.L.: Sure. Well, quite simply, I was not allowed to do what I was capable of doing. I was there to do a technical task, taking care of histories and physicals, which was ridiculously simple, with a group of people who had what were called acute psychiatric illnesses. It was the same as in medical school where I felt that my own skills would have been best employed in really finding out what was bothering people, rather than running lab tests. . . .

D.G.: I'd like to interject a point here relevant to Peter's feeling of oppression. It's so indicative of the kind of services that are delivered to psychiatric patients that hospital administrations would literally rather spend more time and money trying to get histories and physicals than they would on any attempt to do any kind of therapy. Here is a psychiatric setting, and they spend more time worrying about your ingrown toenails or your athlete's foot than they do trying to talk to you about what's really going on. At best they do a rather cursory talking to you, fill you up with medication, and write the discharge summary at the same time they do the initial interview.

STUDENT: Peter gave us a view of the program as it began through the hospital hierarchy. You were part of the hierarchy, Peter, and you had an "in." But what about Joy—how did you get involved?

J.M.: I guess it started when Peter would come to our Thursday night meetings and talk about what was going on at the hospital. I started going out to some planning sessions. Peter asked Danny and me and some other people to go to mental health planning meetings with him out at the hospital, kind of as consultants. He wanted us to talk about our experience at the rap center, because the rap center at its best was a good model of a community psychiatric center. At those planning meetings I sort of got turned on, but I was still very reluctant to get involved because the hospital atmosphere was so rigid. . . . I had been going down to J Ward on weekends with Danny and Peter, working with people who were having what gets labeled as "acute psychotic experience"—people who were either on acid or just having what the shrinks call "fresh breaks"; I saw them as people who were farther out than we are, or farther in, or in unusual states of consciousness. Anyway, we'd let Al Johnson, the head shrink on weekends, know when we'd be coming in; he'd pick out some people whom he'd judge as "appropriate" for Danny and me to work with, and then refrain from zonking them out—medicating them with the usual massive doses of phenothiazines. And though in some ways the experience was really rich for me and I think I helped some people, I didn't like working in an institution. I found it very oppressive.

On the other hand, I saw that I couldn't do radical psychiatry in a vacuum. That is, whether I was working with my groups in Berkeley or working with people on J Ward, I knew that so much of what was hurting people, myself included, had to do with what was going on with the world outside them. And when an opportunity presented itself to work in that "real" world, I simply couldn't turn my back on it. My strongest impulse was to get involved working with Peter to organize the day-care program. My status was "volunteer therapist." Peter and I co-led a therapy group. Nobody at the hospital knew anything about radical psychiatry, and at that early stage in the game I wasn't about to tip our hand. I was just "that strange-looking hippie woman who wore floor-length Indian dresses and no brassière, come to help out that doctor man who'd been commissioned by Leonti Thompson to change things. And Peter's a doctor, so he must know what he's doing; he certainly wouldn't bring in an incompetent therapist, even if she *does* dress kind of weird. . . ."

STUDENT: Joy, how did you view the hospital, how did it seem as a psychiatric or liberating situation? Did it have any of the elements that you perceive to be important in bringing about people's liberation?

J.M.: No. The first problem we were confronted with was the traditional hierarchy, with a male psychiatrist on top and a woman social worker under him. I think both of them freaked out under our pressure for community-patient participation. [Both of them left the hospital three or four months after we started.] I didn't see anything going on at the hospital that was liberating. Here, I'll read you an excerpt from a journal I started last summer, which may give you a feel for my experience of the hospital:

131]]]

"It is a sterile, airless institutional green room. There are nine or ten men and one woman sitting around a long table talking.

"Peter and I walk in. I make eye contact with one man who sits at the head of the table. No one else seems to notice us. No one moves to make room for us at the table.

"But outside the circle of people rimming the table there are two chairs, against the wall.

"We sit close so our thighs and shoulders touch. I am aware of the integrity of my being, my sexuality, the beauty of my serene face, my relaxed graceful body, and how natural my body feels sitting close to Peter, whose face also is serene, whose body is also open, unselfconscious, naturally postured as a child —belly relaxed and round, breathing easy, thighs apart. . . .

"I look at the faces around the table. Their expressions go from bored to anxious to depressed to hostile to vacant or glassy-eyed.

"Sometimes someone says something sort of funny and sometimes someone laughs. Too hard. Nervously. The bodies of the people appear to be stiff-limbed, rigid, involuted. Living dead. These people are psychologists, psychoanalysts, psychiatrists, and psychiatric social workers. They're planning the lives of people they call The Mentally Ill."

You can imagine how awful, how poisonous that scene felt to me. I'd come from a very unstructured environment at the rap center, and here I walked into a place that was uptight, and had forms, and people had to write stuff in charts, and I wasn't into taking notes on people or stuff like that. . . . I came from a place where people had a lot of physical contact, where stroking was an important element of therapy, whether it was physical stroking or verbal, and I walked into the hospital where people didn't touch each other—either physically or emotionally. They had no permission to touch each other, there was very little real protection. The people were deceived into believing they were protected because they had the walls of the hospital around them, and the hierarchy with doctors around them, but there was nothing I could call growth-producing or liberating human experience. . . .

STUDENT: How did you ease these people out who couldn't cope with your trip, your way of therapy?

D.G.: They eased themselves out.

P.L.: What we did was to engage the patients in a group process that became too hot for the other staff people. There was a lot of shock value, I think, in the fact that Joy is a high school dropout, though eminently well-trained to do therapy, and that shocked the hell out of them. They were O.K. people, they just didn't like intensity. They didn't like really getting into things. So it wasn't like we marched in in a heavy Marxist-Leninist way and said "You're no good—out." It wasn't like that at all. We just made things more intense.

J.M.: They were running a finishing school,[2] as we got to call it, and they didn't dig our ideas about community control. We really wanted to work with the existing staff. We went there with an attitude of affiliating and not ripping anyone off or hurting anyone; and like Peter says, they just couldn't deal with it. The concept of a peer-group organization was just too heavy.

P.L.: Like for instance, we insisted right from the beginning that patients be allowed to attend all staff meetings, and that really freaked the staff.

STUDENT: How do you cope with the fact that it's a county hospital run by a board of directors? What happened with that?

---

[2] Now, some three-and-a-half years later, I'd call it "a finishing school for the powerless."—J.M.

D.G.: Well, having a really good boss has something to do with that. I mean the program chief is a very bright man, and he really wants to do something. He really wants to produce an atmosphere where people are going to get better. So he was willing to go along when we said we wanted patients to come to staff meetings; we don't believe in a system that doesn't include their participation. It's actually a very simple notion, but it's amazing just how the tone of things changes when it actually starts to happen. It doesn't matter how many come, or even if some days nobody comes—just plant the idea that one patient might walk in the door, and the whole way people conduct their business gets changed.

STUDENT: Do they come?

D.G.: Yes. By no means do all of them come, though I'd say around twenty percent show up at some of the staff meetings. But the idea is that you can't get away with all those mystifying trips. You can't say things like "this guy is a chronic undifferentiated schizophrenic."

STUDENT: I want to know how Danny got involved in this whole thing.

D.G.: I guess it started for me when I met Joy. I went to volunteer at the free clinic over a year ago and Joy interviewed me and decided that I was good enough to be her co-therapist. I had just returned from teaching at a very fancy women's school in the East . . . and I thought: "You've gone to school for fifteen years, and you've got a Ph.D. and you're O.K.," and here I was being interviewed by a high school dropout who decided that I was good enough to work with her. I dug Joy, I suppose more because of it than in spite of it. But I think I'd like to talk not only about how I got involved in the hospital thing, but also about how things like what we did can happen. And I'll call them principles of organizing, though they're hardly principles, just thoughts that might be helpful to other people.

To begin with, you have to have allies. So Peter told our affinity group, and we got together and rapped about such things. Joy and I resonated to what he was doing. So we would go out on weekends and do psychiatry with people on this understaffed ward. Why weekends? Weekends were a time when we had a friendly ally in charge. Well, he wasn't really an ally, but he was tolerant.

So another principle is: Have a tolerant or friendly psychiatrist in charge where you want to do your work. Also, on weekends, a lot of the heavy-number chiefs aren't there; so you'll have a lot more flexibility. If you wander around and open a locked door, no one's going to jump on top of you. Also, we were thought to be semi-experts. That is, we had long hair and stuff like that so we must know about drugs, right? And these people knew nothing about drugs. All they knew was that all these scared people were coming in and they didn't know how to relate to them.

So that's another principle: Demonstrate some expertise in a particular area so the various authorities will think they can somehow benefit from your presence. In our case, they looked on us not only as long-haired weirdo freaks but also as people who knew something that could benefit them. And when we went around opening locked doors and talking to people the staff didn't totally freak out. Another principle is: Let them think they are getting a good deal. In fact, they were. There were several of us coming out and working for nothing at that time, helping them perform a service that they were interested in having performed.

But things don't always happen miraculously. It didn't always run so smoothly. Sometimes we had hassles with nurses, we had hassles with the psychiatrist in charge of the ward, but we were polite and friendly. While we really didn't compromise our principles in any sense, or hesitate to do things that we thought were important, we *did* make a conscientious effort to learn people's names and say "hi" and be friendly, offer people a bite of our candy bar, hug each other in their presence. Just being warm, friendly people really did have an effect. As one might expect, some of the most oppressed people who worked on the ward responded to us most quickly. People like technicians, orderlies, aides didn't quite know what to make of us, but they kind of liked us; they were friendly toward us.

So one of the things that resulted was that we felt welcomed on that ward. We were adding to what existed. I'm not sure if that's completely honest. We would open locked wards. Now it turns out one of the reasons they always have locked wards is that all these places are always understaffed. They have all these loony crazy people wandering around causing trouble, singing songs and things of that sort . . . but if people whose job it is to keep order in all of that chaos see you as really trying to help them, they're a hell of a lot less offended by a fairly audacious act like opening a locked door. And if what you do doesn't work and you cop to it and take responsibility for it and say, "Gee, I guess it didn't work when we let Joe out and he ran away," or something like that, and you apologize and say, "I guess we'll have to work out a better system, but I really don't think social isolation is the proper way to treat this person's freak-out," then it becomes a common problem for everyone to solve, rather than a problem of simply establishing a smooth-running show on the ward. The transition from my volunteering on weekends to becoming a paid employee of the county was helped along immeasurably by the fact that they needed a psychologist. This is a touchy subject, and I wish I knew how to engineer such things because it's clear that unless you've discovered a new biological principle of how to live, you have to get paid for your services, and they tend to want to pay "professionals." We really do not have a properly organized principle of how to get hired at these institutions.

STUDENT: What other pressures, besides asking that patients be admitted to staff meetings, did you bring to bear on the people you were working with? What techniques did you use?

J.M.: Some of the most important work we did took place in community meetings . . . most hospitals' "community" meetings are phony, token events—pastimes—having little resemblance to political organizing, much less good psychiatry. Instead, they consist of a bunch of super-zombies (over-medicated and electroshocked patients) who have been herded into a circle where other less-than-super zombies (bored and depressed doctors) try to "analyze the group." The community meetings we insisted on having at Martinez were the exact opposite. While attendance was optional, patients wanted to go, they had real power and nobody was ever bored. In fact, community meetings were absolutely crucial to the life of the program. First, we would talk about *real* things, such as how to make the program work—meaning what to do so that people wouldn't need the program; we worked on getting people off medications, giving and getting strokes, getting meaningful work, setting up happy group living situations, dealing with oppressive hospital policies, and so on. Second, the meetings were divided into two categories, therapeutic and government. Third, *all* workers, not just the doctors, were encouraged to attend —they were needed. Fourth, while there were regularly scheduled meetings, one of each type per week, anyone could call additional meetings if needed. Fifth, staff did not always run meetings. Patients also took responsibility for facilitating.

In addition to community meetings, we instituted Contact raps, instead of the usual intake procedure. I never once wrote a word in anyone's chart. I refused. At every opportunity I criticized the charts and the garbage that was written in them. Sure enough, pretty soon patients were demanding to read their charts. I did a training group in radical psychiatry—at the request of eight of the patients—so patients could learn to lead groups.

D.G.: We pushed the idea of contracts pretty hard. You know: What do you want for yourself? What do you want from us? We would tell people that the oppression and screwed-upness in their lives led them to get into certain unhappy scenes, and that it wasn't our job to put them through a pretzel-making machine and send them back to the same shitwork that drove them crazy.

STUDENT: What kind of contracts did they make up?

J.M.: The same kind as Danny and I get in the group we do here in Berkeley. There's nothing magical about it. Contracts like "I want to get strokes"; "To move away from my parents"; "To stick up for myself"; "To get angry"; stuff like that. So, introducing contracts at the hospital was crucial, too. We introduced every principle and technique of radical psychiatry that we could; at first we used as little rhetoric as possible, except with a few people who could relate to it; and then eventually in big meetings, in the community meetings, other people began to pick up our language and, most important, the ideas behind it.

D.G.: Some of the most oppressed people in mental hospitals are not the patients, but the staff. For example, even nurses, who have some status—because they're not like techs or orderlies—stand up every time a doctor walks into the room. And the nurses frequently got pretty hostile when they saw us with our long hair and heard us talking about liberation. But lately we've been approached by the head of the psychiatric nursing staff to train all her people, herself included, to use radical psychiatry.

STUDENT: I have a friend who's a psychiatrist in a day treatment center in the city and he's definitely a prisoner. He's tried to do things and the reactions he gets are yes, yes, and then nothing gets done. It's driven him crazy—now *he* has to see a psychiatrist!

D.G.: You have to have allies or you will go crazy. That's what Contact is all about.

STUDENT: Well, how do you get the word to people about how to go about doing this in other hospitals? I mean, if other workers don't really know there's been a success, they just feel they're beating their heads against the wall. What can you do to get these other hospitals to get the same thing going somewhere else?

J.M.: Well, one thing we're doing is taping this class so I can do up an article for *The Radical Therapist*, which you could refer your friend to. Also, I think your friend might do well to get involved at the Radical Psychiatry Center here in Berkeley. . . .

P.L.: If you're in a situation like that, like the one your friend's in, you've got to get out—which is what I would have done, except that I found Joy and Danny. And I guess the three of us were like a critical mass, because when we started there were only two other people on the whole staff. Anyone who came in after that, after we started working there, found we were more fun to relate to and had this new idea they were open to, and it got bigger and bigger until the other two left. With a critical mass of people saying, "It's O.K., it's O.K. to make changes," everything goes fine. If you really get into permission with one another, it's very powerful. . . .

J.M.: Yes, we used permission techniques and the concept of permission. We told people they had options. We showed people alternatives. But I think it's important to add here that when leaders go around telling people it's O.K. to change, they must also guarantee protection. I mean that whether you're "doing a therapy group" or organizing a community, it's part of your responsibility to stay with and support the people you've succeeded in turning on, until they become self-supporting. Otherwise, the whole thing becomes a cruel joke. Psychiatric interns and residents do this to ward patients all the time: they come in—lone saviors—try new innovations, offer hope, then duck out when they've "done their time."

When people get to a point in their lives where they've decided to change their death scripts to life scripts, life often gets plenty scary. It's at that point that protection—the reassurance that everything's going to be O.K.—is crucial. That reassurance can be transmitted directly and verbally. It is also communicated, often quite dramatically, by example. Though certainly there were times when Danny, Peter, and I were down, or anxious—getting impatient with waiting for the changes we wanted in the program—we never had any doubt that what we were demanding was right on.

We were always confident that the values we struggled to give expression to—self-determination, community control, loving human relationships—were values that we have a right to pursue because we are human beings. That was also a kind of protection. We had each other for protection—at the hospital and in our affinity group in Berkeley—and so we were able to show others what we meant when we opposed the idea of individualistic solutions like long-term one-to-one therapy or one-to-one political manipulation, and when we talked about Contact and the protection that comes from working with peers in a group.

I can't stress enough that any attempt to organize, or even just to raise consciousness a bit, without the guaranteed protection of allies, is doomed to fail. Lenny Bruce, one of the greatest artists and political commentators of our time, tried to do it alone. He had no protection. Lenny Bruce was suicided by society.

SUMMARY (by Joy Marcus)

*Radical psychiatry and community organizing are interchangeable in their practice.

*The basic theories and techniques of radical psychiatry can be transferred to broader political arenas than therapy groups.

* Just as in effective psychiatry, effective political action requires that people feel permission to: 1) define problems—see, think, feel; 2) be angry; 3) fight back; 4) have vision, use imagination, have fun; 5) work cooperatively; 6) organize; and 7) follow-through.

*Being engaged in a community organizing process is therapeutic for people; in order to take political power we need to rid ourselves of internalized oppression; while being engaged in the process of taking power, we feel more alive and are able to experience ourselves as intelligent and powerful, thus ridding ourselves of old "tapes" about being "crazy," "stupid," "worthless," "weak," "incompetent."

*Effective political action is a good indicator of psychiatric success.

*The most pleasurable kind of organizing occurs when people act in behalf of their own liberation, rather than entering a situation from a markedly one-up (and guilty) position to "Rescue" an oppressed class.

10. RADICAL PSYCHIATRY HISTORY
by Claude Steiner

THE THEORY

The theory of Radical Psychiatry was conceived early in 1969 when I began teaching a course by that name at the Free University in Berkeley. At that time it consisted simply of a series of complaints against establishment psychiatry which had been written into a Manifesto on the occasion of the 1969 annual convention of the American Psychiatric Association in San Francisco, and offered few theoretical or practical alternatives to the oppressive conditions of establishment psychiatry of the times. In the summer of 1969 on the heels of the People's Park uprising in Berkeley, a Free Clinic was established by the medics who had assisted the injured and wounded in the Berkeley streets. Part of the Free Clinic's plan was to include psychological counseling; and a few months after the Free Clinic opened its doors a Rap ("Radical Approach to Psychiatry") Center was started, with welfare and draft interviews, contact rap, street rap, problem solving groups, and a training program.

In the context of the Rap Center's activities, the theory began to develop. I contributed my understanding of group psychotherapy, transactional analysis, and psychiatry in general. Hogie Wyckoff brought with her feminism, radical politics, and Marxist theory. Joy Marcus, also a radical feminist, contributed community organizing theory and skills and poetry. Many others contributed with their criticisms, their struggles, and further theory. Ronald Laing's, Herbert Marcuse's, and Wilhelm Reich's thought became clearly relevant and were adapted into the theory. The theory became a blend of political and psychiatric thought which became applicable to the everyday problems in people's lives. As more people joined the radical psychiatry movement, the theory was applied not only in problem-solving groups but also in their daily lives. Over the next four years sexism, the oppressiveness of monogamy, hetero-sexual and family structures, competition, the uses and abuses of power, affinity and enmity became the focus of the theory resulting in further theory about relation-ships, cooperation, and power.

At approximately the time when we started working at the Rap Center (spring, 1970), Michael Glenn, a psychiatrist in the Air Force stationed in Minot, North Dakota, and a small group of people started the quarterly journal, *The Radical Therapist,* which from its second issue included writings from the radical psychia-trists in Berkeley. Eventually, one whole issue of *The Radical Therapist* (November, 1971) was devoted to the writing from radical psychiatry. This book is a selec-tion of articles from that issue. At the same time, Michael Glenn and the other members of the R.T. Collective moved to Cambridge, Massachusetts and in April, 1972 *The Radical Therapist* changed its name to *Rough Times.*

The change of name was the outcome of a struggle within the R.T. Collective between therapists and radi-cal theoreticians who opined that doing therapy and teaching therapy skills are activities which ultimately oppress people. The new name, *Rough Times,* announced their intentions to concentrate on documenting and attacking the oppressive activities of psychiatrists and allied oppressive institutions.

In January, 1973, a group of radical psychiatrists in Berkeley, including Hogie Wyckoff, Joy Marcus, and myself, started a new journal named *Issues in Radical Therapy* which pursued the editorial goals of the original *Radical Therapist*. This journal (Box 23544, Oakland, California 94623) continues to publish theoretical and practical articles about therapy and radical psychiatry and is now in its second year of publication.

THE BERKELEY RADICAL PSYCHIATRY CENTER (BRPC)

The BRPC had its beginning with a small core of people at the Free Clinic's Rap Center who considered themselves radical psychiatrists. Radical psychiatrists were in the minority at the Rap Center and over a period of time eventually ran into difficulties with the rest of the workers.

On the one hand, the "professionals" became alarmed at the radical anti-establishment psychiatric notions of radical psychiatrists and the increasing trend toward linking psychology and politics and toward revolutionary involvement by radical psychiatrists.

On the other hand, a leveling trend was introduced by counter-culture persons who felt that all hierarchies in an organization should be abolished and who felt that no one was especially knowledgeable or capable in the field of psychiatry, so that no approaches were correct but rather everyone should "do their thing" according to their interests and inclinations. This group reacted against radical psychiatrists, accusing them of being authoritarian and elitist.

A third area from which radical psychiatry was attacked was by persons in movement politics who found fault with radical psychiatrists' points of view on the basis of the intolerant "Lefter Than Thou" criticism (see Chapter 15). This criticism, largely theoretical, discounted the work of radical psychiatrists on the basis of not being sufficiently revolutionary or radical. The Rap Center's business meetings, which were operated by the consensus of anyone who attended, became more and more polemical, less and less effective, and eventually so extraordinarily frustrating that almost no decisions of any significance could be made and only the most banal matters could be discussed and acted upon.

Because of this, the radical psychiatry group had asked to become a separate part of the Berkeley Community Health Project, on equal status with the Rap Center and the Free Clinic. This status was temporarily given; and as radical psychiatry developed further, free now of the different lines of attack upon it, the conflict over its principles and practice grew, and eventually in late 1970 the radical psychiatry group was asked to leave the Berkeley Community Health Project. A few months later the group found a house at 2333 Webster, and with its own space and headquarters began to work hard at its tasks. In a year's time, the Radical Psychiatry Center had grown by leaps and bounds, daily contact raps were held which were heavily attended, a large waiting list for people who wanted to join problem-solving groups developed, about fifty people received training and eventually joined the center as facilitators, and a very well-attended Radical Psychiatry Conference was held in the summer of 1971. (See Chapter 11 for a description of the Center's operation at that time.)

The summer of 1971 was the high point of spirit and enthusiasm at the Radical Psychiatry Center. Everything seemed positive and constructive; it appeared as if the radical psychiatry movement was headed for continuing expansion and growth. Three communal houses had been established in which radical psychiatrists attempted to live by radical psychiatry principles; training programs in Los Angeles, San Francisco, and Sacramento were being held; it appeared that other Radical Psychiatry Centers would be started; and, judging by the positive reception of people plus the great enthusiasm of the workers, it seemed that the radical psychiatry movement would continue to flourish.

However, a split developed within the radical psychiatry community at this point. A group of facilitators who were unhappy about the conditions at the Center held a series of secret meetings in which they discussed important and often valid criticisms of the radical psychiatry community. The secret nature of these meetings was an unexpected violation of the assumptions of cooperation and honesty which were assumed to govern behavior within the community. Until this secret surfaced, unresolved bad feelings and paranoias ran rampant and work in action rap and collective suffered. The new radical psychiatry group was composed of people who felt oppressed within the community. An open meeting was held in which the new group criticized the workings of the Radical Psychiatry Center (see Appendix at the end of the book); following this, the community split into two camps: the New Radical Psychiatry group (comprising about twenty group leaders, most of whom had recently joined the Center); and about thirty others (among them Joy Marcus, Hogie Wyckoff, and myself) who refused to continue to work with the members of the New Radical Psychiatry group.

The split was complete by the fall of 1972, and a struggle ensued over the rights that the two groups had over the house on Webster Street in which the Radical Psychiatry Center operated. The new group wanted to use the house on certain days; the old group did not want to share the house with them. In the end, the house, owned by me, was locked up by us, and both groups had to find other quarters to pursue their activities. In time, the old Radical Psychiatry Center group returned to the house.

The split in radical psychiatry badly weakened what had appeared to be a strong, positive movement. Within the next year, the three original members of the Radical Psychiatry Center—again Joy Marcus, Hogie Wyckoff, and myself—left the Center one after the other, at different times and for different reasons. At the present time, the future of the group is uncertain as to its political and psychiatric directions. Only time can tell what their impact in the radical psychiatry and radical therapy movements will be.

11. AN ANALYSIS OF THE STRUCTURE OF THE BERKELEY RADICAL PSYCHIATRY CENTER (FALL, 1972)

by Members of the Radical Psychiatry Center[1]

The Berkeley Radical Psychiatry Center (BRPC) is a community psychiatry organization with headquarters at 2333 Webster, Berkeley, California 14705. We serve people living in Berkeley and North Oakland.

INTRODUCTION

The BRPC is presently made up of five training collectives, the group members' organization, the Rap press work collective, IRT, a political study group, and problem-solving groups for leaders.

ACTION RAP

The BRPC is open to the public Monday through Friday from 5:30 to 7:30 for Action Rap which is a

---

[1] The principal authors of this chapter (as well as Chapters 12 and 13) are Anita Friedman, Claude Steiner, and Hogie Wyckoff.

drop-in group facilitated by members of each day's training collective.

The Action Rap (formerly called Contact Rap) is overseen by the Head, who is a member of that day's training collective. The Head is responsible for it that day, and is expected to be available to make on-the-spot decisions in extreme situations such as suicide risk, violent behavior, drug overdoses, or any acute psychiatric emergency that may occur. The Head makes certain that Action Rap is a protected situation and that there is a facilitator in each room.

Various things that can happen at Action Rap are: a) people can get information about radical psychiatry; b) people in need of help can sign up for groups and work in Action Rap while on the waiting list; c) people in crisis can get emergency help; and d) people can get strokes. By strokes we mean positive human recognition and contact. People can work in the social context of Action Rap to break down the artificial constraints on people's freedom to love each other (stroke economy) by giving strokes, asking for strokes, accepting strokes that they want, rejecting strokes that they don't want, and by stroking themselves.

We ask people not to come more than twice a week. (We specified this limit because we were overcrowded and weren't able to take care of everyone.) We ask people for contributions to support the BRPC.

The Action Rap usually adheres to the following format:

It starts with an introductory explanation in one central room. The group then divides into different rooms. The general contract is to learn how to overcome our own and each others' mystified oppression. Hopefully, there are not more than fifteen people in each room, preferably ten. We sometimes make contracts, which are work agreements, to do problem-solving in specific areas. In each room at least one group leader

149]]]

acts as a facilitator and gives political and problem-solving information. The facilitator helps people meet each other and creates safety by not letting people verbally or physically attack each other and helps people ask for and get what they want. It is not the facilitator's responsibility to Rescue people in this situation. By Rescue we mean assuming more than half the responsibility for people getting what they want. The general working agreement in radical psychiatry is that we offer options and help people get in touch with what they want so that they can work to get it. It is important to remember that people who are in a psychiatric crisis always take priority, and facilitators should call on the Head in any emergency situation.

The Action Rap is the hub of the BRPC's activities. It takes the place of the intake or screening interview of most psychiatric facilities and gives the newcomer an opportunity to evaluate the BRPC before making any commitment. From Action Rap a person may sign up for and proceed to a problem-solving group or, when necessary, to a one-to-one crisis intervention session.

PROBLEM-SOLVING GROUPS

A major psychiatric activity of the BRPC is problem-solving groups. We solve problems in groups instead of in individual therapy because we feel that teaching people to act collectively is a vital part of our work as community organizers. Problem-solving groups are co-led by two trained radical psychiatrists. The group is made up of eight people who are seeking help. Two observers from training collectives may also be present to learn how a problem-solving group functions and to exchange feedback with the leaders. Their relationship with the group members parallels that of the group leaders in that they do not play with group members while observing/leading the group.

The group work is based on the Principles, Manifesto, and Working Contract of the BRPC. The following are specifics of how we work:

All group members make a contract with the leaders and the group as to what they want to accomplish. The contract should be a simple positive statement that could be easily understood by an eight-year-old.

It is expected that people attend regularly. The group starts and ends on time. People are expected to call ahead if they can't attend. If a person doesn't contact the group for two weeks in a row she or he is no longer considered a member of the group. People are expected to come to group drug-free. This includes psychotropic drugs such as Librium, Elavil, Thorazine, heroin, alcohol, marijuana, etc. However, a reasonable and safe time will be allowed for withdrawal when needed, usually a maximum of a month. If at the time of the meeting a group member is under the influence of a drug, she or he is still expected to attend; however, under these circumstances she or he may be asked not to take up time with ineffectual attempts at work.

People usually sign up to work when they come into group and circle their name if they are in special need. It is the group's responsibility to keep track of time and be sure that everyone gets what they want. If, during the week, people are in trouble they can call other group members or the group leaders for support or information. Through our experience we have found that it interferes with problem-solving when group leaders have sexual or intense social contact with group members. We prefer that members of the same problem-solving group don't have sexual contact because it may make it impossible for them to work in the same group together.

People who join a radical psychiatry problem-solving group while in therapy elsewhere are given one month to choose one or the other. We are unwilling to work with people using other psychiatric services with the exception of body therapies because: a) it is often a contradiction in terms of approach to problems; b) it is a duplication of service in a situation where there exists a scarcity; and c) our experience shows us that it is a difficult working situation.

It is the responsibility of group members to support the center financially but how they do it is up to them.

TRAINING COLLECTIVES

There are five training collectives in radical psychiatry. Each is made up of a maximum of eight radical psychiatrists. Initially, the training collective is led by a radical psychiatrist capable of training others, the goal being for everyone to eventually have equal information, responsibility, and power.

When a training collective achieves information and skills in how to lead problem-solving groups, the leader begins to bring problems from her problem-solving group to the collective to facilitate the process of becoming an equal member. Thus, everyone takes equal responsibility for leadership; and the training group becomes a collective without a designated leader.

The responsibilities of a training collective are: a) supervision and work at the Action Rap of the day; b) training group leaders by the exchange of information, observing each others' groups, self-evaluation, asking for and giving honest feedback and supporting each other; c) actively taking responsibility for all the groups coming out of that collective; and d) participation in and responsiveness to the planning group, and other

BRPC community activities such as Sunday Seminar and Phase II.

People interested in training are advised to go to the different Action Raps to meet the members of the various collectives. New trainees are admitted to preliminary training based on consensus of the training collective. New people in training and radical psychiatrists from the collective work together for at least four weeks in Action Rap. Every session is followed by an exchange of information and feedback. Then people in preliminary training work in the training collective for another four weeks, after which time everyone decides if they feel good about continuing to work together.

TEACHERS' COLLECTIVE

The teachers' collective is made up of the leaders of each training collective and others involved in teaching radical psychiatry. The contract is to learn to teach radical psychiatry and to ask for and give honest feedback about each others' work. Leaders bring problems and information about their collectives to it. When there is no longer a need for a leader in a training collective, its members will send a chosen representative to the teacher's collective.

This is how a training collective looks in action:

One person volunteers to facilitate that meeting. He writes the agenda on a blackboard so everyone can see what needs to be covered. This facilitator then helps the group keep track of the time and works to help the meeting run smoothly.

Based on our experience, we have found that groups work best if people unload held resentments and paranoid fantasies at the beginning of the meeting. After the work of the meeting is completed it is important to leave time for a self-conscious discussion of how people worked together as a group and to exchange feedback and strokes that have not yet been given.

PLANNING GROUP[2]

The planning group is the final decision and policy making body of the radical psychiatry community. It serves to get community-wide consensus on proposals generated in the various collectives. The Center's activities are planned at the bi-weekly meeting. The planning group is composed of two representatives from each work collective and two representatives from the group members' organization. Anyone in a radical psychiatry group or in radical psychiatry training may attend planning group meetings. However, only representatives will have a voice at these meetings. The agenda and minutes of the planning group will be available to anyone who wishes to read them, and representatives of the different groups are expected to post agenda items ahead of the meeting so that those attending will be prepared to deal with them. Decisions of the planning group are hopefully reached by consensus; but in the case of an item that is hotly disputed, the majority vote will carry. Majority and minority opinions will be duly recorded in the minutes. Planning group decisions are taken back to the different groups represented, and the vote of the representatives will be ratified by the whole group. If dissatisfaction with either the vote of the group representative or the total vote is encountered, the matter will be re-opened upon request.

THE SUNDAY NIGHT SEMINAR is a forum for political

---

[2] Planning Group was later replaced by a General Community Meeting held every other Sunday. Proposals were passed by consensus vote, with three "nays" constituting veto power.

and theoretical discussion. It is open only to people in training and their invited guests. This is a good place for people from different collectives to meet each other and exchange information. This forum is open to any interested individual or group. The seminar is led by a facilitator and decisions about scheduling future presentations and discussions are made there. Group members who are invited are asked to consult with their leaders and observers.

PHASE II is a collective of group leaders which concerns itself with the relationships of the BRPC to geographical areas other than our community. It meets weekly and takes its proposals to the planning group.

The group members' organization meets periodically and brings its proposals to the planning group.

ACCESS TO MEETINGS

Action Rap is open to all. Problem-solving groups are closed. Phase II, training collectives, and teacher's collective are open to all persons in training by arrangement.

Planning group is open to group members and leaders in training; anyone else interested may ask to attend. Sunday seminars are open to persons in training and their invited guests. All other community meetings are open to group members unless specified.

12. A WORKING CONTRACT FOR GROUP LEADERS AT THE BERKELEY RADICAL PSYCHIATRY CENTER

1. We believe that in order for Radical Psychiatry to remain relevant and viable it must be open to new ideas and change. All values, theory, and practice, including this contract, are subject to a dialectical process of change based on an ongoing and cooperative dialogue.

2. We are a center serving the psychiatric needs of the Berkeley community in which we live (i.e., people within Berkeley and North Oakland). Our primary interest is in organizing our community, and we consider its needs our first priority. We see ourselves as a "community" center, where we provide for one of our own basic needs.

3. We act as community organizers; that is, we teach problem-solving skills and support people to collectively reclaim political power. We see political power as power to control our own lives and environment.

4. We believe that all our actions are political and that it is not possible to separate our "personal" from our "political" lives. We believe that people have the right to direct their own lives; to assert this right is to use political power. We believe that isolated individuals cannot successfully eliminate their oppression and that there

are no personal solutions possible to political oppression.

5. We are committed to struggle against all unequal and oppressive power relationships. We see ourselves as a part of a larger revolutionary struggle for human liberation.

6. We succeed through collectivity and affinity. We believe that cooperation is essential to our collective strength; we work with people with whom we feel safety and affinity.

7. We communicate radical political values. We believe that in this society people are oppressed. When internalized, this oppression becomes "mental illness." Radical psychiatry makes clear the connection between external oppression and psychiatric disturbance.

8. Throughout our training we take an active part in shaping all our information and skills with each other. We work with a co-leader, take observers into our training collectives and problem-solving groups, and we train others in radical psychiatry.

9. We fulfill the minimum time commitment to radical psychiatry by working in Action Rap at least once a week, by working in a training collective, and by leading groups for at least one year.

10. We acknowledge that there are standards of what is good radical psychiatry. These standards are determined by training collectives. We value problem-solving skills. We achieve these skills by working cooperatively and by committing ourselves to ask for and give honest criticism, feedback, and support from each other and group members.

11. In our work we use contracts which are cooperative work agreements, so that people ask for what they want and work to get it.

12. We work to eliminate power imbalances and equalize power among all people in the radical psychiatry community.

13. Our reward in doing and training others to do problem-solving groups is to see people reclaim their political power and to become active with us in creating social changes. We don't do radical psychiatry for strokes or money from group members.

We don't do problem-solving with people who are in other types of therapy (with the exception of some types of body work), because of scarcity of services and contradictions in theory and practice.

Our experience has taught us that sexual or intense social contact with group members impairs the work of problem-solving groups. We also avoid sexual contact with co-leaders, with the exception of already established relationships.

14. We affirm the Principles and Manifesto of Radical Psychiatry and this Contract in our work. We endeavor to remove the contradictions between radical psychiatry theory and our lives. We actively support the existence of the Berkeley Radical Psychiatry Center.

13. AN ANALYSIS OF THE POLITICAL VALUES OF THE BERKELEY RADICAL PSYCHIATRY CENTER

1. Liberation within an oppressive society is not possible. It is a mystification. People cannot be truly free if this society is not free because social oppression will necessarily impinge on their freedom.

2. We believe that people are by nature unwilling to oppress or be oppressed. The desire for liberation and the energy for the attainment of liberation comes from people's basic nature.

3. We believe that people's problems are political problems. Therefore, we teach radical political values as an integral part of problem-solving. However, we don't encourage people to do things they don't want to do. We use contracts so that they can freely define and ask for the help they want.

4. We don't rescue people. The way out of oppression is to decide to do something about it and act on that decision. Action means work, not the passive consumption of a radical psychiatrist's efforts and skills. The necessity for action is an integral part of radical psychiatry awareness.

5. We support people to take back their power as autonomous human beings. Our goal is to empower people

and to de-empower leadership. We teach people problem-solving skills so that they can learn how to bring about revolutionary change through action. We don't promote pacification and adjustment to the status quo by merely providing people with short-term comfort and good feelings.

6. Alienation = Oppression + Mystification. People are alienated because power over their own lives has been taken away from them in the service of oppression. People internalize oppression by believing that the problem is within them rather than in an exploitative, elitist, and capitalist society, whose interest is in maintaining an alienated and docile population.

7. Oppression + Awareness = Anger. We demystify oppression and give people permission and support to use their emerging anger constructively to fight it—not just oppression which has been internalized but also oppression from the external world.

8. Contact + Awareness = Action → Liberation. Awareness here means radical awareness of political problems. Techniques such as gestalt therapy, transactional analysis, psychodrama, or role-playing do not directly demystify how people are oppressed. These techniques alone can in fact co-opt people's anger and be used in liberal pacification programs by providing contact without awareness or action. Our actions are designed to create stresses within the Psychiatric Establishment, not to relieve it by peaceful coexistence.

9. Unequal distribution of power, wherever found, is a source of oppression. We support those who are in a position of lesser power to become strong.

10. Sex roles oppress all people, especially women. In our society the nuclear family is used as a means of instilling oppressive values. In it children are mystified

and programmed to accept oppression, women are an unpaid labor force at home serving men who serve, in turn, as a production force for the profit of others. Monogamy promotes scarcity of strokes, which perpetuates isolation and alienation and encourages the consumption of "goods."

11. A radical psychiatrist is not merely a counter-culture shrink. We are community organizers. We teach people problem-solving and the value of working together to reclaim their power.

12. Radical psychiatry is free. It is not a product for people to buy because we feel it is wrong to sell people back their humanness. We want to avoid being co-opted and corrupted as a commodity. We wish to provide radical psychiatrists with the means for support from sources other than fees for service from group members.

14. RADICAL PSYCHIATRY AND THE VIETNAM VETERAN by Robert Schwebel

Leading a radical psychiatry group of hospitalized veterans of the Vietnam War helped me understand the devastating effects of imperialist wars on the troops of the aggressors. It also helped me understand more about the nature of psychiatric problems and their remedies.

PSYCHIATRIC DISTRESS FITS THE SITUATION

The psychiatric distress of veterans of the United States military in Vietnam follows plainly and obviously from the experiences of those men. Large numbers of American soldiers were drafted, often against their will. Others, not given the facts, were convinced that they would be fighting for freedom and their brothers and sisters, so they enlisted. Once inducted, soldiers are given the basic messages: "Kill or get killed" and "Don't think and don't feel." American soldiers are taught to risk their lives and ordered to commit crimes against the Vietnamese people. At the gut level, many of these soldiers know there is something wrong with what has happened to them and with what they are doing. Of those that have this intuition or understanding, many become "mentally ill." It is not surprising that because they are either tricked or forced to get into the military, because they are ordered into dangerous situations, and because they are being shot at, many Vietnam veterans arrive in mental hospitals feeling "paranoid"—as if everyone is after them. It is also not surprising that because they have been involved in criminal and dehumanizing activities other Vietnam veterans arrive in hospitals feeling depressed, considering themselves worthless people not entitled to any human emotions and pleasures. It's a vicious circle: people who fear they are no good fear that other people are "out to get them"; and people who fear that other people are "out to get them" fear that they are no good. In all cases, the veterans end up feeling alienated from life and lonely and uneasy. "Mental patients" returning from the war in Vietnam end up hating themselves and hating other people. Just as by understanding their experiences their problems can be understood, so it is that by knowing their problems that their experiences can be understood. One veteran said, "I can't look anyone in the face anymore. I'd rather have come home in a box." Another veteran felt that he had become so ugly in Vietnam that he couldn't bear looking at himself in the mirror anymore.

All paranoia has a basis in reality. Sometimes it is easy to find the basis. For example, there was a twenty-two-year-old soldier who was tripping on acid with four "buddies." Two of them turned out to be police, and they handed him over to the authorities. Instead of arresting him, the authorities demanded that he inform on his friends. When he refused to do this, they made it look like he was informing anyway by having him report to them on a weekly basis so that everyone would notice. Soon his friends thought he was an informer. He became paranoid.

Another veteran became paranoid when he bought a

houseful of furniture on credit from a slick salesman who tricked him. As the terms of the contract unfolded he found himself spiraling into debt. He fell behind on many payments. Soon his phone service was about to be shut off, his car was repossessed, his rent was overdue, threatening lawyers were calling almost daily, and his furniture was about to be taken back.

The person who feels that he doesn't deserve to feel human emotions and pleasures knows that he has been involved in dehumanizing activities. People know when they are doing really bad things. A U.S. soldier was sitting alone in the jungle when he heard a noise in a tree. He turned around and shot into the tree as he had been trained to do, and an eight-year-old child fell down, dead. The young soldier stopped feeling emotions after that.

THE VIETNAM VETERAN AND RADICAL PSYCHIATRY

The military says, "Don't think and don't feel." Without exception, Vietnam veterans have good reason to think and feel that people have been after them and that they have been doing criminal and dehumanizing things. However, most G.I.'s return to civilian life ignoring what they have done and fitting in well in this society. Their ability to love and think is probably severely impaired as a result of their experiences which they must block out. The others—the ones who are overtly bleeding emotionally—are on to something. The Vietnam veteran who is paranoid knows that everyone is after him. The Vietnam veteran who does not have any emotions knows he has done wrong. In most hospital situations there is an attempt made to make people emotionally and intellectually discount their experiences or accept them uncritically. Quite possibly this is why distressed hospital patients often return to hospitals after an apparent recovery. Humans who know something about themselves are reluctant to give up this knowledge. In radical psychiatry groups we do not try to make veterans (or any group members) ignore or forget their experiences. We also don't try to "pig" (put down or attack) people and make them feel guilty. Rather, in a radical psychiatry group we build from an individual's knowledge and feelings and give them a chance to think and love more than they have been doing.

The basic principle of radical psychiatry is that all problems of a psychiatric nature are caused by mystified oppression. Mystified oppression makes people feel alienated. To combat alienation radical psychiatry gets people in contact with one another. To combat mystification radical psychiatry gets people aware of their oppression. And, to combat oppression, radical psychiatry gets aware people together.

AWARENESS AND THE VIETNAM VETERAN

It is very clear that Vietnam veterans have injunctions against thinking, especially about the ways in which they have been oppressed. In order for people to think and talk about things, a safe atmosphere had to be established. The stroke economy was loosened up by doing permission exercises which brought about stroking (giving human recognition and warmth, as defined by Eric Berne). Protection was provided by not permitting "pigging" and "trashing" (group pigging), so that people felt like they could say what they wanted to without fearing attack. Then, certain clear statements were made to the group: "It is O.K. to talk honestly about your own actual experiences," "It is O.K. to talk about how you feel," "It is O.K. to consciously choose your values," "It is O.K. to be scared," "Your gut feelings count," "Your gut intuitions count."

It is amazing how blind people are to really seeing the forces that oppress them. It is exciting to see how quickly, given a chance, they tune in to them. Aside from the individual and unique experiences of the veterans (which we dealt with in group), a common basis for paranoia was found throughout the group. First the draft (not to mention parents and school) and then their commanding officers ruled over the veterans by force. People whom they had trusted turned out to be against them: recruiters with great promises, teachers who told them it would be for freedom, officers who said it would be for their country, parents who said be brave for us, and friends who let them go. And—although they were not oppressed by the Viet Cong—those bullets that flew overhead were real. The oppression that got them into the service and the combat fears of everyday life in the war are what got these men doing the awful things they did. While they had some realization of what they did, they had little or no understanding of how they arrived at doing it.

Leading a group of Vietnam veterans shows the strong injunctions people have against really seeing the ways in which they are oppressed. People with no human pleasures or feelings stay that way because they don't believe they deserve any "goodies." They are aware of what they have done, but not of the ways in which they have been oppressed into doing these things. "Paranoid" people think everyone is after them; and, ironically, this prevents them from clearly figuring out who is oppressing them and zeroing in on that person. However, given an opportunity, people can come to understand the oppressive forces that shape their lives.

The blindness to oppression of the Vietnam veteran has a long history of development. Often, parents teach it to their children. Here are a few examples of how it works:

Two parents have just explained to their kid that she must do all the chores they assign. They have made it clear that she is to be "on duty" continually and subject to the whims, schedule, and needs of her parents regardless of her own needs, etc. The conversation continues:

PARENTS: Be good, my little girl, and do what I tell you. (Don't think about it. Good girls don't think.)

KID: I won't do it. (I know oppression when I see it.)

PARENTS: But what I say is in your best interest. You must listen to your parents (i.e., you don't *know*, I do).

KID: I will choose myself.

PARENTS: We love children who do as they are told. (I'll withdraw my love if you are not dependent on me and don't follow my rules. If you think for yourself, you lose my love.)

KID: I'll make up my own mind.

PARENTS: We are doing our best to be good parents. You should love your parents. (Here is something to fog up your mind. "Loving your parents" means doing exactly as they say. Love is obedience.)

Another example occurs when a young child sends out her radar, and observes oppressive behavior. For example, one parent puts down the other parent. The child protests, and the parents respond like this: "You're not being paid to think around here. This is not the concern of young children." (In other words, "Dummy up!") School is yet another institution that teaches blindness to oppression. At the same time as kids are oppressed in the classroom, they are taught about a world which exists without oppression.

CONTACT AND THE VIETNAM VETERAN

Along with increased awareness, the group provides an opportunity for emotional contact. In the group, people get together and stop hating themselves and hating other people.

Probably the most remarkable thing about the group making contact was the utter state of stroke starvation that the men suffered from. They gave and received few strokes. Yet, they easily learned to do stroke/permission exercises and benefited greatly from them. In one exercise developed by Claude Steiner a free stroke economy is proclaimed. Everyone is free to ask for, accept, offer, reject, or decline to give strokes. In a related exercise, called "Trash the Stroke Economy," developed by a training group collective in radical psychiatry, a circle is formed and one person at a time goes into the center. That person is free to ask for or offer to give strokes to anyone. People on the outside are free to reject or accept strokes and give or decline to give strokes when asked. The stroke starvation was so severe among the veterans that we often started meetings by doing back rubs for one another. When one new group member heard about the back rubs he said, "I don't want people walking all over me and pounding on me." However, this typically hard veneer was covering a very needy person who soon readily accepted strokes. This is often the case with Vietnam veterans.

168]]]

TRASH AUTHORITY: AN EXERCISE

Most veterans suffered from the authoritarian control they lived under in the military. A fear of authority and an accompanying rigidity was not uncommon. Because they often had not had an opportunity to be on their own, many veterans still relied on their families. Few of the veterans had had an opportunity to choose their own values.

I developed an exercise to meet this problem: People in the group make up unreasonable rules. Then, other members of the group break various rules. The person who made up each rule tells the others to stop breaking her or his rule and why. The group flatly refuses to stop what they are doing and then explains why also. (This exercise is good for anyone who went to school in this country.)

A: No touching.

(People in the group start touching each other.)

A: People will think you are gay.

GROUP: Touching doesn't necessarily mean that I'm gay; and, anyhow, people can be gay if they want to be.

A: Keep your distance.

GROUP: I would rather be close.

A: People will think you are weak.

GROUP: They're wrong.

A: Keep to yourself.

GROUP: No, I don't want to do it alone. I *want* to be close.

A: It doesn't look good to me.

GROUP: That's *your* problem!

B: New rule: address everyone as sir or madam.

(Everyone in group starts calling each other by first names.)

B: Respect status. Respect authority.

GROUP: I reserve my respect for things I think are worthwhile.

B: Don't assume familiarity.

GROUP: I want to be close and have human relationships.

B: I'm running the show.

GROUP: I'm not one-down to you.

B: People should keep their distance.

GROUP: I will choose my closeness.

B: That's the way it is around here.

GROUP: Then it's time for a change.

C: A new rule: both feet must be kept on the floor.

GROUP: Breaks rule, etc.

D: A new rule: keep quiet!

GROUP: Breaks rule, etc.

STRUGGLE

In radical psychiatry it is felt that people should not "pig" themselves, and that guilt does not benefit anybody. This is not to say that bad experiences should be ignored or discounted. There are many things that Vietnam veterans may have done in their war experiences about which they will *never* feel good, even after they stop "pigging" themselves about them. Often they have done irreversible damage as part of the United States military. However, veterans can learn from their experiences and put their knowledge to use. They can talk about what they have been doing and become part of a movement which helps make it so that no other people will be cast into the roles they were in and forced to do the things they have done. They can feel better as part of a force which aims at preventing invasions like the one of Vietnam. Permission to be involved in a social struggle can be important in helping a veteran to feel like he is recovering some of his humanity which was ripped off in Vietnam.

Much of the potency developed by group members in radical psychiatry is directed against the oppression which immediately threatens a person. People leave groups feeling capable of handling most problems. In contrast with this defensive potency, social involvement is a chance to take the offensive and strike out against oppression. It serves the function of helping people feel better about bad things they have done by trying to end the roles which oppressed them. Involvement in a social struggle is a good way to feel a part of the human race. Alienation from the human race is not uncommon, especially among Vietnam veterans. To rejoin the human race is to work with other people for a world which is better for everyone, where people can think and love to their full potential.

15. RADICAL PSYCHIATRY AND MOVEMENT GROUPS PLUS A POSTSCRIPT by Claude Steiner

Radical psychiatry's main goal is to help human beings overcome alienation. Because alienation requires contact with other human beings in groups, it is important that radical psychiatry provide guidelines for the healthy functioning and survival of groups. When people who are interested in radical changes organize groups, they quite naturally wish to organize them along lines which differ from the authoritarian and alienating basis on which oppressive, establishment groups are usually organized. As a consequence, the structure of such groups is usually uncertain and indeterminate, and the cohesiveness of such groups against external attack is weak. There are two types of attacks upon movement groups which have become classic examples: one of them is the leveling of hierarchies; the other is the game "Lefter Than Thou."

LEFTER THAN THOU[1]

It is a phenomenon completely familiar to everyone who has worked in a radical organization that in the

---

[1] This game was first detected by Hogie Wyckoff, who also provided its name.

course of events it often happens that one or more people will attack the leadership by professing to be more revolutionary or more radical than that leadership. Since it is always possible that this is the actual state of affairs—namely, that the leadership of the group has become counter-revolutionary—many an organization has been totally torn apart by this kind of argument; in many cases, organizations that were doing true and valuable revolutionary work.

How is one to distinguish between a situation in which a splinter group is for some reason or another attacking the leadership illegitimately, and one where such a group is, in fact, justified in its attacks?

I would like to cast the illegitimate attack of the leadership of a group by a splinter group in the mold of a Bernian game. The game is called "Lefter Than Thou." The thesis of the game is that a group of people doing revolutionary work which has a certain amount of momentum always includes a subgroup of people with revolutionary aspirations who are nevertheless incapable of mustering either the energy or the courage to actually engage in such activities.

"Lefter Than Thou" players are persons who are dominated by an extremely intolerant and demanding conscience (or Parent) on the one hand and are not able to mobilize their scared Child to do any work on the other. Criticism of the activities of the group and the decisions of the leaders becomes a substitute for revolutionary work. This criticism occurs, usually, at meetings where work would ordinarily be discussed, and it always replaces effective action. "Lefter Than Thou" players are either effective in dismembering the organization, in which case they wind up without a context in which to work; or else they are expelled from the organization by the effective leadership of it, and find themselves again in a situation in which no work can be done.

In both cases, they have a clear-cut justification for their lack of activity, and this is the payoff of the game.

It is a hallmark of "Lefter Than Thou" players that they are angry, often "Angrier Than Thou"; it is quite possible, however, to distinguish the anger of a "Lefter Than Thou" player from the anger of a person who is effectively reacting to his oppression.

"Lefter Than Thou" players are most always children of the middle class. On this basis it is easy to see why a group of black militants can hardly be accused of playing "Lefter Than Thou" while a group of white college students who accuse these black militants of not being radical enough is suspect.

Whether a person plays "Lefter Than Thou" or not can be determined by making a simple assessment of how much revolutionary action they take other than at meetings over, say, a period of a week. It will be seen that, if observed closely, the activity of a "Lefter Than Thou" player occurs mostly in the form of an itellectual "head trip" at meetings and hardly ever in the real world. "Lefter Than Thou" players will excel in destructive arguments, or sporadic destructive action when sparked or impelled by others. It will also be seen that they lack the capacity to gather momentum in creative or building work and that they lack the capacity to work alone due to the extreme intransigence of the Pig Parent in their head which will defeat, before it is born, every positive, life-giving effort.

It appears, therefore, as if that extraordinarily divisive game "Lefter Than Thou" is played by persons whose oppression has been largely oppression of the mind. This form of intellectual oppression, a Calvinist "morality of the intellect," is usually accomplished in a liberal context in the absence of societal or familial application of force—a context in which action or force is actually disavowed, so that the chains that bind the person are strictly psychological or within the head, yet most paralyzing indeed. When anger is felt it is not expressed physically but in the form of destructive talk.

Movement groups are especially vulnerable to destructive talk as their leaders are often in awe of and mystified by intellectual accomplishment. It must be remembered that a game has to be played by the Victim as well as the Persecutor; the Victim in this case being the leaders of the group under attack who, ordinarily, are more than willing to submit to the persecution of the "Lefter Than Thou" player. This willingness to respond to "head trips" and intellectual arguments is a characteristic of certain cultural subgroups, so that while a "Lefter Than Thou" player would be scoffed at and ignored in a very clearly action-oriented movement group, "Lefter Than Thou" players have a capacity to affect the decisiveness of the guilt-ridden intelligentsia.

This game is a liberal, intellectualized form of the aggressiveness that has been observed among the oppressed poor and the blacks. It is a well documented fact that crimes against persons occur mostly between members of oppressed subcultures. Frantz Fanon in *The Wretched of the Earth* illustrates how the savage, homicidal, and capricious criminality that has been observed among Algerians dissolved when the war of liberation became established. The supposed fact that Algerians are born criminals, such being taught even to Algerians by the faculty of Algiers, was not only *not* a fact but a mystification of their oppression. The actual fact of the matter is that the oppressed, when they have no access to their oppressors, either because their oppression is mystified or because their oppressors are not within reach, are likely to wind up at each other's throats. "Lefter Than Thou" is a case of the frustrated and mystified oppressed seizing the throats of their own brothers and sisters because of an incapacity to engage in positive creative revolutionary action.

The measure of a revolutionary's worth is the work

that she or he does. When a person questions the effectiveness of the leadership of a group or the work of a group, the first question to that person should be, "What work are *you* doing?" It will be found that in most cases the critic is a person who is doing very little or no work. If that person is, in fact, contributing a great deal of work outside of the discussions at meetings, then the challenge of the validity of the leadership's goals and methods is again open to consideration. Thus, the demystification of a critic's actual work output is a very important tool in the maintenance of a cohesive movement group.

Another usual attack upon movement groups which is also quite effective is "leveling."

LEVELING, HIERARCHIES AND LEADERSHIP

The greatest single evil in mankind is the oppression of human being by human being. Oppression ordinarily expresses itself in the form of hierarchical situations in which one person makes decisions for others. It has been the wish of many to eradicate this greatest of all evils from their lives. In order to do so, some people have completely leveled hierarchical situations and have attempted to function socially in the total absence of leadership, with the hope of building a society without hierarchies in which the greatest evil—oppression— cannot find a breeding ground.

With the specter of the worst pig, authorization hierarchy, haunting them, people have attempted to work in organizations which have been leveled of all hierarchies. In my opinion, such organizations, when they involve more than about eight persons, have an extremely low chance of survival. When "levelers" enter an organization and impose willy-nilly a no-hierarchies principle, they usually bring about the ultimate destruction of the group.

I will attempt here to demonstrate the fallacy of leveling of hierarchies, as well as to present an alternative to leveling which, I believe, is capable of making rational use of the valuable qualities of leadership in people, while at the same time preventing that extension of leadership into oppression which is such a scourge upon humankind.

First, let me define some terms:

I will call "oppression" the domination force or threats of force of one person by another.

I will call "leveling" a situation in which, at least publicly, no leader is recognized and no hierarchy is allowed in a group, even though leadership and hierarchy may in fact exist.

I will call a "hierarchy" a situation in which one human being makes decisions for other human beings.

I will call a "leader" a person in a group who is seen as possessing a skill or quality which causes others to wish to learn or profit from that quality.

Hierarchies come in a great variety of forms—from the murderous hierarchies in a capricious war to the mother-child hierarchy, including the hierarchies between teacher and student, man and woman, black and white, master and slave, factory owner and exploited worker, foreman and journeyman, craftsman and apprentice. Some of these hierarchies are alienating and dehumanizing. Others are not. To relate to all hierarchies as if they were all dehumanizing and evil is a great error, bordering on mindlessness. Hierarchies should be analyzed in terms of whether they affect human beings well or badly.

There are at least three human hierarchies which are of obvious value, and whose leveling would clearly not profit humankind.

The first and most basic hierarchy is the hierarchy between mother and child. Here, one person makes decisions for another person; and yet it is difficult to see how leveling this hierarchy would be of any advantage. When this mother-child or parent-child hierarchy is extended beyond its fruitful and natural reach—namely, when it is imposed by force or threats of force and beyond the period in which the child needs parental protection and when it is extended to large aggregations of people—then this parent-child hierarchy becomes the model for the military, the great corporations, and so on.

Another such is the hierarchy between a human being who is in great physical pain or need (the sick, the hungry, the wounded, the deranged) and another human being who has the means to fulfill that need. When a person is in dire physical need he may wish that another human being make decisions for him. Again, this natural hierarchy, which is conducive to well-being, can be extended into one that is damaging, as has been the case with the hierarchy that has been created by the medical profession and the attending psychiatric and other mental health professions. Again, the continuation of the need beyond necessity, the continuation of ministration beyond necessity, and the encouragement of the preservation of the hierarchy even in the absence of physical need have resulted in a hierarchical medical establishment which at this point may be doing more against human health than for it. This may sound startling; but if one separates medical knowledge, which is vast and potentially helpful, from medical activity, which is self-serving and oppressive, one can see that the medical establishment is not only not fully serving humanity but holding back potential help from it.

A third hierarchy is based on differences of skill between human beings, in which one person who can be considered a craftsman is sought out by another person who wishes to learn her craft. This hierarchy in which one person places himself below the other in knowledge is desirable to both. The apprentice, by recognizing his need to learn and by riveting his attention to his master, is likely to acquire a skill more quickly and more thoroughly than a student who questions her master's knowledge. On the other hand, a teacher who is given attention and recognition by an apprentice finds in his teaching the greatest reward for his life effort. Both the craftsman and the apprentice profit from this process; and it is hard to see how either of them, especially the student, is damaged by it. Again, this natural hierarchical situation can be extended beyond its necessity, so that certain persons are forever kept in an inferior position to others with respect to their skill. This, of course, is the basis for most universities and professional schools and is again an example of where a natural hierarchy can be extended into an oppressive and evil one.

It is characteristic of humanizing hierarchies that they are, first, voluntary; and, second, bent upon their own destruction of self-dissolving.

All three of the above-mentioned beneficial hierarchies can be extended into oppressive ones. The tendency toward dehumanizing hierarchies that may exist in human beings can be overcome by human beings who decide that they wish to do so. That very same tendency can also be empowered by the human intelligence, as has been done, to the point of building monstrous hierarchies which may now consume us. As human beings we have the choice between mindlessly extending natural hierarchies to the point that they will devour us, or equally as mindlessly leveling and abolishing them; or, on the other hand, using our intelligence, wherever it suits us, to create groups with humanizing beneficial hierarchies when needed.

I wish to postulate an intelligent principle of authority which discriminates between hierarchy and oppression and which, I hope, will be useful to people working in Movement organizations.

The first principle of human hierarchies is that they be voluntary and that they be self-dissolving; that is, that the eventual historical outcome of the group's work be to make the hierarchy unnecessary.

The second principle of human hierarchies is that leaders shall be responsive and responsible.

In order for a hierarchy to be voluntary it cannot involve oppression or coercion by force or threats of force. As a consequence, no one shall use force or threats of force in any situation relating to human beings within a movement or an organization of which they are members. Intimidation of group members by psychological means ("pigging") must be avoided by developing an atmosphere of mutual protection between group members.

Responsive leaders are leaders who are available for criticism by group members. Thus, leadership can be extended only as far as it remains possible for all group members to make extended face-to-face contact with the leaders.

Finally, a responsible leader is one who feels the impact of his or her actions and takes responsibility for them. This is a human quality which can only be assessed by observation. Responsibility is judged from the leader's previous actions and can only be ascertained over a period of time during which his or her work is open to scrutiny and during which the important quality of responsibility is observed.

The same kind of guilt that operates in the leadership when faced with "Lefter Than Thou" players comes into effect when confronted with a leveler.

The self-doubt of a leader is the greatest aid to the leveler. Oppressors don't respond to such attacks at all; but good leaders are prone, because of their basic wish to be responsive and responsible, to allow the attacks of a few to vitiate their useful work for the many. Thus, when faced with such attacks, leaders should responsibly investigate their work and responsively obtain feedback from all the group's members before abdicating their leadership. Only if this analysis reinforces the levelers' arguments should a leader allow that most precarious process, leveling, to occur in the group.

A POSTSCRIPT (1974)

As the editor of this anthology and the originator (some say "father") of Radical Psychiatry, I feel compelled to make a few final statements which come to mind upon rereading this final chapter.

The years between 1969 and 1973, when I finally extricated myself from the position of leadership at the Berkeley Radical Psychiatry Center, have been the most exhilarating, traumatic, dramatic, informative, discouraging, and ecstatically happy, as well as unhappy, years of my life. Looking back, I feel that I've learned a great deal about the processes that govern the formation and development of movement groups and the pressures impinging upon their leaders.

The most important lesson I've learned is in relation to power—and the almost inevitable quandary in which a leader finds herself or himself after whatever movement she or he has originated gains some momentum. My position at the Radical Psychiatry Center after it became a strong organization was very much like the position of the father of an adolescent. I was deeply loved for my good deeds and violently hated for my misdeeds, at times by the same people. And it appeared that as long as I held any power within the radical psychiatry community, I would not be able to live in peace within it. I could not be seen as an equal by others because I had, in fact, a great deal of power. I was not able to give up this power because people relied on it, even as they resented my having it; and also because I did not really know how to give it up effectively. For instance, I was a skilled and experienced therapist, but people resented the manner in which I taught my skills. The only thing I knew to do was to stop teaching, which was in turn resented. Or, I personally held title to the building which housed the Center. This was resented, but the organization was not financially capable of taking it off my hands, nor were they willing to move to a different location. Because I was committed to the eventual equalization of power between all members of the community, I did not hold on to my position as I probably could have, had I wanted to. On the other hand, the ever-increasing stream of criticism and dissatisfaction expressed to me by members of the community as I relinquished my powerful position within it (criticism which they had harbored secretly and had never expressed) became persecutory toward me in magnitude and succeeded in causing me to want to abandon my place within the community altogether.

This process was extremely painful. In retrospect, I wish I had left earlier and thus subjected myself to less pain. The outcome of an earlier departure would not have, in my mind, been to the Center's detriment. I believe now that persons who start organizations should plan how they will take their leave from them before they are forced out; or, heaven forbid, before they find themselves misusing their power in order to hold on to their position. I believe that their main contribution is the forbearance of the wounds sustained in their struggle with their brothers and sisters within the movement. The Radical Psychiatry Center and the Radical Psychiatry Movement, together with the Radical Therapy Movement, have made a profound impression on the psychiatric and mental health professions by now. On the whole, I am satisfied with my contribution to it.

To the people that I struggled with, the people that I loved and benefited, the people that I hated and hurt, I say: "When everything is said and done, the question that remains is simply: 'Have we succeeded in diminishing the oppressive misuse of power by the psychiatric establishment?'; and if the answer is yes, let's congratulate ourselves, one and all."

I believe the answer is: Yes! and I praise us for our accomplishments. Our work continues as the oppression, mystification, and alienation of the people has only begun to be lifted.

Venceremos!

—Claude Steiner
April, 1974

Appendix

APPENDIX A Résumé of the Criticisms of Radical Psychiatry Made by the New Radical Psychiatry Group (November, 1971)

CHANGE

Eight or nine months ago some important changes took place in radical psychiatry: training groups became collectives; we went from being radical psychiatrists to community organizers; and affinity became an important concept. The separation between work and our personal lives became blurred. Using rules learned in intimate relationships we began working on building a utopian community. Our personal lives became a revolutionary testing ground, especially in the sexual areas. The decisions to change were made by a small in-group, yet everyone was *expected* to conform.

POWER

How did it come about that *one group* has the *power*? This evolved as a natural process first by doing together, then sleeping, and ultimately living with one another. People began to look alike and move together. They had the power of getting strokes from each other; they could all vote as a block; they had the power of influence and quick communication. They had the power of allegiance based on sexual relationships. This in-group had created standards for living for the out-group just as in outside society where one group dictates and the rest of the people are isolated individuals. The in-group labels people, calls them "passive power players," "lefter than thou players," "liberal," and makes them feel not O.K. It has become hard to get into training groups and difficult to start a group. Diversity and creativity are stifled. It has become difficult to have criticism heard.

The initial structure of radical psychiatry was based on a teaching hierarchy with the teaching collective at the top and action rap at the bottom. This was a natural hierarchy based on knowledge and expertise; but those at the top of the hierarchy now have power which they mystify and which they are not invested in giving up.

We all agree on the Manifesto, Principles, and Working Policy. In the last four or five months there have been no serious innovations. The in-group did a good job of teaching skills and principles, but these skills and principles have been learned now, and they (the in-group) are no longer needed in that position. The skills have been equalized, but the in-group does not want to give up power or move in a dialectic for change.

The in-group has been putting more energy into solving problems for the in-group than in doing problem-solving groups. We want to put therapy ahead of our personal lives. The in-group has created new unstated demands which are no secret—having Child affinity and putting energy into our lives as a higher priority than therapy.

Radical psychiatry has become anti-creative as a result of the power structure. New ideas have been overlooked, or ideas that are suggested have not been heard and have been defended against.

The foundation of radical psychiatry is only dealt with from the top. Behavior control has become instituted. (For example, "Don't point.") People talk alike;

they use the same jargon. There are token changes (like changing the name of stamps to "held resentments"). Paranoid fantasies have become used to control deviant behavior. The statement, "I can't work with you," used to be the beginning of a dialogue and work on mediation. Now it is the end of dialogue. It has become established party line. It has become unsafe to act independently and creatively in radical psychiatry. The fear is to be considered uncooperative or competitive.

PRELIMINARY TRAINING

There is no one clear way to get into preliminary training and training collectives. People attempting to get in are not told what the process is. They feel judged and tested. The burden for initiating all moves is put on people seeking training. They are made to feel powerless and feel pressured to adapt. They feel confused, alone and unsupported, which causes empowering and alienation.

Group members have a difficult time getting into training collectives. They also are oppressed by values in radical psychiatry. They are told that there is only one way to end oppression. Values and ideals are pushed on group members. The assumptions about relationships are anti-monogamous. Values and rules about groups are not explained or encouraged to be questioned. Group members can't play in the same space as group leaders or get training. Leaders do not talk about their own problems or admit they have problems. Group members are told if they don't like it they can leave.

CRITICISM AND COMMUNICATION

People with criticism have been labeled "lefter than thou players," "destructive forces," "uncooperative."

This labeling destroys the dialectic process as it prevents criticism. The biggest offenders are those in power in the in-group. They get strokes from each other, are one-up, and consider themselves better. Issues that they do not like are considered "head trips" and "piggy." There is only one form of criticism allowed: "this feels bad"; and if you don't use it you're told to leave or shut up.

Communication barriers are being used to maintain power. There is horizontal communication, but little vertical access. This maintains the power structure in radical psychiatry. Outsiders can think they've become insiders, but they are still outsiders. For instance, group members asked for a sheet explaining rules about problem-solving groups, but there was very little energy put into this. Group leaders isolate themselves so they don't see the effects of their power.

In action rap there is a lid put on spontaneous feelings. Anger has become "pig," and laughter has become "gallows." In regard to our jargon, we tell people to wait and get used to it. This encourages empowering and adapting. We discount fresh perspectives and reinforce stock responses. The facilitator in action rap will say "I support you," meaning that he gives permission without any real human caring or actual protection. Facilitators maintain power by this double message which is a verbal message not backed by feelings. The facilitator in action rap may be uptight, but says it's O.K. for other people to be open.

SELF-CRITICISM IN RESPONSE TO THE CRITICISM OF THE NEW RADICAL PSYCHIATRY GROUP

Distribution of power in the radical psychiatry community is uneven and mystified. Some people have more power than others. Some sub-groups have more power than others. Power resides in strokes, communication, money, affinity, etc. Equalizing power among the various spheres of interest in the radical psychiatry community is essential.

Homogeneity or lack of diversity colludes with empowering. Any homogeneous group becomes empowered by those who see themselves as different from it. We need to share things other than radical psychiatry. There are things outside of radical psychiatry modes that people can give each other.

We need to create a sense of *safety, openness,* and *desire for change* so that criticism is freely given, as well as desired, heard, and implemented.

We have to figure out how to work with antagonistic criticism, and we have to learn to distinguish antagonistic criticism from cooperative criticism.

We have to work on being open to and encouraging feedback and critical feedback of action rappers, group members, and leaders-in-training. We have to make an all-out effort to encourage people to write so as to better disseminate ideas.

Group members need more access to information, specifically radical psychiatry theory.

We have to evaluate the relationship between group members and group leaders and between action rappers and group leaders.

This means, specifically, in terms of strokes, since strokes are power, especially physical strokes, sharing social space, sharing play space.

The stroke economy within the community as well as in relationship to people outside the community needs to be demystified. The relationship between strokes and power needs to be demystified and dealt with.

Often, sexual strokes are empowered. Thus, nonsexual relationships are considered deficient in some way. There's a lack of emphasis and encouragement of brother-to-brother, sister-to-sister, and brother-to-sister relationships.

TRAINING AND PRE-TRAINING

Training and pre-training need heavy criticism, analysis, and change. Pre-training, especially, has developed sloppily and with a great lack of self-criticism and discipline. Much work is needed here.

Should group members be in training at the same time that they are in group?

It's important to watch for the problem or unwillingness to share power in the area of preliminary training. This problem happens a lot, specifically in the relationship between people already in collective and preliminary trainees, and needs to be worked on.

We have to make slots during specific collective periods and problem-solving groups for talking straight. Paranoid fantasies have been used to include much more than paranoid fantasies because of a lack of place for feedback, hunches, intuitions, thoughts, questions, Pig messages, etc. Anger and Pigging has been delivered in the form of stamps at the beginning of meetings. Ritualizing transactions in this way needs to be re-evaluated and re-structured.

Our use of specialized language and specialized ways of relating (stamps, paranoias, no pigging) often isolates us from other people. Our expectations that all our strokes be gotten from people within the community and not from people outside isolates us and is a discount of other people. We don't give enough support to people who work in radical psychiatry who get strokes from people who do not work in radical psychiatry.

CONCLUSIONS

The above self-criticism, a great deal of which comes from and coincides with the New Radical Psychiatry Criticism Seminars, does not necessarily spell out any insoluble differences between them and us.

However, there is one basic political difference between the two groups that we've been able to ascertain from doing an evaluation of their criticism. Primarily the difference manifests itself in terms of how the two groups want to practice radical psychiatry.

The New Radical Psychiatry group seems to want to relate to each other around work only. That is, working in training collective, doing problem-solving groups, doing action rap, and having seminars, but not beyond.

We, on the other hand, want to learn, teach, develop, and *live* Radical Psychiatry. We want to build a supportive, therapeutic, political community in which radical psychiatry theory is practiced. We want to build personal, political, and working affinity, while the New Radical Psychiatry group believes work affinity is all they want. It is because of this very basic difference that we don't want to work with them any longer.

We do not believe that it is necessary to be able to work with everyone to create revolutionary change. It is possible for there to be many parallel struggles in the Radical Therapy Movement.

Index